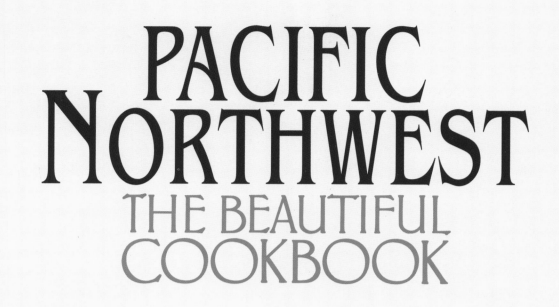

PACIFIC
NORTHWEST
THE BEAUTIFUL
COOKBOOK

Seared Sea Scallops with Roasted Red Pepper and Polenta (recipe page 104)

AUTHENTIC RECIPES FROM THE PACIFIC NORTHWEST

PACIFIC NORTHWEST

THE BEAUTIFUL COOKBOOK

CONSULTING EDITOR AND FOOD TEXT
KATHY CASEY

REGIONAL TEXT
LANE MORGAN

FOOD PHOTOGRAPHY BY
E. JANE ARMSTRONG

SCENIC PHOTOGRAPHY BY
JOHN CALLANAN

CollinsPublishersSanFrancisco
A Division of HarperCollinsPublishers

First published in USA 1993
by Collins Publishers San Francisco

Produced by Weldon Owen Inc.
814 Montgomery Street
San Francisco, CA 94133 U.S.A.
Phone (415) 291-0100   Fax (415) 291-8841

Weldon Owen Inc.:
President: John Owen
Publisher: Jane Fraser
Senior Editor: Anne Dickerson
Editorial Assistant: Jan Hughes
Copy Editor: Carolyn Miller
Proofreader: Lisa Conrad
Production: Stephanie Sherman, Mick Bagnato
Design: Tom Morgan, Blue Design
Design Concept: John Bull, The Book Design Company
Map: Mike Gorman
Illustrations: Diana Reiss-Končar

Recipe Writers:
Kathy Casey (Western Washington)
Gwenyth Caldwell Bassetti and Donna
    Boechler (Eastern Washington and Idaho)
Greg Higgins (Oregon)
Christina Reid Orchid (Islands)
Kasey Wilson (British Columbia)

Photography Assistant: Greg DeBoer
Food Stylists: Diana Isaiou, Kathy Casey, Phyllis
    Bogard, Jane Morimoto, JoAnne Naganawa,
    Carol Ladd
Food Stylist Assistants: Charlene Nomaguchi, Ann
    Manly, Teresa Domka

Library of Congress Cataloging-in-Publication Data:

Casey, Kathy.
    Pacific northwest the beautiful cookbook : authentic
recipes from the Pacific northwest / consulting editor
and food text [by] Kathy Casey ; regional text [by]
Lane Morgan ; food photography by E. Jane
Armstrong ; scenic photography by John Callanan.
        p.   cm.
    Includes index.
    ISBN 0-00-255151-9 : $45.00
    1. Cookery, American—Pacific Northwest style.
2. Northwest, Pacific—Description and travel—
1981-   I. Title.
TX715.2.P32C37   1993
641.59795—dc20   92-41019
                                       CIP

Manufactured by Mandarin Offset, Hong Kong
Printed in Hong Kong

A Weldon Owen ◆ Production

*Pages 2–3: Nicknamed the "Emerald City," Seattle shows off
its cosmopolitan skyline.*

*Right: Baker, one of the original towns on the historic Old
Oregon Trail is now a logging and cattle town that celebrates
its wild West beginnings with an annual rodeo.*

*Pages 8–9: Grangeville, Idaho, is a gateway to some of the
state's richest wilderness areas. Over three million acres of
mountains, lakes and rivers surround this pastoral setting.*

*Pages 10–11: Rib Eye Steak with Ha Cha Cha Barbecue
Sauce and Frizzled Onions (recipe page 128).*

*Pages 14–15: Fields of blooming tulips, iris and daffodils
create carpets of vibrant colors across the fields around Mt.
Vernon, Washington in the early spring.*

Spiced Pancakes with Whipped Cream and Summer Fruit (recipe page 224)

CONTENTS

INTRODUCTION 17

VANCOUVER ISLAND
AND THE SAN JUAN ISLANDS 24

APPETIZERS, SOUPS AND SALADS 32

VANCOUVER AND BRITISH COLUMBIA 68

FISH AND SHELLFISH 76

WESTERN WASHINGTON 112

MEAT, POULTRY AND GAME 120

EASTERN WASHINGTON,
EASTERN OREGON AND IDAHO 156

VEGETABLES, GRAINS AND PRESERVES 164

WESTERN OREGON 202

DESSERTS, COFFEE AND BEVERAGES 210

ACKNOWLEDGMENTS 250

AUTHOR INFORMATION 250

GLOSSARY 251

INDEX 254

This mural in Chemainus, Vancouver Island, depicts the early pioneers and the development of the town's logging industry.

INTRODUCTION

Since the beginning, the Pacific Northwest has been known for its beauty and its food. The Kwakiutl nation of northern Vancouver Island named one stretch of beach Having Coho Salmon. Other spots, more than one, the Kwakiutl called Having Everything Right: beauty, roots, berries, fish. Olalla, a community in western Washington, was named for the berries that grew there, while Camas and Wapato, east of the Cascade Mountains, commemorate gathering spots for edible roots.

The diverse landscapes of the Pacific Northwest— ocean beaches and inland coves, steaming volcanos and rolling hillsides thick with wheat, rain forest moss and desert tumbleweed—provide an equivalent diversity of great food. The same wild mushrooms, fresh berries, oysters and crab that four-star restaurants use in their signature dishes are available to residents with a few spare hours to forage.

Long before food professionals began to debate the characteristics of Northwest cuisine, the ambitious native cultures of the north Pacific—Kwakiutl, Haida, Bella Coola, Tsimpsian and others—based their wealth on an abundance of seafood and their prestige on feasts that went on for days. From their villages and fish camps on Vancouver Island and the mainland coast, they caught and preserved tremendous numbers of salmon, halibut, smelt, shellfish and other seafood, including whale. Their techniques for grilling salmon and steaming clams and oysters are still beach-fire favorites today. Their powerful and sophisticated artwork, one of the cultural glories of the Northwest, is another legacy of the abundance of food their land provided: They had the time and security for elaborate creative projects.

East of the Cascade Range, tribes depended more on salmon, which traveled hundreds of miles up the Fraser and Columbia rivers and their tributaries. The great fishing sites at Kettle Falls and Celilo Falls, where fishermen speared the giant Chinooks as they thrashed and leaped up the rapids, became centers of native commerce. Tribes came from all over the Northwest to trade oil for obsidian, salmon for buffalo robes, preserved salmon eggs for dried berries.

The first Europeans to visit the area were seeking furs and sovereignty, but at the same time, they needed food. The first written reviews of Northwest food were highly favorable. William Clark of the Lewis and Clark expedition found smelt, taken from the Columbia River and spit-roasted in the native style, to be "superior to any fish I ever tasted." Columbia River salmon were "of an excellent flavor," he wrote, although the explorers eventually tired of an all-fish diet and began purchasing dogs to eat.

Once commercial farming began, Northwest produce received its own chorus of praise. "The various culinary vegetables are in great profusion, and of the first quality,"

Mount Hood is the highest mountain in Oregon at 11,239 feet and is second only to Japan's Mount Fujiyama as the world's most climbed glacier-covered peak.

wrote John Kirk Townsend after a trip to the Oregon Country in 1834, a statement that is just as true today. The first gardens were planted to feed the crews of sailing vessels and the traders and trappers associated with the Hudson's Bay Company. One of the first crops was the potato, which coastal Indians had received from the early Spanish explorers, who had acquired it from the Indians in South America.

The commercial potential of Northwest food was apparent, and much of the best soon went for export. Northern California had already decimated many of its oyster beds, so boatloads of tiny Olympia oysters from the Willapa and Samish bays were shipped to San Francisco, where they sold for twenty dollars a plate in the 1850s. Due to overharvesting, and the slow-growing Olympias' inherent fragility, the price is about the same today, if you can find them at all.

Sturdier Pacific oysters have largely replaced the Olympias, and gourmets seek out custom breeds such as the Westcott Bay Petites of San Juan Island. Most oysters eaten in the United States come from Washington in jars, but Northwesterners are privileged to have theirs fresh.

Clams were another staple, once so numerous that settlers plowed them from the sand with horse teams and praised them in song, as in "The Ballad of the Old Settler": "No longer a slave to ambition, I laugh at the world and its shams, when I think of my happy condition, surrounded by acres of clams." Coastal residents were likewise pleased to be surrounded by acres of mussels, by hidden troves of giant geoducks, and by waters rich with crab, shrimp and dozens of species of fish. Today, the ode to clams is the familiar theme song of a famous chowder house.

Fishing is a favorite pastime in the Northwest, especially around Idaho's Lake Coeur d'Alene famous for its 14 varieties of rainbow trout.

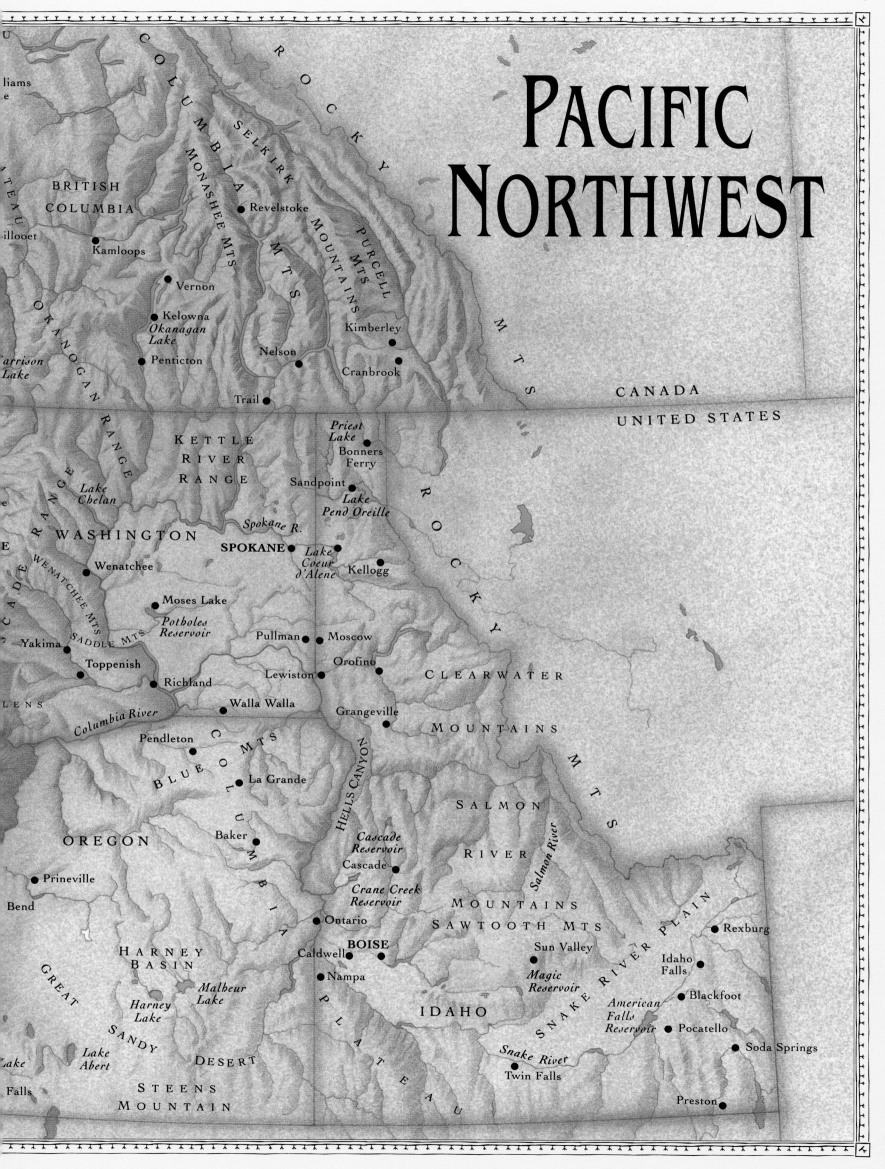

PACIFIC NORTHWEST

BRITISH
COLUMBIA

Revelstoke

Kamloops

Vernon

Kelowna
*Okanagan
Lake*

Kimberley

Penticton

Nelson

Cranbrook

Trail

CANADA

UNITED STATES

*Priest
Lake*

Bonners
Ferry

KETTLE
RIVER
RANGE

Sandpoint

*Lake
Chelan*

*Lake
Pend Oreille*

WASHINGTON

Spokane R.

SPOKANE

*Lake
Coeur
d'Alene*

Kellogg

Wenatchee

Moses Lake

*Potholes
Reservoir*

Pullman   Moscow

Orofino

CLEARWATER

Yakima

Toppenish

Lewiston

Richland

Walla Walla

Grangeville

MOUNTAINS

Columbia River

Pendleton

SALMON

Baker

RIVER

Salmon River

OREGON

*Cascade
Reservoir*

La Grande

Cascade

MOUNTAINS

Prineville

*Crane Creek
Reservoir*

SAWTOOTH MTS

Rexburg

Bend

Ontario

BOISE

Sun Valley

Idaho
Falls

HARNEY
BASIN

Caldwell

*Magic
Reservoir*

Blackfoot

GREAT

Nampa

*American
Falls
Reservoir*

Pocatello

*Malheur
Lake*

IDAHO

Soda Springs

*Harney
Lake*

SANDY

*Lake
Abert*

DESERT

Snake River

STEENS
MOUNTAIN

Twin Falls

Preston

19

The fertile, rolling hills of the Palouse Country in southeastern Washington create a sea of color as crops near the harvesting season.

Once canneries and railroads made it possible to transport perishable seafoods, the Northwest became the world's main supplier of salmon. Built on the water's edge in bays all up and down the coasts, canneries created their own communities of Chinese, Native American and European workers, who labored twenty hours a day in season, gutting and cleaning and packing an avalanche of fish. Iowans who had never seen a live salmon could at least admire the painting on the Rod and Reel brand label for sockeye, packed in Blaine, Washington. Railroad connections also opened up markets for frozen salmon and halibut.

The railroads changed Northwest farming. Formerly restricted to storage crops like wheat and produce for the local market, the area soon became a major producer of apples, pears, peaches, berries, potatoes, onions, milk, cheese and on and on—a list that now totals well over one hundred commercial crops.

The seacoasts and fertile valleys west of the Cascades were obvious sites for settlement and for farming. The vast stretches of the inland Northwest took more time to gain full appreciation, but they are now the heart of the area's agriculture. Irrigation turned thousands of acres that were marginal and thousands more that were frankly desert into some of the most productive farmland on the continent. Northwest wheat, legumes, apples and potatoes found markets all over the world. The racing waters of the Columbia, dancing with giant salmon, were replaced by a series of dam-created lakes traversed by boats and barges piled with grain. Agriculture became the region's largest industry, replacing timber and fishing and holding its own even against industrial giants like the Boeing Company. The wild salmon have dwindled from the "nearly inconceivable" numbers noted by Lewis and Clark to an endangered remnant.

The quality of Northwest crops was evident from the start; the quality of the region's cooking took longer to develop. Settlers were preoccupied with taming and developing their immense new country; they had little time for menu planning. Much of the Northwest's best food was exported to San Francisco or New York, while status-conscious restaurants in Seattle, so as not to seem provincial, served Maine lobster and French champagne.

Great Northwest meals became the province of inspired home cooks, many of whom were immigrants from villages where cooking was valued but food was scarce. Set down in the bounty of the Northwest, they knew just what to do. Young Angelo Pellegrini, later to become a noted food writer and an authority on Shakespeare, astonished his college classmates with lamb roasted with artichokes. Other Italian immigrants filled the stalls of Seattle's Pike Place Market when it began in 1907. Italians coming to the Walla Walla Valley brought seeds for a large, sweet onion that could be eaten raw with crusty bread and butter. Their grandchildren now prosper growing Walla Walla Sweets.

Japanese settlers west of the Cascades established many of the vegetable and berry farms that fed Seattle, Tacoma and Vancouver, and also introduced teriyakis and tempuras to the roster of seafood dishes. Moon snails and seaweed, both ignored by Anglo beachcombers, showed up on Japanese tables in the new country, along with the wild matsutake mushrooms of the Cascade foothills. Chinese restaurants at first were established and patronized by the mostly male residents of nineteenth-century Chinatowns, but eventually they found a wider clientele for their hot and sour soups, dim sum and noodles.

Nordic fishermen did not convert their new neighbors to lutefisk, but pickled herring and gravlax became part of the Northwest repertoire. African-Americans drawn to Seattle and Portland to work in defense plants during World War II brought the secrets of great barbecue to bear on Northwest pork and chicken. Latino

Totem poles, carved to proclaim clan status and ancestry, are part of a rich Native American/Canadian tradition in the Northwest.

Gastown, named after saloon keeper "Gassy" Jack Deighton, has preserved its mid-nineteenth century heritage when it was known as the hub of Vancouver.

workers, who came first as migrant labor and later as permanent residents, established tortilla factories and pepper farms.

As Portland, Seattle and Vancouver, B.C. prospered as international ports in an increasingly global economy, Northwest city life—once mocked for its provincial, stay-at-home flavor—became more cosmopolitan. Another influence was the Century 21 Exposition of 1962, a world's fair that introduced Korean, Indonesian and other previously unfamiliar cuisines to Seattle diners.

When gourmet cooking became a national preoccupation, the Northwest's culinary advantages—a tremendous variety of high-quality food and a fertile mix of ethnic traditions—became apparent. Locally grown daikon, cilantro and Asian pears began to show up in supermarkets alongside carrots and potatoes. Restaurateurs began to concentrate on the freshest and purest of local ingredients, supporting local specialty growers and—in at least one case—having hand-picked wild greens shipped to their door by UPS.

Cooks at the Shoalwater in Seaview, Washington, picked tasty snails off the Long Beach Peninsula greenery. Innisfree, in the Cascade foothills, served cream from the owners' own Jersey cow. On Vancouver Island, Sinclair Philip dove for shellfish within view of his Sooke Harbour House kitchen. The Northwest wine and beer industries rapidly achieved national stature, and became companions to serious intent in the kitchen.

Parts of the Northwest were still pioneer country well into the twentieth century. Boston baked beans and Southern corn bread were already cookbook standards at a time when the local favorites in the Pacific Northwest were Indian meals of smoked salmon and baked camas. Many culinary traditions are only now being established, and the excitement over Northwest cuisine is in part a

Roadside stands and U-pick farms are a common sight along Northwest highways during the summer months, promising sun-ripened fruits and vegetables.

The largest oceanfront dunes in the world, Oregon Dunes National Recreation Area provides wetland breeding grounds for over 400 species of wildlife.

Vancouver's natural environs are easily accessible; here, visitors hike the Capilano Suspension Bridge, a swaying footbridge that spans the Capilano River 230 feet below.

commercial recognition of what good family cooks have known for generations: The best and most creative cooking celebrates good ingredients rather than disguising mediocre ones.

The new interest in the best local foods has encouraged a second wave of culinary pioneers. While commercial fishing has dwindled due to overharvesting and loss of habitat, specialty fishing operations that provide top-quality, line-caught wild salmon have created a market for "designer fish." Similarly, while development has paved over much of the farmland in valleys around Puget Sound, a new generation of farmers grows high-ticket salad greens and vegetable specialties on plots not much bigger than a suburban backyard. Gourmet entrepreneurs turn out ever-lengthening shelves of dried cherries, goat and sheep cheeses, cranberry conserves, estate wines and wheat-based ales, flavored vinegars and pickled shallots.

Food co-ops and farmers' markets exemplify the contrasts in Northwest agriculture today. In the Moscow, Idaho, co-op, bins of locally grown organic rye and lentils, the most basic of crops, share space with tubs of Northwest salsa and wild huckleberry jam. At the Columbia Basin Farmers' Market, communal Hutterite farmers sell bread and pies next to newcomers with basil and eggplants. Down the road from the market site in Moses Lake are some of the biggest irrigated farms in the Northwest, which produce potatoes for French fries on several continents.

The concerns of agribusiness—geared for export—and of small-scale local growers do not always coincide, but the variety of farm sizes and styles is one of the strengths of Northwest agriculture, giving it a resiliency that not all farming regions can match.

For those who are lucky enough to know its attributes, the Pacific Northwest remains a culinary paradise, a place where some young children know where to gather mussels for seafood linguine and when to check beneath the alders for the first chanterelle of autumn. People who have never bought a cookbook or set foot in a gourmet restaurant will debate the merits of razor clams versus steamers, or of commercial blueberries (fat and sweet, a flavor full of sunshine) versus wild huckleberries (tiny, blue-black morsels with a taste so intense that a sliver of pie is enough).

Now such great debates, all the more satisfactory because both sides win, are a sport for visitors as well. Northwest markets and restaurants take pride in presenting the magnificent foods this land provides so generously.

THE ISLANDS

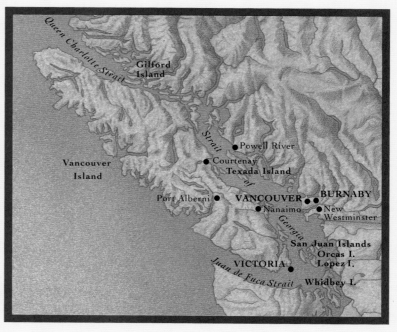

THE ISLANDS

From the rainy northern reaches of Vancouver Island to the sun-bleached American San Juans, the island life has long attracted self-sufficient Northwesterners. Vancouver Island, much the largest of the group, parallels the British Columbia coastline for nearly three hundred miles. Its sheltered eastern shore looks back to the mainland across the humped silhouettes of dozens of channel islands. The population is centered to the south, around the provincial capital of Victoria, and to the east where towns that began by mining coal and other minerals now depend on forestry, fishing and, increasingly, tourism.

The ocean coast of Vancouver Island is much wilder, a rain forest pummeled by the storms of the North Pacific and on calm days often wrapped in fog. The communities on the west side grew up in the coves and inlets that provide some protection from the weather. One of them, a native village at Nootka Sound, was for a time in the late eighteenth century the most famous port on the Pacific Coast, the center of the lucrative sea otter trade. It was also the site of the first meal served to Europeans on Vancouver Island, a feast of porpoise, seal, whale and other meats provided by Maquinna, a Nootka leader, to Capt. James Cook in 1782.

For the Native Canadians and the European explorers, the water was the only highway. Even today, the road ends at Tofino on the west side, less than halfway up the island.

Previous pages: One of the most spectacular and intricately linked archipelagos in the world, the San Juan Islands were formed by glacial activity. Left: The century-old Hotel de Haro on San Juan Island has long been a favorite destination resort for vacationers in search of a quiet, bucolic refuge.

BRUCE HANDS

27

To get to jewels like Warm Springs Cove, where you can sit in a natural rock pool at the base of a steaming waterfall while the Pacific surf splashes your toes and the horizon swings up to swallow the sun, you need a boat or plane.

The forested spine of the island is part of the Insular Mountains, a mostly submerged range that also breaks the surface to the north to form the Queen Charlotte Islands. This section of the island is sparsely populated, occupied primarily by an uneasy pairing of provincial parks and logging operations.

Like Dick Wilson of Hotsprings, the earlier native inhabitants of Vancouver Island and the inhabited gulf islands depended mostly on seafood. They collected clams and oysters on the beach, netted salmon in the rivers, and built canoes as long as European sailing ships to go out after whale and halibut. The Europeans brought seeds for their own favorite foods. The first garden was attached to a Spanish outpost at Nootka Sound, and yielded artichokes and chard as well as more plebian onions, potatoes and cabbage.

Full-scale farms began after the settlement of Victoria and spread up the eastern side and into some central valleys of the island. Hay and pasture, sheep and poultry, dairying and some vegetables are the major crops. Sheep thrive on the dryer Gulf Islands to the east, and lamb barbecues are a feature of island social life.

Victoria was the first city on Vancouver Island and is still by far the largest. It was established in 1843 as a Hudson's Bay Company headquarters, "a perfect Eden in the midst of the dreary wilderness of the northwest coast," wrote James Douglas, the usually impassive Hudson's Bay official who surveyed the site. When the Treaty of 1846 put the HBC headquarters on the Columbia River in American hands, Victoria became the company's base, and in 1849 the island became a Crown Colony with a mandate for growth. British settlers arrived to farm, and Scottish miners to work the seams of coal along the Strait of Georgia at Nanaimo. The next impetus to settlement was the Fraser River gold rush, which doubled the population of Victoria in 1858. Victoria was the only source of supplies and port of entry for the region, and it was overwhelmed.

In 1862, Victoria was incorporated as western Canada's first city. The surrounding farm communities of Cowichan, Chemainus, Alberni, Comox, Saanich and Sooke were developing with the construction of market roads. To a greater extent than eastern Canada, which had had generations to develop a separate identity, Victoria and the surrounding communities took on a strongly British flavor from its influx of new immigrants. British food and British farming predominated, creating a legacy that is still apparent in orchards with traditional English apple varieties such as Cox's Orange Pippin, in fast-food outlets selling Cornish pasties, in tearooms featuring Devonshire cream and in pubs serving genuine stouts and porters.

Island settlement was by no means entirely British, however. A substantial number of the early gulf island settlers were black (as was James Douglas) and Japanese, with both groups hoping to find in a new country an equality that had been denied them in more settled areas. Black Americans were among the twenty-nine people who landed on Saltspring Island in 1859. The Estes family, Sylvia

Opposite: Ferries provide a vital link between the islands and the mainland; here, two young commuters take in the view on the upper deck of one of the many ferries that traverse the waters daily.

The San Juan Islands were named by Gonzalez Lopez de Haro, who sailed into de Fuca's strait in 1790 and christened the island chain after his patron saint.

BRUCE HANDS

The sculpting power of the surf is illustrated by the gnarled driftwood scattered along the island shores.

and Louis and their two children, arrived the next year with fifteen dairy cows, which they had to lower into the water with ropes so the cows could swim ashore. The family moved into a cabin without a door or a roof and within a year had thirty head of cattle, 180 quarts of wheat from a one-quart sowing, butter and enough milk to share their production with the traveling minister.

Before long, food on the islands of British Columbia had evolved in two directions: formal colonial and community potluck. The Empress Hotel, opened in 1908, exemplifies the colonial traditions: afternoon high tea, tea dances, a Boar's Head parade at Christmas. At Sooke, to the west, Sooke Harbour House has the same gentility—a decanter of port is found in each guest room—combined with an emphasis on the freshest of regional foods in inventive combinations. The roe from sea urchins collected off the rocks nearby is served with a rinse of locally made apple cider, while the distinctive B.C. golden mantle oysters are clothed in a purée made of garden carrots and fish stock.

These meals are served mostly to well-heeled visitors. Islanders themselves, especially those in outlying areas, are more oriented toward the family dinner and the community get-together. Islanders always have been self-sufficient in both their food and their entertainment. "On Tuesday I salted half the deer, made some butter and planted out the tomatoes," Arthur Spalding wrote in 1893 to his wife, who had left South Pender Island to have a baby within reach of a doctor. "Next morning Long and I went over and helped Gerry slash an opening from Bott Bay to his house. Poker in the evening."

The Spaldings and their neighbors held work parties, called bees, to divide the labor of turning forest into field. "A lot of the fellows turned up for the bee: ...we killed a sheep to feed them on," wrote Spalding during a subsequent baby-induced separation. The gulf islands today attract visitors who want to sample the homegrown life. Fishing lodges, farmers' markets and roadside stands keep tourists in touch with local bounty, and many island lodges and restaurants maintain their own kitchen gardens. Main dishes lean toward the local specialties: seafood and lamb.

The San Juans are the southern continuation of the Gulf Islands of British Columbia. Nearly eight hundred islands make up the San Juan archipelago, ranging from Orcas, the largest at fifty-eight square miles, to tide-washed rocks that support only a fringe of seaweed. A state ferry service links the biggest islands—Shaw, Lopez, Orcas and San Juan—as well as the Canadian port of Sydney on Vancouver Island. The rest are accessible by private boat or plane. In summer the waters are crowded with everything from oceangoing yachts to fleets of kayaks.

With their red-earth bluffs, twisted madrona trees and

innumerable secluded coves, the islands are irresistibly beautiful. An additional attraction for residents of the western Washington mainland is that the islands have about half the average rainfall of the Seattle area. But although life here may be idyllic, it is generally not particularly remunerative. Native tribes used the islands as rest stops and fishing bases, but a lack of fresh water precluded most permanent residence until the advent of well-drilling technology. It still limits development today, to the relief of many who want to preserve the San Juans' tranquil character. From the start, island settlers have responded to the lure of the place, and then searched for ways to finance their decision.

Many started out by farming, although only Lopez has enough level ground and fertile soil to make agriculture really attractive. In the days of the Mosquito Fleet steamers that stopped at the island docks and delivered produce to markets on Puget Sound, Lopez was a thriving farm community. In 1930 at the close of the Mosquito Fleet era, it had 134 farms and its own creamery.

Today residents on all the islands are dedicated and innovative gardeners, but the main harvesting is done at sea. "As long as the tide goes out, you won't starve," says one Orcas Island resident. The days are gone when purse seiners off Lopez would sometimes have nets so loaded with salmon that they couldn't lift them into the boats, but salmon fishing continues on a restricted schedule. Reef net fishing, a native technique that originated in the San Juans, is still practiced by some commercial crews, both Native American and white. Using small boats with a distinctive spotting tower in the front, fishermen and -women spread their nets from boat to boat, siting them to intercept the salmon that hug the shores seeking the scent of their natal streams.

Established in 1843 as a Hudson's Bay Company headquarters, Victoria is now a mecca for tourists from all over the world who come here to sample its visual and culinary delights.

Another bountiful fishery in the early days was herring. One of the first settlers on Waldron Island was Eduard Graignic, a French sailor who jumped ship in Victoria in the 1870s. He and the family he raised on Waldron fished by lighting beach fires at night to attract the herring, and then rowing around the bedazzled fish with their nets. Graignic made enough by this method to finance a visit back to Paris. Fishing for dogfish—small, ugly sharks that abound in Northwest waters—was another source of income during World War II, when their livers provided a substitute for cod-liver oil.

Waldron has never had a ferry, so its residents are experts at making their own entertainment on the island. The annual Fourth of July picnics on Waldron in the forties were such occasions. "Lizzie would go to the dock a few days before the Fourth and put up a notice in Mr. Crum's old store that there would be a picnic on Lysle Beach," wrote Waldron's most famous chronicler, June Burns. "The long picnic tables would be spread with white tablecloths and fried chicken, new peas and potatoes and beets and carrots and fresh garden salads, baked beans and roasts of whatever animals had been butchered that week, moist homemade cakes, fresh churned butter, milk, and cream."

The meal she describes is not only traditional and abundant, but strictly seasonal, an island necessity in those days. The chickens would be from that spring's hatch, the new potatoes and peas planted according to the local rule of "in by Washington's birthday, out by Fourth of July." Baby beets and carrots were ready, but not yet corn, green beans or tomatoes. The butter and cream came from recently freshened cows, thriving on the early summer grass.

Limestone mines and cannery work, along with fishing, provided much of the cash income in the San Juans in the first decades of the twentieth century, but tourism is the biggest business now. By ferry, plane or private boat, visitors come to see small-town charm in incomparable settings. Bicyclers circumnavigate the hilly island roads, while kayakers explore the coves and small islands offshore. And food is part of the allure. Most of the remaining island farms are now oriented toward the tourist market. Produce stands sell gourmet lettuces, zucchini blossoms and other exotica to local restaurants and to camping and boating cooks. Herbs are a popular crop, responding well to the nearly Mediterranean soil and climate, and the islands' first winery opened on San Juan in 1992.

The water is still more fertile than the land, however. Clams, crabs and oysters are all staples of the boater's dinner. Commercial divers work the rocky sea bottom, harvesting sea cucumber and sea urchins for Asian markets.

Although Orcas, San Juan and—to some extent—Lopez have acquired considerable hustle and bustle in the form of T-shirt shops, espresso bars and even supermarkets, less developed islands like Shaw, which has one small store run by Franciscan nuns, and Waldron still require self-sufficiency and improvisation. If you forgot to get the sherry for the marinade, you can't just run down to the corner. But self-sufficiency is not the same as isolation. The Shaw Island Women's Club, for example, hosts an ambitious series of cooking and food classes each year, featuring chefs from around the Northwest. With a garden in the backyard, seafood in abundance, wild mushrooms in the forest and the latest techniques at their fingertips, island cooks can create their own Northwest cuisine without supermarket distractions.

Appetizers, Soups and Salads

Dungeness crab, on display at Pike Place Market in Seattle, are a local favorite.

APPETIZERS, SOUPS AND SALADS

Remember when, years ago, party food and appetizers meant platters of cocktail sausages and heavy dips with chips? Much has changed since then, and the food at today's cocktail party is far more varied and interesting, reflecting our current way of cooking and eating. In recent years, more appetizers began showing up on restaurant menus, prompting a sampling approach to meals, and bite-sized foods have become the party nibbles of choice.

Northwest entertaining is somewhat casual and the cuisine is definitely *not* just about salmon. Appetizers may be tiny smoked oysters or radishes straight from the garden dipped in coarse salt. The cheese might be Oregon's traditional sharp Tillamook Cheddar cheese, or exotic, handmade sheep or goats' milk cheese with such flavorings as dried cherries and walnuts or garlic and dill.

At neighborhood pubs and microbreweries, local beers wash down spicy tomato salsas scooped up with fresh tortilla chips, salted roasted hazelnuts and beer-battered Walla Walla sweet onion rings. Fried calamari is a favorite appetizer made from Pacific squid, dipped in seasoned flour or cornmeal then quickly fried and served with a lemony aïoli or a house-made tartar sauce.

Caponata made from the high-summer vegetable harvest is served with roasted garlic and fresh goat cheese spread on toasted herb croutons. In the fall, wild mushrooms are found everywhere from elaborate restaurant appetizers to simple sautés of chanterelles with garlic, herbs and butter.

The abundance of fresh seafood in the Northwest makes it an appetizer favorite. Oyster purists prefer oysters on the half shell eaten right on the beach, adorned with nothing other than a quick squeeze of lemon, a slug of crisp Northwest white wine and perhaps a bite of buttered French bread. For some this is the quintessential oyster experience; others enjoy them with a dollop of zippy cocktail sauce or a splash of vinegary mignonette sauce. Thinly sliced cold smoked salmon with pickled onions, sturgeon caviar and salmon caviar glimmering like big red pearls are often enjoyed at holiday parties with a toast of Northwest sparkling wine.

Native Americans brine then smoke salmon bellies, creating a sweet and salty hard-smoked piece of fish known as squaw candy. Sushi is made from the freshest raw fish, such as a thin slice of the giant geoduck clam topping sticky rice spread with hot wasabi paste with a bite of pickled ginger. Other Asian-influenced appetizers include shrimp-filled egg rolls and barbecued pork with hot Chinese mustard and sesame seeds for dipping. Fresh seasonal vegetables such as asparagus and thin slices of sweet yam are delicious dipped in tempura batter and quickly fried. Vietnamese rice paper, shrimp and cilantro roll-ups, Thai fish cakes and Chinese steamed tiny dumplings with pork filling also have been popular through the years.

Previous pages, clockwise from left: Wild Greens with Red Wine Vinaigrette (page 50), Granny Smith Apple and Yakima Gouda Tartlets (page 38), Eggplant Caponata and Roasted Garlic (page 66), Northern White Bean Soup with Chipotle Crème Fraîche (page 38)

In the sixties and seventies, when crab prices were low, it was common at a cocktail party to see an appetizer of cream cheese topped with cocktail sauce and a pound of fresh Dungeness crab meat! All this was scooped up on crackers. Now it's more common to see crab meat stretched in a hot dip with artichokes and Parmesan cheese.

The Norwegians and Swedes brought us pickled herring, pickled beets and the smorgasbord, along with Scandinavian nibbles such as Swedish meatballs. Traditionally these are prepared with minced onion sautéed in butter, then combined with ground beef, ground pork and sometimes ground veal, and seasoned with salt, pepper, nutmeg and allspice. These tiny meatballs are served plain, or topped or accompanied with a white sauce for dipping.

Nothing warms the soul and fills the senses better than the aroma of homemade soup wafting through the house and steaming the windows. Favorite Northwest varieties, both depending on flavorful, slow-simmered stocks, include rich asparagus soup and a cold-curing chicken and noodle.

The French word *palouse* means "grassland country," and this is the name of the lush, rolling-hill farmlands of eastern Washington and northern Idaho. It is here that the United States' lentil crop is grown. From this area come hearty soups such as Palouse lentil and slow-simmered split pea with smoked ham hocks, warming dishes for drizzly, chilly winter nights.

Seafood chowders, oyster stews and bisques stir up fervent debates here. Northwesterners can be quite set in their ways when it comes to clam chowder, for example. Usually it's white, at least we can agree on that, but when it comes to the thickness, the type of clams, the seasoning—to dill or not to dill—the discussion can become heated. Oyster stew, a Christmas Eve tradition, is another dish that can be controversial, but most people will agree on using the freshest just-shucked oysters available and barely warming them until their edges just curl in the milk or cream or half & half.

These days there is no excuse for serving a salad of iceberg lettuce with a few token slivers of red cabbage,

Walla Walla, Washington, is known for its "sweet," delicious onions cultivated only in this area.

Wild mushrooms thrive in the damp forest beds near Princeton, British Columbia.

what with the variety of beautiful greens available in Northwest stores and farmers' markets. Most also are easily grown in the home garden, and others could be growing wild right outside your back door. From the nutty arugula that grows wild in eastern Washington to nasturtium blossoms, salads today are bright and interesting combinations of flavors. European and Asian varieties of greens grow well in the temperate Northwest climate, so many small farmers specialize in exotic-green mixes. Fruits, smoked meats and poultry, seafood and roasted nuts are popular salad additions. Dressings are usually simple emulsions of good oils and vinegars, with berry vinegars being favored. But also popular is a creamy blue cheese dressing made with Oregon blue cheese, buttermilk and sour cream.

Seattle has a famous salad: the Crab Louis. Although no one knows who Louis was (prounounced "Louie"), the salad is thought to have been created there (or in San Francisco). A bed of crisp greens topped with a mound of fresh Dungeness crab meat (and sometimes sweet bay shrimp), hard-cooked egg halves, cucumber slices, tomato wedges and black olives, Crab Louis is traditionally garnished with a lemon wedge and a sprig of fresh parsley and is served with Thousand Island dressing.

Other Northwest salads range from crunchy, celery-seed-flecked cabbage slaws, purple potato salad (made from a variety of potato that is actually purple in color) and thick-sliced vine-ripened tomatoes with fresh basil, to mom's macaroni salad, brimming with chunks of king crab brought home by a son just back from a season of crabbing in Alaska.

MANILA CLAM CHOWDER

A steaming bowl of clam chowder is real Pacific Northwest comfort food. The small and tasty Manila clam is perfectly tender when not overcooked. Fresh parsley adds a bright and refreshing touch.

4 lbs (2 kg) Manila, butter, or steamer clams

1 cup (8 fl oz/250 ml) water
1 cup (8 fl oz/250 ml) dry white wine
3 garlic cloves, minced
1 bay leaf
½ cup (4 oz/125 g) butter
1 cup (8 oz/250 g) chopped onion
1 cup (8 oz/250 g) chopped celery
1 cup (8 oz/250 g) chopped carrot
1–4 garlic cloves, chopped

Left to right: Granville Island Chowder, Manila Clam Chowder

◙ Scrub the clams well to remove any grit; discard any clams that are open and do not close when handled or that have a broken shell.

◙ In a large stockpot, place the clams, water, wine, garlic and bay leaf and cover with a lid. Bring to a boil over high heat, reduce heat to medium, and steam the clams until they open, about 8–10 minutes.

◙ Remove the lid and set the clams aside to cool. Strain the clams and reserve the cooking liquid. Remove the clam meat from the shells and reserve.

◙ Melt 4 tablespoons of the butter in a large pot. Add the onion, carrot, celery and garlic and sauté over medium heat for 5 minutes. Add the herbs, reserved cooking liquid, pepper and potatoes; cover and continue to cook for 10 minutes or until potatoes are just tender. Add the half & half.

◙ In a small bowl, blend the milk and cornstarch together. Stirring briskly, add the cornstarch mixture to the chowder and continue stirring as the chowder thickens slightly. Add the reserved clams and heat through. Keep warm over very low heat; do not let boil.

◙ Just before serving, stir in the fresh parsley. Garnish each serving with ½ tablespoon of the remaining butter.

SERVES 6 AS A MAIN COURSE, 8 AS AN APPETIZER

British Columbia

GRANVILLE ISLAND CHOWDER

Vancouver's Granville Island Public Market opened for business in July 1979. Since then, locals and tourists have been lured by the splendid array of Pacific seafoods and succulent meats, exotic fruits and vegetables, and an endless variety of other foods and even flowers. Vancouverites cook many different versions of this chowder, depending on which fish and shellfish are available from the fishmonger at the Market.

6 bacon strips
1 onion, chopped
3 garlic cloves, minced
1 green bell pepper (capsicum), thinly sliced
2 carrots, thinly sliced
2 tablespoons chopped fresh parsley
4 cups (32 oz/1 kg) peeled, seeded and coarsely chopped
    fresh or canned tomatoes
3 cups (24 fl oz/750 ml) bottled clam juice
1½ cups (12 fl oz/375 ml) dry red wine
1 tablespoon fresh thyme, or 1½ teaspoons dried thyme
salt and freshly ground pepper to taste
2 cups (10 oz/300 g) diced peeled potatoes
2 lb (1 kg) mixed fresh shellfish and boneless fish such as
    peeled large shrimp, scallops, crab meat, salmon and
    snapper or other firm, white-fleshed fish fillets, cut
    into pieces

◙ Cut the bacon into 1-in (2.5-cm) pieces. Fry until crisp in a heavy pot or Dutch oven. Add the onion, garlic, green pepper, carrots and parsley, and cook over medium heat for 10 minutes, stirring occasionally.

◙ Add the tomatoes, clam juice, red wine, thyme, salt and pepper, and bring to a boil for 1 minute. Lower the heat, cover the pan, and simmer for 20 minutes. Add the potatoes, cover, and simmer for 30 minutes, or until the potatoes are tender.

◙ Add the shellfish and fish, and cook, stirring gently, just until the fish turns opaque, about 5 minutes.

SERVES 6–8

1 teaspoon dried thyme
1 teaspoon dried tarragon
½ teaspoon ground white pepper
6 cups (30 oz/900 g) cubed peeled potatoes
3 cups (24 fl oz/750 ml) half & half (half milk and half
    cream)
1 cup (8 fl oz/250 ml) milk
2 tablespoons cornstarch (cornflour)
½ cup (¾ oz/20 g) minced fresh parsley

Northern White Bean Soup with Chipotle Crème Fraîche

This bean soup, like all legume soups, will benefit by being made a day or two ahead and reheated to fully develop its flavors. The chipotle crème fraîche garnish adds a smoky note to the soup. Chipotle chilies are available in cans, packed in adobo sauce. If you can't find chipotle chilies, substitute a jalapeño and add some cilantro to the cream.

4 smoked bacon slices, cut into ¼-in (6-mm) strips
1 lb (500 g) dried Northern white (haricot) beans, soaked
    overnight in water to cover
1 carrot, finely diced
1 onion, finely diced
3 stalks celery, finely diced
2 tablespoons minced garlic
1 tablespoon chopped fresh sage
1 tablespoon chopped fresh thyme
10 cups (80 fl oz/2.5 l) chicken stock (see glossary)
salt and pepper to taste
Chipotle Crème Fraîche (recipe follows), optional
1 red bell pepper (capsicum), julienned (optional)

◼ In a large saucepan over medium heat, cook the bacon strips until crisp, about 7–10 minutes. Add the beans, onions, carrots, celery, garlic and herbs; sauté until the vegetables are tender and the onions are translucent, 5–7 minutes.

◼ Add the chicken stock and bring to a simmer. Reduce the heat to low. Cover and continue cooking over low heat, stirring every 30 minutes. Cook until the beans are completely tender, 2–3 hours. Adjust the seasonings with salt and pepper to taste if needed.

◼ Serve garnished with swirls of chipotle créme fraîche and bell pepper, if you like.

SERVES 6–8

CHIPOTLE CRÈME FRAÎCHE

◼ In a blender or food processor, combine ½ cup (4 fl oz/125 ml) crème fraîche or sour cream, 1 tablespoon minced chipotle chili, and 1 teaspoon paprika. Blend until smooth and thoroughly combined.

MAKES ½ CUP (4 FL OZ/125 ML)   *Photograph on pages 32-33*

Granny Smith Apple and Yakima Gouda Tartlets

Because of their firm flesh and tangy flavor, Granny Smith apples are perfect for baking. In this recipe, the classic combination of apples and cheese is enhanced by a flaky crust. Prepare the shells and filling ahead of time, then assemble and bake the tartlets just before serving.

PASTRY SHELLS

3 cups (12 oz/375 g) all-purpose (plain) flour
½ teaspoon salt
2 teaspoons sugar
⅔ cup (6 oz/180 g) cold lard
⅓ cup (3 oz/90 g) cold unsalted butter
5 tablespoons cold water

FILLING

1 tablespoon unsalted butter
3 large Granny Smith or other tart green apples, peeled,
    cored and coarsely chopped
1 tablespoon minced fresh thyme, or ¼ teaspoon dried thyme
6 oz (180 g) grated Yakima or other Gouda cheese, about 1½ cups

◼ In a food processor, combine the flour, salt and sugar. Process for 2 seconds. Cut the cold lard and butter into ½-in (1.5-cm) pieces. Add to the flour and process by pulsing the machine until the mixture resembles coarse crumbs. Add the water gradually and process until the dough forms a ball or sticks onto the blade. Divide the dough in half and gently form into a ball.

◼ Or, to make by hand: Measure the flour and sugar into a medium bowl. Cut the butter into the flour with a pastry blender or 2 knives until the mixture is the texture of course meal. Sprinkle the water a tablespoon at a time over the mixture while blending quickly with a fork. Gather the dough lightly together with your fingers to form a soft ball, working quickly so the dough will stay cold.

◼ Press the ball flat, wrap in plastic, and refrigerate for at least 1 hour.

◼ Roll the chilled dough on a pastry cloth or a lightly floured board, working from the center towards the edges, to a 1/8-in (3-mm) thickness. Using a 3-in (7.5-cm) round cutter, cut the dough into circles.

◼ Center a circle of dough over each 2½-in (6.5-cm) tartlet pan, and, beginning at the center, work toward the edges and up the sides, pressing the dough lightly into the tin with your fingertips. Push the dough against the edge of the tin to trim off the excess dough. Prick the bottom of the shell with a fork. Refrigerate until cold and firm.

◼ Preheat an oven to 400°F (200°C). Bake the shells for 5 minutes, then reduce the heat to 350°F (180°C) and bake until light brown, about 3–5 minutes more. Remove from the oven and set aside, leaving the oven on.

◼ Melt the butter in a saucepan, add the apples and thyme, and cook over low heat until slightly soft but not mushy, about 5 minutes. Remove from the heat.

◼ Place 1 tablespoon of the apple filling in each shell and press down lightly to flatten the mixture. Top with grated Gouda cheese.

◼ Bake at 350°F (180°C) for about 10 minutes, or until the cheese is melted and the shells are light brown. Let cool slightly and serve warm.

MAKES 48 TARTLETS   *Photograph on pages 32-33*

Spiced Onion and Ale Soup

Dark ale gives this hearty soup a sweet richness. Serve it in front of the fire on a damp winter evening. Try it with garlic croutons, a sprinkling of sharp Cheddar melted on top, and, of course, a hearty ale to wash it down.

2 tablespoons butter
4 yellow (brown) onions, cut into thin slices
1 cup (6 oz/170 g) diced smoked ham
3 tablespoons minced garlic
¼ teaspoon ground allspice
1 tablespoon chopped fresh thyme, or 1 teaspoon dried thyme
¼ cup (2 fl oz/60 ml) Dijon mustard
1½ cups (12 fl oz/375 ml) pale ale
8 cups (64 fl oz/ 2 l) chicken stock (see glossary)
2 tablespoons cornstarch (cornflour) mixed with ½ cup (4
    oz/125 ml) cold water
salt and pepper to taste
2 cups (8 oz/250 g) grated sharp Cheddar cheese
½ cup (3oz/60 g) sliced green (spring) onions

◼ In a large, heavy saucepan or Dutch oven over medium heat, melt the butter and cook the onions, ham, garlic, allspice and thyme, stirring frequently until the onions are evenly caramelized, 10–15 minutes.

◼ Add the mustard, ale and chicken stock and bring to a simmer for 15–20 minutes. Whisk in the cornstarch and water mixture and boil gently for 4–5 minutes to thicken. Reduce the heat to a low simmer and add salt and pepper.

◼ Serve garnished with grated Cheddar and green onions.

SERVES 6–8

Shrimp Wonton Soup with Vegetable Flowers

SHRIMP WONTON SOUP WITH VEGETABLE FLOWERS

A light, satisfying soup with the fanciful touch of vegetable flowers. Chopped chicken, pork or crab may be substituted for the shrimp.

WONTONS

6 oz (185 g) raw shrimp meat
1 teaspoon soy sauce
1 teaspoon minced fresh ginger
¼ teaspoon salt
1 tablespoon egg white
1 garlic clove, minced
2 tablespoons minced green (spring) onion
2 tablespoons minced red bell pepper (capsicum)
16 wonton skins

SOUP

4 green (spring) onions
8 cups (64 fl oz/2 l) rich chicken stock (see glossary)
1 tablespoon soy sauce
1 tablespoon slivered fresh ginger
2 Chinese *lop chong* sausages, thinly sliced (optional)
wontons (above)
4 large shrimp, sliced in half lengthwise
2-in (6-cm) piece zucchini (courgette), sliced into 8 flowers*

2-in (6-cm) piece yellow summer squash (vegetable marrow), sliced into 8 flowers*
2-in (6-cm) piece carrot, sliced into 8 flowers*
2 fresh shiitake mushrooms, thinly sliced, about ½ cup (2 oz/60 g), optional
4 fresh cilantro (coriander) sprigs
4 sprigs of enoki mushrooms (optional)

◙ To make the wontons: Place the shrimp, soy, ginger, salt and egg white in a blender or food processor. Chop until well combined. Transfer the mixture to a small bowl and mix in the garlic, green onion and red pepper. Divide the filling among the wonton skins, placing about 1 teaspoon of filling about 1 in (2.5 cm) from one corner of each skin. Dip your fingers into water and lightly dampen the outside edge of the wontons. Fold up 1 corner of a wonton to cover the filling, then fold it over again. Turn the wonton so that the triangle is toward you. Dampen the left corner of the wonton with a little water. Fold the right corner over and affix it to the left corner, then pull stuffed center towards you. Repeat to fold all of the remaining wonton. Refrigerate until needed.

◙ To make the soup: Cut the green part off the green onions and cut into thin diagonal slices. Cut the root end off the white part of the green onions. Make 4–5 lengthwise cuts through each onion without going all the way through to the end. Spread the pieces apart and place the onions in ice water to open up.

◙ In a large pot, combine the chicken stock, soy sauce and ginger. Bring to a boil and drop in the Chinese sausage and wontons. Cook for 3 minutes, then drop in the shrimp, zucchini, squash, carrot and shiitake mushrooms. Boil for approximately 2 more minutes, or until the wontons are tender.

◙ Divide the soup among 4 bowls and garnish with cilantro sprigs, enoki mushrooms, sliced green onion and vegetable flowers.

SERVES 4 AS A LIGHT ENTRÉE, 8 AS A STARTER

* *To make the vegetable flowers, cut four to six ⅛-in (3-mm) channels down the sides of the vegetable pieces with a channel knife or paring knife, then slice into flowers.*

Western Washington

SPICY SQUASH BISQUE WITH ROOT VEGETABLES

Organic or home-grown squash are best for this recipe because their flavor is much more pronounced and sweet. For a hearty main-course meal, add slices of smoked sausage to the bisque, and accompany with Winter Greens with Spicy Walnuts, Apples and Cranberry Vinaigrette (recipe on page 64) and hot corn muffins.

4–6 orange winter squashes, about 5–6 in (13–15 cm) in diameter
4 tablespoons (2 fl oz/60 ml) olive oil
1½ cup (12 oz/375 g) diced onion
2 garlic cloves, minced
4 cups (about 1¼ lb/625 g) cubed sweet winter squash and/ or pumpkin
1½ teaspoons ground cumin
1 teaspoon coriander seed, crushed
¼ teaspoon ground nutmeg
1 teaspoon cardamom seed, crushed
¼ teaspoon cayenne pepper
1 bay leaf
1½ teaspoons salt, or to taste
3½ cups (28 fl oz/800 ml) rich chicken stock (see glossary)
¾ cup (6 fl oz/180 ml) sour cream
⅓ cup (1½ oz/45 g) corn kernels
½ cup (4 oz/125 g) julienned carrots
⅓ cup (3 oz/90 g) julienned parsnips

⅓ cup (2 oz/60 g) thin-diagonal-cut celery
1 small leek, white part only, thinly sliced into rounds
2 green (spring) onions, thinly sliced on the diagonal

◙ Preheat an oven to 350°F (180°C). To prepare the squash bowls: Cut the top one third off of the squashes. Scoop out the seeds and loose fiber thoroughly. Place the lids back on the squash. Place the squash on a baking sheet and bake for 30 minutes, or until the flesh is tender. Set aside.

◙ To make the soup: Meanwhile, in a large, heavy saucepan, heat 2 tablespoons of the olive oil over medium-high heat; add the onions and sauté for 2–3 minutes. Add the squash, garlic, spices and seasonings. Sauté for another 2–3 minutes. Add the chicken stock and bring to a boil. Turn down the heat, partially cover the pan, and simmer for approximately 15–18 minutes, or until the squash is very tender.

◙ Remove from the heat; remove and discard the bay leaf. In a blender or food processor, carefully purée the hot soup in small batches with the sour cream. Pour the processed soup back in the pot and keep warm.

◙ To serve the soup: In a large skillet, place the remaining 2 tablespoons of olive oil and heat over medium-high heat. Toss in the vegetables and sauté quickly until tender, about 2–3 minutes. Divide the soup among the warm cooked squashes or soup bowls, and mound a few vegetables in the center of each serving. Garnish with green onions.

SERVES 4–6

Spicy Squash Bisque with Root Vegetables

SPRING ASPARAGUS SOUP

This light, creamy asparagus soup is easy to prepare, yet elegant enough for a special luncheon; or serve it with country baked ham and fresh biscuits for a springtime Sunday dinner.

2 lb (1 kg) trimmed fresh asparagus
¼ cup (2 fl oz/60 ml) olive oil
1 cup (8 oz/250 g) diced yellow (brown) onions
½ cup (4 oz/125 g) diced shallots
1½ cups (7½ oz/330 g) peeled and diced russet potatoes
5–6 cups (40–48 fl oz) chicken stock (see glossary)
about 1 cup (8 fl oz/250 ml) heavy (double) cream
salt and freshly ground white pepper to taste

◼ Remove the tips from half of the asparagus, reserving the stalks. Blanch the tips in boiling water until bright green, about 30 seconds. Remove the asparagus from the water and plunge them into cold water, drain, and set aside. Cut the remaining asparagus and reserved stalks into pieces.
◼ Heat the olive oil in a large saucepan, add the onions and shallots, and cook over moderate heat until the onions are translucent, about 5–7 minutes. Add the potatoes and asparagus and cook until the asparagus turns bright green. Add the chicken stock and bring just to a boil. Reduce the heat and simmer for 20 minutes, or until the potatoes and asparagus are tender.
◼ Purée the soup in batches in a food processor until smooth. Return the soup to the saucepan and heat to steaming. Add the cream to the desired thickness and heat thoroughly; do *not* boil. Adjust the seasoning to taste.
◼ Garnish with asparagus tips to serve.

SERVES 6

Top to bottom: Spring Asparagus Soup, Chilled Bing Cherry Soup

CHILLED BING CHERRY SOUP

Deep garnet Bing cherries are perfect for this summer-evening soup, which is both tart and sweet. A simple entrée such as grilled fish or chicken could follow, making an elegant little meal.

2 cups (16 fl oz/500 ml) water
1 cup (8 fl oz/250 ml) Muscat or sweet Riesling wine
2–3 tablespoons fresh lemon juice
1 teaspoon grated lemon zest
¾ cup (6 oz/185 g) sugar
4 juniper berries, crushed
4 peppercorns
6 whole cloves
1 cinnamon stick
6 cups (3 lb/1.5 kg) pitted Bing cherries
1 tablespoon cornstarch (cornflour)
6 tablespoons (3 fl oz/90 ml) sour cream

◼ Add the water, wine, lemon juice, lemon zest, sugar and spices to a medium stockpot and bring to a boil. Add the cherries and bring to a boil again. During the last 5 minutes of cooking, mix the cornstarch with 1 tablespoon water; whisk into the hot liquid. Cover the pot with a lid and remove from the heat. Allow the cherries to steep for at least 30 minutes.
◼ Strain the cherries from the juice, reserving the juice and the cherries. Discard the cinnamon stick, cloves, juniper berries and peppercorns. Reserve 18 of the whole cherries. In batches, purée the remaining cherries in a food processor until smooth. Add the reserved juice; chill.
◼ Serve well chilled in cold bowls. Garnish each bowl with 3 whole cherries and a swirl of sour cream.

SERVES 6

PALOUSE LENTIL SOUP

Most of the lentils grown in the United States come from the rolling-hill region of eastern Washington and northern Idaho called the Palouse. Lentils are high in fiber and low in fat, and fit all the requirements for today's healthful diet. Served with a green salad and bread, this thick, hearty soup makes a main course.

5 oz (155 g) diced pepper bacon or smoked bacon
1 cup (8 oz/250 g) finely diced yellow (brown) onion
1 cup (6 oz/180 g) finely diced celery
1 cup (8 oz/250 g) finely diced carrot
2 garlic cloves, minced
2 teaspoons fresh marjoram, or 1 teaspoon dried marjoram
1¼ cups (7½ oz/230 g) dried lentils
6–7 cups (48–56 fl oz/1.5–1.8 l) chicken stock (see glossary)
1 bay leaf
salt and freshly ground pepper to taste

◼ In a large, heavy saucepan or Dutch oven, sauté the bacon over moderate heat until crisp and brown. Remove the bacon from the pan and set aside. Add the onion, celery, carrot, garlic and marjoram and cook for about 5 minutes, or until the onion is translucent.
◼ Add the lentils, chicken stock and bay leaf, and bring just to a boil. Reduce the heat to low and simmer until the lentils are tender, about 30 minutes. Taste and adjust the seasoning. If the soup becomes too thick during cooking, add more chicken stock.
◼ Garnish with pepper bacon.

SERVES 6–8

Top to bottom: Palouse Lentil Soup, Scotch Broth

SCOTCH BROTH

This hearty homemade soup makes a memorable meal served with crusty bread and a salad. Scotch broth lends itself to ahead-of-time cooking and will keep in the refrigerator for 3–4 days. Thin with chicken stock if necessary.

STOCK

1½–2 lb (750 g–1 kg) lamb blade (shoulder) steaks or other
    lean lamb with bones
flour seasoned with salt and pepper
3 tablespoons olive oil or vegetable oil
½ cup (4 oz/125 g) *each* chopped carrot and onion
½ cup (3 oz/90 g) chopped celery
2 large garlic cloves, minced
1 teaspoon sugar
6 cups (48 fl oz/1.5 l) water
¼ cup (⅓ oz/10 g) chopped fresh parsley
1 bay leaf
one 3-in (7.5-cm) sprig fresh thyme, or ½ teaspoon dried thyme
¾ teaspoon salt
8–10 whole peppercorns

½ cup (3 oz/90 g) pearl barley
2 large carrots, diced

1 small white turnip, julienned
salt and pepper to taste
parsley and grated lemon zest for garnish

◼ Trim the meat of any fat and dredge the meat lightly in the seasoned flour. Heat the oil in a heavy skillet, add the meat and bones, and brown well. Transfer to a soup kettle.
◼ In the same skillet, sauté the chopped carrot, onion, celery and garlic in the meat drippings for 1–2 minutes. Sprinkle the sugar over the vegetables and continue to cook, stirring constantly. The vegetables should caramelize slightly but not burn. Add the vegetables to the meat and bones.
◼ Stir about 1 cup (8 fl oz/250 ml) of the water into the skillet, scrape up the drippings, and pour them over the meat and vegetables. Add the remaining water, parsley, bay leaf, thyme, salt and peppercorns. Cover and bring to a boil. Reduce the heat and simmer slowly for 2 hours or until the meat is tender.
◼ Strain the stock and degrease. Remove the meat from the bones, dice, and reserve. Combine the strained stock and pearl barley in the soup kettle and cook for 30 minutes. Add the reserved meat and diced carrots and turnip, and cook an additional 20 minutes, or until the vegetables are tender. Adjust the seasonings.
◼ Serve garnished with fresh parsley and a pinch of lemon zest.

SERVES 4–6

ROASTED SPICY NORTHWEST NUTS

These roasted nuts have just enough "zip" to make you come back for more. Roast them in big batches and store them for the holiday season.

1 lb (500 g) walnut halves and pieces
1 lb (500 g) hazelnuts
⅓ cup (4 fl oz/125 ml) honey
1½ teaspoons ground ginger
1½ teaspoons ground coriander
½ teaspoon cayenne pepper
1 tablespoon kosher salt

❖ Preheat an oven to 375°F (190°C). In a large roasting pan, toast the walnuts and hazelnuts for 5 minutes in the preheated oven, stirring once or twice. While the nuts are toasting, heat all the remaining ingredients except the salt in a small saucepan over medium heat. Bring the mixture to a low boil and remove from the heat.

❖ Remove the nuts from the oven, leaving the oven on. Pour the honey mixture over the toasted nuts and stir thoroughly to evenly coat all the nuts. Return the nuts to the oven and toast for 15–20 minutes more, stirring once or twice. Break a few of the nuts in half to see if they are golden brown inside. When they have reached this stage, remove the nuts from the oven and sprinkle the kosher salt evenly over them. To prevent them from sticking together, stir the nuts every 5 minutes for the first 15 minutes, then every 10 minutes until they are completely cool.

❖ Store in an airtight container.

MAKES 2 LBS (1 KG)

YAKIMA BEEFSTEAK-TOMATO SALSA WITH FRESH TORTILLA CHIPS

The El Ranchito tortilla factory, restaurant, and Mexican import store in Zillah, Washington, is a favorite stop for tourists and a busy hub for the Mexican-American community. El Ranchito's excellent tortillas, which are distributed throughout the Pacific Northwest, make delicious chips, especially when served with this bright-red fresh salsa made with local beefsteak tomatoes in season. On a hot night, serve this vibrant dip with freshly fried chips as a first course in place of soup or salad.

SALSA

2 large roasted red bell peppers (capsicums) or 3 Anaheim (mild green) chili peppers (see glossary)
3 large or 6 small ripe beefsteak tomatoes
1 large firm cucumber
1 white onion
2 garlic cloves, minced
¾ cup (1 oz/30 g) chopped fresh cilantro (coriander)
3 tablespoons fresh lime juice
¼ cup (2 fl oz/60 ml) seasoned rice wine vinegar
1 teaspoon ground cumin
salt and pepper to taste

TORTILLA CHIPS

1 package (12) fresh corn tortillas
oil for frying

❖ Cut the tomatoes in half, remove the seeds and excess juice, and chop. Peel and chop the cucumber and onion. Mix the tomatoes, cucumber and onion in a large bowl. Add the garlic to the mixture and stir in the cilantro, lime juice, vinegar and cumin.

❖ Peel the charred peppers, remove the seeds and ribs, chop, and add to the salsa. Add salt and pepper to taste. Chill.

❖ Cut the tortillas into sixths. Heat about 3 in (7.5 cm) of oil to 375°F (190°C) in a deep, heavy pan (a cube of bread will brown in 1 minute at the correct temperature). Fry the chips for 1–2 minutes, or until golden. Drain on paper towels.

MAKES 4 CUPS (32 FL OZ/ 1 L) SALSA AND 72 CHIPS

Clockwise from left: Yakima Beefsteak-Tomato Salsa with Fresh Tortilla Chips, Roasted Spicy Northwest Nuts, and Beer-Battered Walla Walla Onion Rings

BEER-BATTERED WALLA WALLA ONION RINGS

The original seeds of the famous sweet onions of Walla Walla reportedly were brought from Spain in a soldier's coat pocket. These large, mild onions are a summer favorite in the Northwest.

Batter for Microbrew Beer–Battered Fish (recipe on page 98)
½ cup (2 oz/60 g) all-purpose (plain) flour
½ teaspoon salt
2 large, symmetrical Walla Walla Sweet onions or other mild white onions, sliced ⅓ in (8 mm) thick and separated into rings
vegetable oil for frying

▧ Prepare the batter and set aside.
▧ Place the flour and salt in a sack. Add the onion rings and shake gently to dredge with the flour.
▧ Heat 2–3 in (5–7.5 cm) of vegetable oil to 350°–375° F (180°–190°C) in a deep, heavy pan (a cube of bread will brown in 1 minute at the correct temperature). Dip the onion rings in the batter and fry in batches until golden, about 2 minutes.
▧ Drain on paper towels and serve immediately.

SERVES 4

Islands

OYSTERS ON THE HALF SHELL WITH HOWDY BEACH COCKTAIL SAUCE

The inlets and backwaters of the San Juan Islands hide many little coves where the wild oyster flourishes. Howdy Beach is an ideal spot for a picnic beginning with fresh oysters and this spicy sauce.

HOWDY BEACH COCKTAIL SAUCE

2 cups (16 fl oz/500 ml) ketchup (tomato sauce)
1/2 cup (4 oz/125 g) chopped red (Spanish) onion
4–6 crushed garlic cloves
½ cup (4 fl oz/125 ml) fresh lemon juice
1 jigger (3 tablespoons) tequila (optional)
4 tablespoons (2 fl oz/60 ml) horseradish
2 drops Worcestershire sauce
2 drops Tabasco (hot pepper) sauce

4–6 oysters per person
lemon wedges

◙ To prepare the sauce: In a medium saucepan, blend all of the sauce ingredients and simmer over low heat for 20 minutes. Do not allow to boil.
◙ Stir occasionally with a wooden spoon. Remove from the heat and let cool. Store in the refrigerator in an airtight glass or plastic container for up to 3 weeks.
◙ To shuck the oysters, begin by rinsing them with cold water to remove grit and sand. Place an oyster on a flat hard surface with the rounded side down. Using a towel or a glove, hold the oyster against the work surface with your left hand. With your right hand holding an oyster knife, insert the blade at the hinge of the shell and twist to lever the oyster open. Continue pushing the blade between the shells, cutting the muscle.
◙ Discard the top shell and wipe the edge of the bottom shell free of debris. Cut under the muscle by moving the blade between the oyster and the shell. Try to disturb the oyster and its liquor as little as possible. Repeat to shuck the remaining oysters.
◙ Serve immediately on cracked ice with cocktail sauce and lemon wedges.

MAKES 3 CUPS (24 FL OZ/750 ML) SAUCE

Oysters on the Half Shell with Howdy Beach Cocktail Sauce

Calamari with Lemon Aïoli

CALAMARI WITH LEMON AÏOLI

Squid season is marked every fall by swarms of midnight harvesters who gather on docks around Puget Sound with buckets and flashlights, hoping for a good catch of this tasty sea creature.

AÏOLI

1 egg
1 egg yolk
3 roasted garlic cloves (recipe on page 66)
3 garlic cloves
⅓ cup (3 fl oz/80 ml) fresh lemon juice
1 cup (8 fl oz/250 ml) good olive oil
salt to taste
grated zest of 1 lemon

1 cup (4 oz/125 g) all-purpose (plain) flour
1 tablespoon cornstarch (cornflour)
1 teaspoon salt

½ teaspoon ground white pepper
peanut (groundnut) oil for frying
2 lb (1 kg) small squid, cleaned and cut into ¼-in (6-mm) rings
lemon wedges for garnish

▨ To make the aïoli: Place the egg, egg yolk, garlic and lemon juice in a blender or food processor and process for 3 minutes, or until smooth and creamy. While the machine is running, gradually drizzle in the olive oil. After the aïoli thickens, stir in the salt and lemon zest. Refrigerate for at least 1 hour before use so the flavors can marry.
▨ Blend the flour, cornstarch, salt and pepper in a medium bowl.
▨ In a deep, heavy skillet, heat the oil to 350°F (180°C). Dredge the squid rings, a few at a time, in the flour. Shake off the excess flour and sauté the squid in the hot oil until barely golden, about 2 minutes. With tongs or a slotted spoon, remove the squid and let drain briefly on paper towels. Repeat until all the squid is cooked.
▨ Serve on warm plates with wedges of lemon and the aïoli in little ramekins for dipping.

SERVES 6

Oregon

PICKLED SALMON

A classic Northwest tradition—especially when you're up to your ears in fresh salmon. This is an instant hors d'oeuvre to pull from your fridge on short notice. Serve it with Walnut-Stout Bread (recipe on page 176) and a cold mug of pilsner.

2 lb (1 kg) salmon fillet, skinned and cut into 1-in (2.5-cm) cubes
1 cup (8 oz/250 g) kosher salt
4 cups (32 fl oz/1 l) distilled white vinegar
4 cups (32 fl oz/ 1 l) water
½ cup (4 fl oz/125 ml) olive oil
1 large onion cut into ¼-in (6-mm) slices
½ cup (3 oz/90 g) pickling spices
½ cup (4 oz/125 g) sugar
6 garlic cloves
2 large fresh rosemary sprigs
2 large fresh dill sprigs
2 jalapeños (hot green) chili peppers, split lengthwise

◨ Place the salmon pieces in a single layer in a nonaluminum container; sprinkle them evenly with the kosher salt. Let sit for 45 minutes at room temperature. Rinse and drain them.
◨ Place the salmon in a large saucepan and add cold water to cover the fish by 2 in (5 cm). Bring to a low simmer over medium heat and remove from the stove. Let sit for 5 minutes, then drain off the poaching liquid.
◨ Mix all of the remaining ingredients together in a large bowl. Add the cooked salmon and gently toss it with this mixture. Transfer the contents of the bowl to an earthenware crock or casserole.
◨ Cover and refrigerate for 24 hours. Pickled salmon will keep in the refrigerator for up to 1 week.

MAKES ABOUT 2 LB (2 KG)

Western Washington

PICKLED HERRING WITH SOUR CREAM AND CUCUMBER

Scandinavians brought pickled herring to the Pacific Northwest, and it's still a favorite here. Pickled salmon (see recipe above) could also be used in this recipe. Serve with crackers or toasted bread rounds as an appetizer or on a smorgasbord.

2 jars pickled herring in wine 9 oz (280 g) each, drained
3 tablespoons sour cream
1 tablespoon red wine vinegar
1 teaspoon sugar
¼ teaspoon ground black pepper
¼ teaspoon celery seed
½ cucumber
½ red (Spanish) onion, thinly sliced

◨ Place the herring, sour cream, vinegar, sugar, black pepper and celery seed in a bowl and toss together. Cut the cucumber in half lengthwise and scoop out the seeds, then cut it in half lengthwise again to form long strips. Cut the strips into ¼-in-(6-mm)-thick slices and add to the herring along with the red onion. Toss well.
◨ Chill well before serving.

SERVES 6–8

Left to right: Pickled Salmon, Pickled Herring with Sour Cream and Cucumber

Oregon

WILD MUSHROOM FILO PACKETS

We're blessed with a profusion of wild mushrooms in the Pacific Northwest, but these appetizers will work well with cultivated varieties as well. Don't be afraid to improvise with both fresh and dried mushrooms.

1 tablespoon minced garlic
1 tablespoon chopped fresh thyme, or 1 teaspoon dried thyme
2 tablespoons shallots or onion, minced
3 tablespoons olive oil
2 lb (1 kg) mixed wild mushrooms, sliced
½ cup (4 fl oz/125 ml) dry white wine
1 teaspoon paprika
1 cup (4 oz/125 g) freshly grated Parmesan cheese
1 teaspoon salt
½ teaspoon ground black pepper
1 cup (6 oz/180 g) sliced green (spring) onions
1 egg
½ cup (4 oz/120 g) butter, melted
½ package filo dough, about 28–30 sheets, cut in half to form 8-by-12-in (20-by-30-cm) rectangles

◫ In a large saucepan over low heat, sweat the garlic, thyme and shallots in the olive oil until the garlic is soft, about 3–5 minutes. Add the sliced mushrooms, raise the heat and sauté for 8–10 minutes. Add the white wine and paprika and cook the mixture until nearly all the liquid is boiled away, 5–10 minutes.
◫ Transfer the mushroom mixture to a large bowl and add the Parmesan, salt and pepper, green onions and the egg; blend thoroughly.
◫ Preheat an oven to 375°F (190°C). Place a sheet of filo dough on a clean dry surface, brush lightly with melted butter, place a second sheet on top and brush it lightly also. Drop 2 tablespoons of the mushroom filling about 2 in (5 cm) from one short edge of the dough, centered between the long edges. Fold each long edge to center, overlapping slightly and enclosing the filling. Fold the nearer short edge up over the filling, then continue folding the rectangle containing the filling over and over to take up the remaining dough. You should end up with a rectangle approximately 2-by-3½-in (5-by-8.5-cm). Repeat until all the filling and the filo dough have been used.
◫ Place the packets, flap down, on a lightly greased baking sheet. Brush remaining melted butter over the packets. Bake in the preheated oven for 10–15 minutes, or until golden brown and crisp.

SERVES 6–8

Western Washington

CRAB-STUFFED MOREL MUSHROOMS

If you're an experienced mushroom hunter, here's a delicious way to feast on your finds. Or look for morels at farmers' markets and specialty foods stores. If fresh morel mushrooms are not available, substitute white button, crimini, or fresh shiitake mushrooms.

STUFFING

½ cup (2 oz) coarsely chopped fresh morel mushrooms, or ½ oz (15 g) dried morels, soaked in warm water for 30 minutes
1 cup (4 oz/125 g) coarsely chopped white button (cultivated) mushrooms
4 teaspoons fresh lemon juice
4 tablespoons (2 oz/60 g) butter

¼ cup (1½ oz/45 g) minced celery
¼ cup (2 oz/60 g) minced onion
1 tablespoon minced garlic
1 large green (spring) onion, minced
1 teaspoon chopped fresh lemon thyme or thyme (optional)
¾ cup (6 fl oz/180 ml) heavy (double) cream
8 oz (250 g) fresh or frozen Dungeness crab meat
¼ teaspoon salt
dash of Tabasco (hot pepper) sauce
3 tablespoons minced fresh parsley
⅓ cup (1½ oz/45 g) freshly grated Italian Parmesan cheese
½ cup (2 oz/60 g) dry bread crumbs
12–15 large fresh morel mushrooms, cut in half and stems trimmed, or 1 lb (500 g) large white button (cultivated) mushrooms, stemmed
½ cup (4 fl oz/125 ml) dry white wine

◫ Preheat an oven to 425°F (220°C). To make the stuffing: In a food processor, place the ½ cup morels, white mushrooms and lemon juice and process until minced.
◫ In a large skillet, melt the butter over medium-high heat. Add the minced mushrooms, celery, onion, garlic, green onion and lemon thyme. Cook this mixture, stirring often, until almost all the liquid has evaporated, about 2–3 minutes. Add the cream and cook until reduced by half, lowering the heat as needed. Add the crab and cook for about 1–3 more minutes, or until almost all the liquid has evaporated.
◫ Remove from the heat and stir in the seasonings, parsley, cheese and as many bread crumbs as needed to make a moist but not dry mixture. Let cool.
◫ Stuff the mushrooms with the mixture, dividing it evenly among them. Sprinkle the tops with some of the leftover bread crumbs. Place a single layer of mushrooms in a baking dish. Pour the white wine around the mushrooms and bake in the preheated oven for 14–17 minutes, or until the mushrooms are tender. Serve immediately.

SERVES 8–10

Islands

WILD GREENS WITH RED WINE VINAIGRETTE

As soon as spring appears, so do the market gardeners. From cities and villages around the Sound they bring trays of carefully tended and foraged greens to the farmers' markets. The stunning variety and abundance are an inspiration to salad makers. Because of their vivid flavor and delicate texture, these unusual lettuces require only a simple dressing to enhance their distinctiveness.

8 cups (1⅜ lb/685 g) washed and dried mixed greens such as red leaf, butterhead, arugula, mâche (corn salad), watercress, mizuna, endive, escarole, frisée, amaranth, burnet, lemon balm, dandelion, radicchio, miner's lettuce and chicory (curly endive)
¼ cup (⅓ oz/10 g) chopped fresh parsley or mild fresh herbs
½ cup (4 fl oz/125 ml) olive oil
½ cup (4 fl oz/125 ml) extra-virgin olive oil
⅓ cup (3 fl oz/80 ml) good red wine vinegar
1 garlic clove, minced
salt and freshly ground black pepper to taste

◫ Tear large leaves into bite-sized pieces and leave smaller leaves whole. Place in a large nonaluminum bowl with herbs.
◫ In a separate container, whisk the olive oils and vinegar together. Add garlic and season to taste. Stir to blend.
◫ Drizzle the dressing onto the greens a little at a time. Gently toss the greens. Add only enough dressing to lightly coat the leaves. Reserve the remaining dressing for later use.
◫ Serve the greens immediately on chilled plates.

SERVES 6–8 *Photograph on pages 32-33*

Top to bottom: Crab-Stuffed Morel Mushrooms, Wild Mushroom Filo Packets

MINI SCALLION BISCUITS WITH SMOKED SALMON SPREAD AND PICKLED ONIONS

This smoked salmon spread can be made up to 2 days in advance and kept covered in the refrigerator. Let it come to room temperature before serving. If available, salmon eggs, sometimes called salmon pearls, make a delicious garnish for the biscuits.

1 small red (Spanish) onion, quartered lengthwise and thinly
    sliced crosswise
¼ cup (2 fl oz/60 ml) seasoned rice wine vinegar
2 cups (8 oz/250 g) all-purpose (plain) flour
2 teaspoons baking powder
1¼ teaspoons salt
¼ teaspoon dry mustard
¼ teaspoon ground black pepper
⅓ cup (3 oz/90 g) vegetable shortening
2 large green (spring) onions, minced
1 tablespoon minced fresh parsley
¾ cup (6 fl oz/180 ml) plus 1½ tablespoons milk
Smoked Salmon Spread (recipe follows)
24 small fresh dill sprigs for garnish

☒ Preheat an oven to 425°F (220°C). In a medium bowl, toss the onion and vinegar. Cover and set aside to marinate for at least 30 minutes or up to 3 hours.
☒ Into a large bowl, sift the flour, baking powder, salt, dry mustard and black pepper together. Cut in the shortening with a pastry cutter or 2 knives, then stir in the green onions and parsley. *Lightly* stir in enough milk with a fork to make a soft dough. Turn the dough out onto a lightly floured surface.
☒ Lightly pat the dough out to a ¾-in (2-cm) thickness. Sprinkle the dough with a little flour. Cut into 15 rounds with a 1½-in (1.5-cm) biscuit cutter. (Do not twist the cutter when cutting dough.)
☒ Place the biscuits, sides touching, on a greased baking sheet. (Note: The biscuits can be prepared up to this point, then refrigerated up to 4 hours before baking.)
☒ Bake for about 18–20 minutes, or until golden.
☒ Let the biscuits cool for about 10 minutes. Split the biscuits in half horizontally. Spread the biscuit bottoms with smoked salmon spread and top each with a little of the pickled onion and a dill sprig. Arrange the biscuits on a serving platter, replace the top half of the biscuits slightly askew, and serve immediately.

MAKES 15 BISCUITS; SERVES 6–8

SMOKED SALMON SPREAD

4 oz (125 g) cream cheese at room temperature
3 oz (90 g) thinly sliced cold smoked salmon
½ teaspoon prepared horseradish
1 teaspoon fresh lemon juice
½ teaspoon minced fresh dill

☒ In a food processor, combine the cream cheese and half of the smoked salmon and process until smooth. Add the horseradish and lemon juice and process, scraping down the sides as necessary, until smooth. Add the dill and process until incorporated.
☒ Transfer the spread to a small bowl. Mince the remaining salmon and stir it into the spread until blended.

MAKES ¾ CUP (7 OZ/220 G)

WHIFFIN SPIT SPOT PRAWNS WITH ANISE HYSSOP MAYONNAISE

The extensive use of fresh garden herbs is a hallmark of Northwest cuisine. Ranch cooks and farm wives have always had a patch of fresh herbs by the back door, some for medicinal purposes, others to brighten a meal on a dreary day. Today savvy restaurateurs and creative chefs are using fresh herbs in remarkable new ways.

1 bottle good Northwest microbrewed beer (12 oz /375 ml),
    or other local beer
4 cups (32 fl oz/1 l) water
6 garlic cloves, crushed
1 bay leaf
6 whole cloves
6 peppercorns
24 large spot prawns or other large shrimp in the shell,
    about 1½ lb (24 oz/750 g)
Anise Hyssop Mayonnaise (recipe follows)

Left to right: Mini Scallion Biscuits with Smoked Salmon Spread and Pickled Onions, Whiffin Spit Spot Prawns with Anise Hyssop Mayonnaise

▨ Bring all the ingredients except the prawns to a boil in a large stockpot. Let the mixture bubble for 2 minutes (for flavors to infuse), then add the prawns and cover with a tight-fitting lid.
▨ Return the pot to a boil and cook for about 2 minutes, then remove from the heat and let the prawns steep for 10 minutes.
▨ Drain the prawns and rinse them with cold water. Refrigerate until ready to serve. If preferred, the prawns may be peeled before serving.
▨ Serve on chilled plates with anise hyssop mayonnaise for dipping.

SERVES 6

ANISE HYSSOP MAYONNAISE

1 shallot, coarsely chopped
2 tablespoons seasoned rice wine vinegar
2 tablespoons dry white wine
½ cup (2 oz/60 g) coarsely chopped fennel bulb
2 large egg yolks
1 tablespoon fresh lemon juice
1 tablespoon Pernod

1 teaspoon salt
¾ cup (6 fl oz/180 ml) peanut (groundnut) oil
¾ cup (6 fl oz/180 ml) mild olive oil
¼ cup (⅓ oz/10 g) coarsely chopped anise hyssop or fresh basil leaves

▨ In a small saucepan, place the shallot, vinegar, white wine and fennel. Over medium heat, simmer the mixture for 10 minutes, or until the shallot and fennel are tender and the liquid is reduced by half.
▨ In a blender or food processor, place the egg yolks, lemon juice, Pernod and salt. Process until the yolks are pale yellow, about 4 minutes.
▨ With the machine on high speed, pour in the warm fennel mixture. Process until smooth, another 4 minutes, then add the oils in a slow, steady stream. The mixture will start to thicken as you reach the halfway point.
▨ After the oil is incorporated, add the anise leaves and pulse a few times to finely chop the leaves. Refrigerate for 1 hour so the flavors can marry.

MAKES 2 CUPS (16 FL OZ/500 ML)

GREEN CHILI CORN CAKES WITH STURGEON CAVIAR

The slight nip of green chilies complements the sweetness of the cornmeal in these delicate cakes paired with salty caviar. Serve a good sparkling wine to complete the trio of tastes.

1 cup (8 fl oz/250 ml) milk
1 egg
2 tablespoons melted butter
½ cup (3½ oz/100 g) minced canned or fresh-roasted, peeled mild green chili peppers
½ cup (2 oz/60 g) all-purpose (plain) flour
½ cup (3 oz/90 g) cornmeal (yellow maize flour)
2 teaspoons baking powder
½ teaspoon salt
½ teaspoon ground cumin
½ cup (4 fl oz/125 ml) crème fraîche or sour cream
2 oz (60 g) Columbia River sturgeon caviar or other caviar
lime wedges for garnish

▨ In a medium bowl, whisk together the milk, egg, melted butter and green chilies. Gradually blend in the dry ingredients, mixing thoroughly between additions to avoid lumps.
▨ Cook the corn cakes by dropping ⅛ cupfuls (1-oz portions) onto a lightly buttered nonstick pan or griddle over medium-high heat. Turn carefully with a spatula when small bubbles come to the surface and the bottoms are golden brown, 3–5

minutes. Cook until browned on the second side, about ½–1 more minute, and serve topped with crème fraîche and a dollop of caviar, and garnished with lime wedges to sqeeze on top.
MAKES 26–28 PANCAKES; SERVES 6–8

NEW WESTMINSTER SALMONBELLIES

The following dish is said to have originated in New Westminster, one of B.C.'s oldest cities. In the seventies, New Westminster salmonbellies was the favorite appetizer served at a now-defunct Vancouver restaurant. The dish lives on, however, in many homes in British Columbia and across Canada.

1½ cups (375 g/12 oz) cooked tiny (bay) shrimp
¾ cup (6 fl oz/180 ml) heavy (double) cream, whipped
2 teaspoons minced fresh dill
1 tablespoon prepared horseradish
salt and freshly ground white pepper to taste
6 thin slices cold-smoked salmon (lox)
2 tablespoons salmon roe for garnish (optional)
6 fresh dill sprigs for garnish
2 lemons, cut into wedges, for garnish
single chive flowers for garnish

Top to bottom: Green Chili Corn Cakes with Sturgeon Caviar, New Westminster Salmonbellies

Bloody Caesar Cocktail

In a medium bowl, combine the shrimp, whipped cream, dill and horseradish. Season lightly with salt and white pepper.

Spread the shrimp filling on the smoked salmon slices and roll them up in a cone shape.

Garnish with salmon roe (if you like), dill sprigs, lemon wedges and chive flowers.

SERVES 6

British Columbia

BLOODY CAESAR COCKTAIL

The Bloody Caesar is a Canadian variation on the Bloody Mary. This authentic version is made with Clamato, a clam and tomato juice blend. Some creative bartenders modify the recipe by using pepper vodka for a spicier taste, or by garnishing the glass with pickled asparagus spears, cooked skewered prawns, or colossal olives instead of the traditional celery stick. They may also frost the rim of the glass by rubbing it with a lemon wedge, then dipping the rim in celery salt before adding the cocktail ingredients.

4–6 ice cubes
2 tablespoons (1 fl oz/30 ml) vodka
½ cup (4 fl oz/125 ml) Clamato juice
2 dashes of Worcestershire sauce
dash of fresh lemon juice
2 drops Tabasco (hot pepper) sauce
freshly ground pepper to taste
dash of celery salt (optional)
1 leafy celery stick for garnish

Fill an 8–12-oz (250–375-ml) highball glass or tumbler with ice cubes and add the vodka, Clamato juice, Worcestershire sauce, lemon juice and Tabasco. Season with a few grindings of pepper.

Stir gently to combine and garnish with a celery stick.

MAKES 1 COCKTAIL

British Columbia

THAI CUCUMBER SALAD

Thai food–lovers have a great variety of restaurants to choose from in Vancouver. This classic Thai salad goes well with a spicy meal.

1 large English cucumber
¼ cup (2 oz/60 g) minced sweet onion
2 tablespoons seasoned rice vinegar
1 tablespoon minced fresh cilantro (coriander)
3 tablespoons shredded carrots
2 tablespoons chopped peanuts

■ Slice the cucumber crosswise into thin rounds. Toss the cucumbers in a bowl with the onion, vinegar, cilantro and carrots. Sprinkle the peanuts over the top, cover and refrigerate. Serve within 2–3 hours.

SERVES 4

British Columbia

SUMMER MELON AND PRAWN SALAD WITH CHUTNEY-LIME DRESSING

A delightful combination of fresh prawns from the Steveston fishing docks in Richmond, British Columbia, and cooling melons from the fruit and vegetable stands that dot the area.

¾ cup (6 fl oz/180 ml) mayonnaise
¾ cup (6 fl oz/180 ml) sour cream
¼ cup (2 fl oz/60 ml) fresh lime juice
¼ cup (2 fl oz/60 ml) minced mango chutney
1 tablespoon curry paste, or 4 teaspoons curry powder
2 medium cantaloupes (rock melons)
1 large honeydew melon
1 lb (500 g) cooked prawns, peeled and deveined
fresh mint leaves for garnish

■ In a small bowl, combine the mayonnaise, sour cream, lime juice, chutney and curry to taste. Chill.
■ Peel and seed the melons. Cut the melons into geometric shapes or slices. Add the melon and prawns to the mayonnaise mixture and toss gently.
■ Serve garnished with fresh mint.

SERVES 6–8

British Columbia

SESAME CAESAR SALAD

A new twist on the classic Caesar salad, still a favorite on Pacific Northwest tables.

CROUTONS

½ cup (4 fl oz/125 ml) olive oil
1 teaspoon Asian (toasted) sesame oil
4 cups (8 oz/250 g) ½-in (1.5-cm) French bread cubes
¼ cup (⅓ oz/10 g) chopped fresh cilantro (coriander)

3–4 heads romaine (cos) lettuce
SESAME DRESSING

¼ cup (2 fl oz/60 ml) fresh lemon juice
2 egg yolks
1 anchovy fillet, minced (optional)

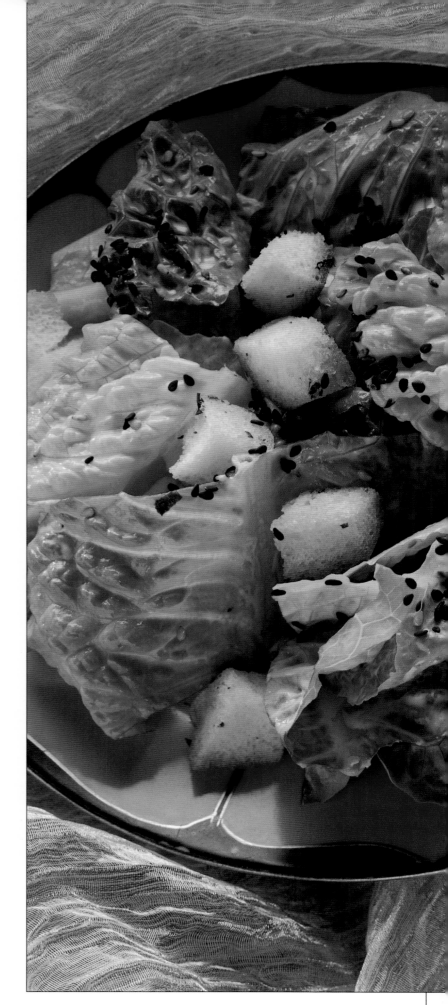

¼ teaspoon Tabasco (hot pepper) sauce
2 garlic cloves, minced
2 tablespoons Dijon mustard
3–5 tablespoons sour cream
1 cup (8 oz/250 ml) plus 3 tablespoons olive oil
3 tablespoons freshly grated Parmesan cheese
¼ cup sesame seeds, toasted
salt and freshly ground pepper or fresh lemon juice to taste
1 tablespoon black sesame seeds (optional)

Clockwise from left: Sesame Caesar Salad, Thai Cucumber Salad, and Summer Melon and Prawn Salad with Chutney-Lime Dressing

◼ To make the croutons: Add the olive oil and sesame oil to a skillet over moderate heat. Add the bread cubes and cilantro and stir for several minutes, or until they are crisp and golden. Spread on paper towels to cool.

◼ Remove and discard the tough outer romaine leaves. Wash the lettuce leaves and dry them well. Tear the leaves into bite-sized pieces, place them in a bowl, and refrigerate.

◼ To make the sesame dressing: Place the lemon juice, egg yolks, anchovy fillet, Tabasco sauce, garlic, mustard and sour cream in a blender or food processor and process until smooth.

With the machine running, slowly add the oil in a thin, steady stream; it will thicken like whipping cream. Add the Parmesan cheese. (If you are using a blender, you may have to prepare this recipe in 2 batches.)

◼ Pour the dressing over the lettuce and toss to coat. Add the toasted sesame seeds.

◼ Taste and add more salt and pepper if necessary, or drops of lemon juice. Garnish with croutons and black sesame seeds.

SERVES 10–12

Pears, Prosciutto and Bitter Greens with Roasted Shallot Vinaigrette

Oregon

PEARS, PROSCIUTTO AND BITTER GREENS WITH ROASTED SHALLOT VINAIGRETTE

This fall-and-winter salad teams the salty tang of prosciutto with the sweetness of ripe pears. Toasted hazelnuts or walnuts may be substituted for prosciutto, if you like.

ROASTED SHALLOT VINAIGRETTE

6 whole shallots, peeled
⅔ cup (5 fl oz/160 ml) olive oil
3 tablespoons Dijon mustard
1 tablespoon chopped fresh thyme, or 1 teaspoon dried thyme
freshly ground black pepper to taste
¼ cup (2 fl oz/60 ml) red wine vinegar
salt to taste

8 cups (9 oz/250 g) mixed bitter greens, such as mizuna, raddichio, endive, arugula and purple kale
6–8 thin slices prosciutto
4 ripe pears, halved and cored

■ Preheat an oven to 400°F (200°C).
■ To make the dressing: Place the shallots and olive oil in a small baking pan or ovenproof casserole and roast until tender and evenly browned, 20–25 minutes. Remove from the oven and let cool for 15 minutes.
■ Remove the shallots from the pan and reserve the oil. Mince the shallots and place in a bowl with the mustard, thyme and black pepper. Whisk these ingredients until combined, then gradually whisk in the reserved olive oil to thoroughly emulsify the mixture.
■ Thin the olive and herb mixture by gradually whisking in the vinegar. Add salt.
■ Toss the greens with half of the vinaigrette and arrange on individual salad plates. Garnish each salad with a slice of prosciutto lightly rolled into a rosette. Thinly slice the pear

halves and arrange the slices over each bed of salad greens.
■ Serve with additional dressing and freshly ground black pepper on the side.

SERVES 6–8

Oregon

SPINACH SALAD WITH STRAWBERRIES AND POPPY SEED–BERRY VINAIGRETTE

Light and refreshing, this salad is perfect on a hot summer afternoon. Use some luscious June strawberries, and try making your own berry vinegar.

VINAIGRETTE

2 tablespoons poppy seeds
2 tablespoons Dijon mustard
2 tablespoons honey
1 cup (8 fl oz/250 ml) canola or safflower oil
⅓ cup (3 fl oz/80 ml) seasonal berry vinegar (recipe on page 193)

2 bunches spinach, stemmed
2 cups (12 oz/375 g) strawberries, stemmed and quartered
1 cup (8 oz/250 g) thin-sliced fresh button (cultivated) mushrooms
½ cup (3 oz/90 g) thinly cut green (spring) onions
½ cup (2 oz/60 g) sliced almonds, lightly toasted

■ To make the vinaigrette: Place the poppy seeds, mustard and honey in a small bowl and gradually whisk in the oil until all the oil is used and the mixture is the consistency of mayonnaise. Gradually whisk in the berry vinegar to thin the mixture to the consistency of heavy cream.
■ Place the leaves of spinach in a serving bowl. Toss with the strawberries, mushrooms, green onions, almonds and enough vinaigrette to moisten them.
■ Serve on salad plates and pass the extra vinaigrette.

SERVES 6–8

Spinach Salad with Strawberries and Poppy Seed–Berry Vinaigrette

Western Washington

SEATTLE CRAB LOUIS

Seattleites say the original Crab Louis was invented by a chef at the grand old Olympic Hotel in Seattle. Some disagree about the correct ingredients for this dish, arguing for and against hard-cooked eggs, sweet pickle relish, and chopped black olives.

LOUIS DRESSING

1 cup (8 fl oz/250 ml) mayonnaise
¼ cup (2 fl oz/60 ml) chili sauce
3 tablespoons chopped black olives
2 teaspoons minced fresh parsley
1 tablespoon minced green (spring) onion
½ teaspoon Worcestershire sauce
1 tablespoon fresh lemon juice
1 teaspoon cider vinegar
1–2 dashes Tabasco (hot pepper) sauce
2 tablespoons sweet pickle relish
salt to taste

4 heaping cups (6 oz/185 g) iceberg or butter lettuce, cut into
    bite-size pieces
4 large whole lettuce leaves
1 lb (500 g) fresh or frozen Dungeness crab body and leg meat
4 hard-cooked eggs, cut in half
12 tomato wedges
12 cooked asparagus spears or cucumber slices
12 pitted ripe black olives
4 lemon wedges
4 flat-leaf (Italian) parsley sprigs

▨ In a small bowl, combine all the dressing ingredients and blend. Set aside.
▨ Place the large lettuce leaves on individual chilled plates. Divide the shredded lettuce among the lettuce leaves and top with the crab meat. Divide the cooked eggs, tomato wedges, asparagus or cucumber slices and black olives among the salads.
▨ Garnish with lemon wedges and parsley sprigs. Pass the dressing on the side.

MAKES 1¾ CUPS (14 FL OZ/425 ML) DRESSING; SERVES 4

Oregon

GARDEN GREENS WITH BAY SHRIMP AND ROGUE RIVER BLUE CHEESE DRESSING

Oregon blue cheese is a product of the rich milk from the dairy cows of the lush Rogue River Valley. If you can't get Oregon blue in your area, substitute your favorite blue-veined cheese. Make sure the shrimp are fresh and sweet and the tomatoes are vine-ripened, if possible.

DRESSING

2 cups (16 fl oz/500 ml) buttermilk
1 cup (8 fl oz/250 ml) sour cream
2 tablespoons prepared horseradish
2 teaspoons Tabasco (hot pepper) sauce
8 oz (250 g) Oregon or other blue cheese, crumbled
salt and pepper to taste

SALAD

1 head red leaf or red oak leaf lettuce
1 head butter lettuce
1 head radicchio (optional)
1 lb (500 g) tiny peeled cooked (bay) shrimp
2 large ripe red tomatoes, cut into wedges
1 bunch radishes, thinly sliced

1 cucumber, cut into thin slices
1 lemon, cut into wedges

▨ To make the dressing: In a large bowl, place the buttermilk, sour cream, horseradish, and Tabasco; whisk until the mixture

Left to right: Garden Greens with Bay Shrimp, Seattle Crab Louis, and Rogue River Blue Cheese Dressing

is smooth. Add the crumbled blue cheese and mix to evenly distribute the cheese in the dressing. Add salt and pepper, and refrigerate.

▨ Wash the lettuces and dry them well. Tear the leaves into bite-sized pieces. On each individual salad plate, arrange a bed of the mixed greens. Divide the bay shrimp among the salads. Garnish with the tomatoes, radishes, cucumber and lemon wedges. Pass the blue cheese dressing on the side.

SERVES 6–8

61

Summer Ceviche

Islands

SUMMER CEVICHE

The islands of Puget Sound are one of the last places in the Pacific Northwest where small fishing fleets market their catch daily. They are a perfect source of fish for ceviche, which requires the freshest seafood available.

1 cup (8 fl oz/250 ml) fresh lime juice
½ cup (4 fl oz/125 ml) seasoned rice wine vinegar
2–4 garlic cloves, mashed
1 red (Spanish) onion, slivered
1 lb (500 g) fresh-shucked scallops
1 lb (500g) fresh halibut, cut into 1-in (2.5-cm) cubes
1 red bell pepper (capsicum), seeded and diced
1 small cucumber, peeled, seeded and diced
1 small papaya, peeled, seeded and diced
¼ cup (⅓ oz/10 g) minced fresh cilantro (coriander)
2 tablespoons minced fresh lemon balm or mint
1 head butter lettuce
1 fresh lime, cut into 6 wedges

☒ Place the lime juice, vinegar, garlic and onion in a nonaluminum bowl. Add the scallops and halibut and toss lightly to coat with the dressing.
☒ Marinate, covered, in the refrigerator for at least 4 hours or overnight, tossing occasionally.
☒ Thirty minutes before serving, add the pepper, cucumber, papaya and herbs. Chill.
☒ Serve on leaves of butter lettuce with wedges of lime for garnish.

SERVES 6–10

ROASTED PEPPER, CORN AND ARUGULA SALAD WITH GOAT CHEESE CROUTONS

Arugula grows wild in some parts of Washington and is considered by some to be a weed. Its rich, nutty flavor is complemented by a dressing of virgin olive oil and balsamic vinegar.

1 green bell pepper (capsicum)
1 red bell pepper (capsicum)
1 yellow bell pepper (capsicum)
2 ears (cobs) fresh corn, husked
2 teaspoons Dijon mustard
1 garlic clove, minced
3 tablespoons balsamic vinegar
2 teaspoons fresh lemon juice
¼ cup (2 fl oz/60 ml) extra-virgin olive oil
¾ teaspoon salt

freshly cracked black pepper to taste
¼ cup (⅓ oz/10 g) chopped fresh basil
12 slices baguette ½-in (1.5-cm) each, lightly toasted
6 oz (185 g) fresh goat cheese (chèvre)
4–6 cups (⅓–½ lb/155–250 g) tightly packed torn arugula

◩ Roast the peppers over hot coals or under a broiler (griller), turning often, until the skin is charred and totally blistered. Place in a paper bag, close the bag, and let sit for 15 minutes. Peel, seed, and thinly slice the peppers.
◩ Grill or broil the corn, turning when each side is lightly browned. Cut the corn from the cob.
◩ In a large bowl, whisk the mustard, garlic, vinegar and lemon juice together. Slowly whisk in the oil. Season with salt and pepper and toss in the basil, roasted peppers and corn. Set aside.
◩ Preheat a broiler (griller) if necessary. Spread the toasted baguette slices with goat cheese and place under a broiler or on the grill for 1 minute, or until the cheese is warm.
◩ Add the arugula to the roasted pepper mixture and toss well. Divide among individual salad plates and garnish with the warm goat cheese croutons.

SERVES 4–6

Roasted Pepper, Corn and Arugula Salad with Goat Cheese Croutons

Top to bottom: Country Bread Salad with Roasted Vegetables, Winter Greens with Spicy Walnuts, Apples and Cranberry Vinaigrette

COUNTRY BREAD SALAD WITH ROASTED VEGETABLES

This salad makes a bright addition to a picnic basket, as it holds up well. Be sure to serve at room temperature.

TOASTED BREAD

4–5 thick slices rustic French or Italian bread, cut into 1-in (2.5-cm) cubes, about 4 cups
3 tablespoons olive oil
2 tablespoons chopped fresh parsley
1 tablespoon chopped fresh basil, or 1 teaspoon dried basil
1 tablespoon chopped fresh thyme, or 1 teaspoon dried thyme
2 garlic cloves, minced
⅓ cup (1½ oz/45 g) freshly grated Parmesan cheese

ROASTED VEGETABLES

2 cups (16 oz/500 g) cherry tomatoes
1 small zucchini (courgette), cut into ½-in (1.5-cm) slices
1 small yellow summer squash (vegetable marrow), cut into ½-in (1.5-cm) slices
1 Japanese eggplant (aubergine), cut into ½-in (1.5-cm) slices, or 1 cup (8 oz/250 g) diced Italian (globe) eggplant (aubergine)
1 red (Spanish) onion, cut into ½-in (1.5-cm) slices
3 tablespoons olive oil
salt and freshly ground black pepper to taste

¼ cup (⅓ oz/10 g) chopped fresh chives (optional)
2 tablespoons capers
1 teaspoon Dijon mustard
⅓ cup (2.5 fl oz/.75 ml) olive oil
1 tablespoon red wine vinegar
fresh arugula leaves or other salad greens (optional)

◩ Preheat an oven to 500°F (260°C). To make the toasted bread: In a large bowl, toss the cubed bread with the olive oil, parsley, basil, thyme, garlic and Parmesan cheese. Spread on a baking sheet and toast in the preheated oven for 5–8 minutes, or until lightly crisped and golden. Let cool (leave the oven on).
◩ To make the roasted vegetables: In a medium bowl, toss the cherry tomatoes, squashes, eggplant and red onion with the olive oil and season well with salt and pepper. Spread all the vegetables except the tomatoes out on a baking sheet and roast in the oven for 2–3 minutes. Add the tomatoes and roast for 4–5 minutes longer, or until the vegetables are lightly browned and the eggplant is tender. Let cool.
◩ In a large bowl, combine the toasted bread, cooled roasted vegetables, chives and capers. In a small bowl, whisk together the Dijon, olive oil and vinegar. Drizzle over the salad, toss, and serve on a bed of fresh arugula or greens, if desired.

SERVES 4–6.

WINTER GREENS WITH SPICY WALNUTS, APPLES AND CRANBERRY VINAIGRETTE

A bright, festive salad to serve during the holidays. Add smoked chicken or turkey to serve as a main course. If crisp, refreshing Asian pear apples (a cross between an apple and a pear) are available, they make an excellent alternative to the apple.

CRANBERRY VINAIGRETTE

⅔ cup (2 oz/60 g) fresh or frozen cranberries
¼ cup (2 oz/60 g) sugar
½ cup (4 fl oz/125 ml) Cranberry Sage Vinegar (recipe on page 188) or cider vinegar
1 teaspoon Dijon mustard
¼ cup (2 fl oz/60 ml) fresh orange juice
¾ cup (6 fl oz/180 ml) vegetable oil
¼ teaspoon salt
freshly cracked black pepper to taste

SPICY WALNUTS

1½ teaspoons butter, melted
⅛ teaspoon cayenne pepper
⅛ teaspoon ground cinnamon
2 tablespoons honey
¼ teaspoon salt
½ cup (2 oz/60 g) coarsely chopped walnuts

1 head butter lettuce, leaves separated
4 cups (6 oz/185 g) mixed winter greens such as kale, escarole (curly endive), romaine (cos), torn
1 red apple, cored and sliced into ⅛-in (3-mm) wedges
½ small red (Spanish) onion, thinly sliced

◩ To make the vinaigrette: Place the cranberries, sugar and vinegar in a small saucepan and cook over medium heat until the cranberries pop, about 4–5 minutes. Remove from the heat and let cool. Purée the cranberry mixture in a blender.
◩ Pour the purée into a medium bowl, and whisk in the mustard and orange juice. Gradually whisk in the oil a little at a time. The dressing should become smooth and emulsified. Season with salt and pepper. Refrigerate until needed.
◩ To make the spicy walnuts: In a small skillet, combine all the

walnut ingredients and toss well to coat. Cook over medium heat until the nuts are lightly browned. Remove from the heat and let cool, stirring frequently to keep the nuts from sticking together. ◼ Arrange the butter lettuce on individual salad plates. In a large bowl, combine the winter greens, apple and spicy walnuts. Toss with enough of the cranberry vinaigrette to coat lightly. Divide among the lettuce beds. Top the salads with the sliced red onion and pass the extra vinaigrette.

SERVES 4–6

British Columbia

Tojo's Shrimp Dumplings with Hot Mustard Sauce

A specialty of Vancouver's Tojo's Restaurant, these shrimp dumplings make a wonderful appetizer. They may be made ahead and refrigerated or frozen.*

6 dried shiitake mushrooms
½ lb (250 g) peeled raw shrimp
1 lb (500 g) fresh or frozen Dungeness crab meat or surimi
1 carrot, minced
1 onion, minced
1 tablespoon soy sauce
3 tablespoons mirin or dry sherry
¼ cup (2 fl oz/60 ml) sake
1 tablespoon sugar
4 cups (32 fl oz/1 l) vegetable oil
Japanese yellow mustard, powdered hot mustard or
  Dijon mustard
water as needed

◼ Place the dried mushrooms in a bowl of warm water and soak for 30 minutes. Drain the mushrooms and remove the stems. Mince the mushrooms.
◼ Place the shrimp in a food processor and process until a paste is formed. Add the crab meat or surimi and vegetables to the shrimp paste and process for about 10 seconds, then add the

*Top to bottom: Barbecued Pork Tenderloin with Plum Sauce,
Tojo Shrimp Dumplings with Hot Mustard Sauce*

soy sauce, mirin, sake and sugar, and process just until the ingredients are combined. Cover the mixture and place in the freezer for 5 minutes to chill.
◼ In a deep, heavy pot, heat the oil to 425°F (220°C) (a cube of bread dropped in the oil will brown in 1 minute). Using 2 tablespoons, shape the chilled mixture into compact ovals by transferring from one spoon to the other. Use a third tablespoon to place the shrimp ovals in the hot oil. Cook for 4–5 minutes, or until golden brown. Remove the dumplings with a slotted spoon, drain on paper towels, and keep warm in a very low oven. Repeat to cook the remaining dumplings.
◼ Combine the powdered or prepared mustard with enough water to make a smooth dipping sauce.
◼ Serve hot with the mustard dipping sauce, or let cool completely and freeze.

MAKES ABOUT 24 DUMPLINGS

* *Before serving, defrost frozen dumplings and place in a preheated 350°F (180°C) oven for 10 minutes, or until heated through.*

British Columbia

Barbecued Pork Tenderloin with Plum Sauce

A tasty appetizer for any season. Homemade plum sauce complements the flavor of pork.

1½ lb (750 g) pork tenderloin (whole fillet)
⅓ cup (3 fl oz/80 ml) honey
1 cup (8 fl oz/250 ml) soy sauce
freshly ground pepper to taste
hot mustard
sesame seeds, toasted
Plum Sauce (recipe follows)

◼ Place the tenderloins in a shallow, nonaluminum container. Spread the honey evenly over the tenderloins. Add the soy sauce to the pan and sprinkle the meat with pepper. Cover and marinate for 2 hours, turning the meat several times during this period.
◼ Light a fire in a charcoal grill with a cover. Place the tenderloins on the grill over medium-hot coals (reserve the marinade), and sear briefly on all sides. Cover the grill and cook the tenderloins, turning them several times and brushing with the marinade, for 20–30 minutes, or until the meat is pale pink when the tenderloins are cut into, or an instant-read thermometer inserted in the center of a tenderloin reads 150°–155°F (65°–70°C).
◼ Transfer to a plate, cover with plastic wrap, and refrigerate overnight, or until very cold.
◼ Transfer the tenderloins to a cutting board and cut crosswise into slices about ¼ in (6 mm) thick. Arrange on a platter and serve with hot mustard, toasted sesame seeds and plum sauce.

SERVES 6

PLUM SAUCE

1½ teaspoons dry mustard
1½ teaspoons cider vinegar
dash of salt
small pinch of dried red pepper flakes
small sliver of garlic
½ cup (4 fl oz/125 ml) greengage plum or apricot jam
½ teaspoon soy sauce
1 teaspoon grated fresh ginger

◼ In a small saucepan, combine all the ingredients and cook over medium heat until the mixture bubbles. Remove from the heat and let cool.

MAKES ½ CUP (4 FL OZ/125 ML)

EGGPLANT CAPONATA AND ROASTED GARLIC

This dip can be made up to 3 days ahead; reheat right before serving. Serve the heads of roasted garlic with cocktail forks for picking out the cloves, and smear on toasted French bread slices, crackers or pita bread crisps. Accompany with fresh goat cheese.

CAPONATA

1 eggplant (aubergine), about 14 oz (440 g), trimmed and sliced crosswise ½ in (1.5 cm) thick
4 tablespoons (2 fl oz/60 ml) olive oil
2 teaspoons kosher salt
1 yellow summer squash (vegetable marrow)
1 zucchini (courgette)
5 white mushrooms, cut into ⅓-in (8-mm) dice
½ red (Spanish) onion, cut into ⅓-in (8-mm) dice
1 tablespoon minced garlic
2 tablespoons dry red wine
1 tablespoon balsamic vinegar
1 jar (6 oz/185 g) marinated artichoke hearts, drained and chopped (liquid reserved)
1 large tomato, cut into ¼-in (6-mm) dice
¼ teaspoon dried red pepper flakes
⅛ teaspoon ground black pepper
⅓ cup (3 fl oz/80 ml) tomato sauce (puréed tomatoes)
¼ cup (2 oz/ 125 g) finely diced roasted red bell pepper (capsicum) or pimiento (canned sweet pepper) (see glossary)
1 tablespoon drained capers
2 tablespoons minced Calamata olives or black olives
2 tablespoons minced fresh basil
1 tablespoon minced fresh parsley

ROASTED GARLIC

3 heads garlic
1 tablespoon olive oil
1 cup (8 fl oz/ 250 ml) water

◙ To make the caponata: Preheat an oven to 450°F (230°C). Spread the eggplant slices on an oiled baking sheet and brush with 2 tablespoons of the oil. Season with 1 teaspoon of the salt. Bake for 25 minutes, or until tender. Let cool slightly, then chop and set aside.
◙ Meanwhile, slice the yellow squash in half lengthwise. Scoop out the seeds and cut the squash into ½-in (1.5-cm) dice. Repeat with the zucchini. Set aside.
◙ In a large, heavy saucepan, heat the remaining 2 tablespoons olive oil over medium-high heat until the surface is shimmering, 1–2 minutes. Add the mushrooms, onions, diced yellow squash and zucchini. Cook, stirring occasionally, until the vegetables begin to brown lightly, about 4–5 minutes. Add the garlic and cook, stirring, for 1 minute.
◙ Stir in the red wine, vinegar and reserved artichoke liquid. Add the tomato, red pepper flakes, black pepper and the remaining 1 teaspoon salt. Cook, stirring, until the tomato softens, about 3–4 minutes.
◙ Stir in the artichoke hearts, tomato sauce, roasted red pepper, capers, olives, basil, parsley and the reserved eggplant. Reduce the heat to medium-low and cook for 3 minutes, or until thickened.
◙ To make the roasted garlic: Preheat an oven to 375°F (190°C).
◙ Cut the top ½ in (1.5 cm) off of the garlic heads. Place them in a small baking dish, drizzle with olive oil, and add water. Cover with aluminum foil.
◙ Bake for 40 minutes. Remove the foil and bake for 10 more minutes, or until browned and *very* soft, like butter. Remove the garlic from the pan. Serve warm with the warm caponata.

MAKES 6 CUPS (48 FL OZ/1.5 L)   *Photograph on pages 32-33*

ISLAND PICNIC POTATO SALAD

Potato salad made with the richly flavored red Nordland potato has no equal. American-style yellow mustard is the secret ingredient. It gives the dressing a particularly robust bite.

8 large (2 lb/1 kg) unpeeled Nordland or other red potatoes, cooked and cut in 1-in (2.5-cm) cubes
8 hard-cooked eggs, chopped
1 red (Spanish) onion, chopped
1 cup (6 oz/180 g) chopped celery
1 large dill pickle (pickled cucumber), chopped
1 teaspoon dried savory
1 teaspoon celery seed
1 teaspoon salt
1½ cups (12 fl oz/375 ml) mayonnaise, preferably homemade
4 tablespoons American yellow mustard
fresh parsley sprigs and paprika for garnish

◙ Place the potatoes, eggs, onion, celery, pickle, herbs and salt in a large bowl. Toss gently. Add the mayonnaise and mustard and fold with a large rubber spatula until well blended. Chill until ready to serve.
◙ Garnish the salad with parsley sprigs and dust lightly with paprika.

SERVES 6–8

MARINATED WALLA WALLA SWEETS WITH TOMATO WEDGES

When sweet onions are in season, this is an unbeatable combination to serve with grilled meats or as a first course with fresh mozzarella cheese.

MARINADE

1 cup (8 fl oz/250 ml) mild olive oil
¼ cup (2 fl oz/60 ml) seasoned rice vinegar
2 tablespoons fresh lemon juice
salt and freshly ground pepper to taste
2 tablespoons minced fresh basil
2 tablespoons minced fresh parsley

2 large Walla Walla or other sweet white onions, sliced
6 ripe tomatoes, cut into wedges
chopped parsley for garnish

◙ Blend all of the marinade ingredients for 30 seconds in a blender, or beat well with a wire whisk. Pour over the onions. Chill for 1–2 hours.
◙ Arrange the tomato wedges in a salad bowl. Layer the onions on top and pour any extra marinade over.
◙ Garnish with parsley.

SERVES 6–8

Top to bottom: Island Picnic Potato Salad, Marinated Walla Walla Sweets with Tomato Wedges

VANCOUVER AND BRITISH COLUMBIA

For the antithesis of Campbell's extreme making do, a walk through a few Vancouver neighborhoods is instructive. Long famous for its beauty, with beaches and bays glinting before a mountain backdrop, Vancouver also is becoming known for its cosmopolitan choices of food. Few cities provide such varied fare in such a compact area. At least one guidebook is devoted entirely to the offerings of neighborhood restaurants and groceries in Vancouver's Little Italy, Japantown, Chinatown, Little India and Greektown. And that leaves out the Yugoslav, Caribbean and Southeast Asian neighborhoods, not to mention the Central European bakeries and delicatessens scattered throughout town. Many of these neighborhoods have been established for generations, and new arrivals—many currently from Latin America and Hong Kong—add to the mix daily.

The simple choice of a sidewalk snack can become an agonizing decision. Will it be a Chinese almond cookie, baked in the auspicious form of a carp? Buttery petits fours from the downtown shopping street known as Robsonstrasse? A diamond-shaped piece of East Indian candy, made with cooked milk, almonds and rose water and decorated with edible silver leaf? A hazelnut gelato after a cup of cappuccino?

Restaurant decisions are no less daunting, covering dozens of cuisines—including native Northwest—and approaches ranging from solemnly classic to frivolously trendy.

Much of the wherewithal for Vancouver's best meals comes from farms nearby. Despite its increasing urbanization, the lower Fraser Valley is still the center of British Columbia's berry and dairy industries and a

source of many other vegetable crops. The Fraser is an immense river, three thousand miles long from its origin in the Rocky Mountains to its mouth, and at its delta it waters half a million acres of some of the richest farmland in Canada. German Mennonite and Dutch immigrants both found the diked fields congenial, and settled down to dairy farms, berries and vegetables. Schnitzels and veal paprikash are common on local restaurant menus, and the local delis feature Gouda cheeses, Kaiser rolls and Black Forest ham. More recent immigrants to the valley, Punjabi families from northern India who are beginning to dominate the berry industry, support a new influx of restaurants, sweet shops and groceries.

The first vegetable crops raised in the valley were staples: potatoes, turnips, dried peas and cabbage. "I remember when it was potato digging time we'd stay home from school," wrote Willena May Reid of her turn-of-the-century childhood near Langley. "There'd be a fire burning a stump out, and we kids would put a potato in the ashes, come back later, and there'd be a lovely baked potato, mealy and white; just have pepper and salt and butter on it."

The Fraser Valley farm families supplied the fast-growing city of Vancouver. On Thursday nights, farmers in the outlying areas would pack up their goods and start out for Westminster—the market site—by boat or wagon. People living on the Yale Road in Surrey could hear them going by all night long. Island dwellers and others along the river shipped their livestock and produce by river ferry, rowboat and even canoe.

Although the offerings no longer include weaner pigs and live chickens by the crate, some Fraser Valley farmers still bring their produce to market, now located on Granville Island in downtown Vancouver. Their fresh herbs and berries, Asian vegetables and salad greens contribute to the city's reputation as a great place for food-lovers.

Canada's richest farmland, Fraser Valley is home to both small and large farms cultivating berries, vegetables and dairy products. Here, a field of carrots is ready for harvest.

FISH AND SHELLFISH

Sweet Pacific oysters are a Northwest delicacy.

FISH AND SHELLFISH

Pacific Northwest waters contain an unbelievable amount of edible fish and shellfish. They are cast for, jigged for, trolled for, picked, dug for and trapped; then they are prepared in a multitude of ways—steamed, broiled, pickled, grilled, baked, poached, stuffed, pan-fried or stir-fried and some types are eaten raw. Pink-fleshed cutthroat trout found in alpine lakes are dusted in cornmeal and pan-fried over campfires for breakfast. Clams are dug and mussels are picked at the beach. Fishermen and -women test their fly-casting skills along river banks in hopes for a shimmering steelhead. Hood Canal residents swarm to their boats for eight days in May vying to fill their pots with sweet spotted shrimp.

The largest salmon in the Northwest was recorded in the 1930s in Petersburg, Alaska, weighing in at a whopping 128½ pounds. Before the dams were built on the Columbia River, a run of very large salmon called June hogs migrated all the way to the Snake River each year. A booklet put out in 1929 by the Associated Salmon Packers awed its readers by revealing that, placed end to end, the cans of salmon packed after a summer's catch would reach *all the way around the earth at the equator,* with enough left over to stretch from Seattle to New York. I'm sure there are a few Northwesterners who would scream if they ever saw another salmon loaf. Those who grew up in the Northwest with this baked dish of canned salmon, white sauce and bread crumbs are much happier now eating grilled fresh-salmon burgers.

People who grew up by the water once considered salmon a "poor people's" food, with beef being the real treat at the table. Freezers were brimming with frozen salmon, and pantry shelves bulged with the gold cans of a lucky fisherman's catch. Now salmon can be somewhat pricy unless you have a fishing-possessed neighbor, a lucky fishing friend or go fishing yourself. Salmon fishing is the true love of Northwest sportsmen and -women. The thrill of reeling in a good fighter is pleasantly recalled in the ache of your pole arm the next day and is rewarded with a backyard salmon barbecue with all the trimmings. Fresh-brewed sun tea, cold microbrews and a chilled Chardonnay are offered. The season's first sweet corn is grilled then slathered with honey butter, and a pot of slow-cooked baked beans with brown sugar and molasses is put out. The table is spread with platters of dill pickles, sliced beefsteak tomatoes, cucumbers, tiny raw carrots fresh from the garden and fresh salmon brushed with a white wine, herb and butter baste and grilled until just barely done (translucent in the center—the way Northwesterners like their salmon), as friends and family line up to fill their plates.

The native tribes of the Northwest coast dined richly on halibut, flounder, herring, salmon and other fish too numerous to list. The primary Native American food was fish, and the most important fish was the salmon. Native Americans called the five species the "five tribes of salmon": pink, sockeye, king, chum and silver. Stories

Previous pages: Barbecued Salmon with Wine Country Butter Baste (page 82)

are told of rivers so thick with salmon you could walk across their backs. One of the most famous feasts of the Northwest tribes was the potlatch, to which a chief would invite both his enemies and friends to show how wealthy and powerful he and his tribe were. A feature at potlatches was cedar-staked salmon, slow-roasted vertically beside a driftwood fire. Cooked by radiant heat, the salmon was moist and tender, with a lightly smoked flavor. This method is still considered to be the ultimate way to cook salmon.

From January to April, eulachons (Columbia River smelt), also known as candlefish, enter the Columbia River. The Chinook Indians dried these oily fish, inserted wicks in them and used them for lights, thus the name candlefish. Today Columbia River smelt are pan-fried or smoked, and the silver (or surf) smelt, the saltwater species available year-round, is prized by the Japanese for sashimi.

In the seventies, the blue mussels that hung off rocks and pilings, once thought of as too much trouble to harvest, became all the rage. Soon these tasty mollusks started appearing on local menus, and people were flocking to collect them on beaches. Prepared similarly to littleneck clams, they are first debearded (the fuzzy part that attaches them to rocks is pulled off), rinsed and scrubbed well, then steamed open in white wine, garlic, shallots, butter, fresh herbs and a little diced fresh tomato, or in cream with slivers of leeks and fresh tarragon leaves. Clam digging has always been a favorite Northwest pastime, with native littleneck and black-striped Manilas being the popular steamers.

On menus along the coast you will find geoduck burgers and clam fritters, as well as razor clams that have

Specialty seafood unique to the Pacific Northwest includes king clams known as goeducks.

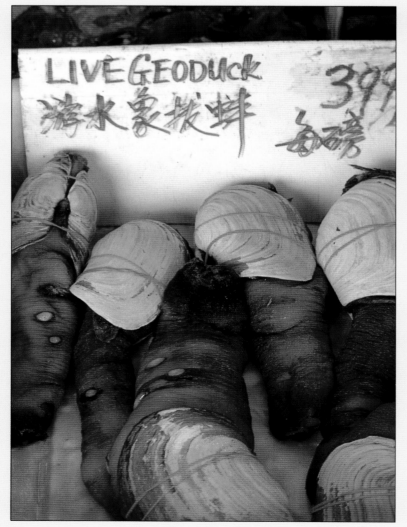

The Fishermen's Memorial Statue, at Fishermen's Terminal in Seattle, was dedicated in 1988 to those whose lives have been lost at sea since the turn of the century.

been dipped in egg and bread crumbs and lightly sautéed in butter, then finished with a quick squeeze of lemon and a sprinkle of chopped parsley. You usually also can find a good fish and chip place frying up lightly battered or breaded pieces of fresh lingcod or halibut fillets, served with French fries and coleslaw, with tartar sauce and malt vinegar on the side to add a little zip.

The Northwest has its share of unusual shellfish species. The giant geoduck clam grows as large as 9 pounds, with the preferred harvest weight being 2 pounds. It lives an average of forty years, with a record age of 135 years, at depths of 4 to 6 feet in the mud of Puget Sound. Named after a Native American word for "dig deep," this giant clam is even the mascot of The Evergreen State College.

Seafood vendors are a favorite destination for local shoppers and tourists looking for the freshest catch of the day.

And does it ever bring big-eyed stares from tourists at Seattle's Pike Place Market, where hoselike geoduck necks hang over a foot long down the sides of iced barrels. The meat is often chopped for flavorful chowders, but the Asian community probably deals with this giant clam best, slicing it thinly, then poaching or stir-frying it with black beans, green onions and garlic.

The Pacific oyster came to Northwest waters by accident: It is believed to have been transported on the bottom of Japanese trade boats. This oyster loved our pristine waters, and in 1991, after 150 years of commercial oyster harvesting, the Pacific coast region was number one in national oyster production for the first time. Pacific oysters as big as tennis shoes can be found on beaches. These "extra larges" are not recommended for raw slurping but they can be cut up and, like smaller ones, dipped in egg, then into cornmeal or bread crumbs, quickly pan-fried and served with lemon wedges and tartar sauce.

The native little Olympia oyster has had some hard times. Between the thirties and forties it became scarce due to pulp mill pollution, which finally forced the Shelton pulp mill to close down in the late fifties. On a 1940s menu from the Poodle Dog restaurant in Fife, Washington, an order of fried Olympia oysters cost sixty cents—so prized that they were the most expensive thing on the menu. It's back again now, thanks to many oyster growers' dedication, hard work and a receptive market.

The unpolluted waters of the Pacific Northwest are a vital ingredient in growing superior oysters. Oysters filter feed about one hundred gallons of water a day. They gain their flavor and other unique characteristics from the water in which they grow. The prime oyster-eating months are December through March, when the oysters do not spawn and are thus plump, crisp and briny. Seafood "guru" Jon Rowley says, "You can tell it's oyster time in the Pacific Northwest when the skies turn oyster gray, which is generally around the first of November."

Oyster farming assures a reliable supply of fresh oysters, and science is working to bring in new varieties. The triploid oyster, also known as the "sexless oyster," was developed at Seattle University in 1985. Genetically engineered to be harvested in the summer, about 75 percent or more of these oysters become sterile and do not spawn in the summer like other oysters do, and therefore they do not become milky or unpleasantly clear.

Sweet Dungeness crab has always been a seaside treat. The best way to enjoy it Northwest style is to cook it on the beach in a pot of boiling seawater. Cook the live crabs for about 15 minutes, cool in cold water, then pull off the back shell and featherlike gills while rinsing the crab clean. Then sit down right there in the sand and start cracking while breathing in the fresh sea air. Dip the luscious meat in melted butter and squeeze on a little lemon, or, as some do, dip it in mayonnaise that has been mixed with chili sauce or cocktail sauce. Serve with a fresh green salad and hot garlic bread and wash it down with a glass of cold crisp Northwest Semillon, and you will find that you haven't a care in the world but just to sit and crack crab.

PAN-FRIED RAZOR CLAMS WITH CITRUS-ROSEMARY BUTTER

Razor clams are a delicacy even in Oregon. Few things can compare to these long, narrow mollusks served hot from the pan. Digging for elusive razor clams is nearly as much fun as eating them.

1 cup (8 oz/250 g) butter at room temperature
4 tablespoons minced fresh rosemary
4 tablespoons minced fresh parsley
2 tablespoons minced garlic
1 tablespoon minced or grated lemon zest
1 tablespoon minced or grated orange zest
2 tablespoons fresh lemon juice
½ teaspoon ground black pepper
2 cups (10 oz/300 g) cornmeal
2 teaspoons salt
½ cup (4 fl oz/125 ml) olive oil
2 lb (1 kg) shucked razor clams
rosemary sprig and lemon wedges for garnish

▨ To make the butter: Place the butter, rosemary, parsley, garlic, lemon and orange zest, lemon juice and pepper in a bowl. Beat until the ingredients are evenly combined, stopping to scrape the sides of the bowl at least once.
▨ Place the butter mixture on a 12-in (1.5-cm) square of plastic wrap or aluminum foil. Shape the butter into a log and roll it inside the plastic or foil; twist the ends to enclose it completely, then roll it to form an even cylinder. Refrigerate the herb butter to firm it for cutting.
▨ Mix together the cornmeal and salt. Dredge the razor clams in the cornmeal mixture, shaking off the excess. In a large skillet, heat the olive oil and sauté the clams in batches over medium-high heat for about 2–3 minutes, or until lightly browned; turn them and cook 1 minute longer.
▨ Serve immediately, garnished with a slice of the rosemary butter, a rosemary sprig and wedges of lemon. Rewrap and freeze any leftover butter.

SERVES 6–8

STEAMED CLAMS IN A THAI CURRY BROTH

When the tides are low, digging native hard-shelled littleneck clams is a Pacific Northwest recreational pastime. Local clams may be steamed traditionally with white wine, garlic, lemon and herbs, or in a more adventuresome way, as in this recipe.

2 teaspoons vegetable oil
1 teaspoon Asian (toasted) sesame oil
1 tablespoon minced fresh ginger
2 teaspoons minced garlic
1 tablespoon minced fresh lemongrass
2 teaspoons fish sauce
½ cup (4 fl oz/125 ml) coconut milk
2 teaspoons soy sauce
1–2 teaspoons Thai red curry paste
1 teaspoon sugar
1 tablespoon fresh lime juice
½ cup (4 fl oz/125 ml) clam juice
2 lb (1 kg) fresh clams in the shell, such as Manila or little-neck, washed

¼ cup (2 oz/60 g) matchstick-cut carrots
¼ cup (2 oz/60 g) matchstick-cut red bell peppers (capsicum), optional
¼ cup (1½ oz/45 g) slivered green (spring) onion
2 tablespoons chopped fresh cilantro leaves (coriander)
lime wedges for squeezing over clams

▨ In a large soup pot or Dutch oven, heat the oils over medium heat. Add the ginger, garlic and lemongrass and sauté for 30 seconds.
▨ Add the fish sauce, coconut milk, soy sauce, Thai red curry paste, sugar, lime juice and clam juice. Bring to a boil and immediately add the clams, carrot, bell pepper and green onion. Cover and steam the clams in the broth for 3–5 minutes, or just until the clams open.
▨ Divide the clams, vegetables and broth among warm bowls. Sprinkle with cilantro and serve with lime wedges.

SERVES 2–4

Top to bottom: Steamed Clams in Thai Curry Broth, Pan-Fried Razor Clams with Citrus-Rosemary Butter

Eastern Washington

BARBECUED SALMON WITH WINE COUNTRY BUTTER BASTE

Each June, partners and staff of Sagemoor Farms in Pasco, Washington, gather with guests to barbecue salmon in the cherry orchard bordering the farm's vineyards above the Columbia River. Green boughs of apple wood, leaves and all, are layered on the coals of a fire made in a deep pit. While the fire builds, slabs of Pacific Northwest salmon are basted and placed on a rack in a covered box, which is then lowered into the pit. The fish cooks slowly in the apple wood smoke, while friends chatter and discuss their estimates as to just when the fish will be done to perfection!

The traditional pit method produces a wonderfully moist fish with just a hint of smoky flavor, but you can simulate this method in any tightly covered charcoal grill. You will need 8–10 green boughs of apple or alder wood with leaves, cut to fit inside the grill under the cooking rack. Although the sweet flavor of wood smoke will be missing, you can also make this dish without the boughs, or use chips of apple wood or alder wood, soaked in water for 30 minutes, then drained and thrown on the fire just before cooking.

½ cup (4 oz/125 g) butter
2 garlic cloves, minced
½ cup (4 fl oz/125 ml) dry white wine
3 tablespoons chopped fresh herbs such as chives, thyme, chervil, basil and parsley
2 teaspoons grated lemon zest
1 whole Chinook or king salmon, 8–10 oz (250–315 g) per person, butterflied with skin intact

◼ Melt 1 tablespoon of the butter over low heat in a small, heavy saucepan. Add the garlic and cook briefly. Stir in the wine and cook until reduced to ¼ cup (2 fl oz/60 ml). Add the remaining butter and stir until just melted. Stir in the herbs and lemon zest. Set aside.

◼ Prepare a fire in a charcoal grill. When the coals are medium-hot, lay 8–10 green apple or alder wood boughs with leaves on the coals. Place the butterflied salmon opened out on a single sheet of heavy aluminum foil, skin side down. Brush the flesh side of the salmon with the butter-wine baste. Pick the fish up in the foil and place it on the cooking rack, foil and all. Immediately cover the grill. Cook for 10–20 minutes, or until the flesh is still slightly translucent in the center, basting once or twice during this time. An instant-read thermometer inserted in the thickest part of the fish should read 140°F (60°C).

SERVES 6–10 *(varies with size of salmon)*   *Photograph pages 76–77*

Islands

CLIFF ISLAND CLAMBAKE WITH FIVE POUNDS OF GARLIC AND A CASE OF WINE

Warm summer evenings on Cliff Island bring together friends and families for a celebration of island life. The pebble beaches and worn logs are nature's backdrop for a different kind of dinner party far from the madding crowd. Everyone pitches in, and in the afterglow of a dazzling sunset, conversation flows like the tide, and great stories begin to unfold in the magic of dusk.

This recipe calls for at least 2 shovels, 6 feet (2 m) of chicken wire, a wire cutter, a long gaff hook or rake, and 5 or 6 clean burlap bags, split at the seams. You can substitute a clean canvas tarp or some big heavy towels for the burlap bags. You will also need

heavy gloves and pliers, enough large rocks to line a large pit, a good amount of dry firewood and wet seaweed, 2 medium pots, and paper cups for the butter.

1 case Northwest microbrewed beer, chilled
5 lb (2.5 kg) small butter or Manila clams
5 lb (2.5 kg) mussels
5 lb (2.5 kg) Pacific Northwest singing scallops in the shell (optional)
3 whole salmon, 10–14 lb (5–7 kg) each, stuffed with 2 heads of garlic each
3 whole rockfish, 4–6 lb (2–3 kg) each, stuffed with fresh sprigs of lovage or parsley
6 whole live Dungeness crabs
25 ears (cobs) corn, husked and wrapped in aluminum foil
8 whole unpeeled red (Spanish) onions
5 lb (2.5 kg) whole unpeeled garlic heads
1 case Muscadet, Sauvignon Blanc or Pinot Gris, chilled
48 fresh oysters in the shell
3 lb (1.5 kg) unsalted butter
4 bunches fresh parsley

Cliff Island Clambake with Five Pounds of Garlic and a Case of Wine

10 lemons
2 cups (16 fl oz/500 ml) raspberry vinegar (optional)

▨ Begin by digging a large trench, about 5 by 12 feet (1.5 by 4 m), and at least 2½ feet (1 m) deep, a couple of feet above the high-tide mark. Hand out beers to all the diggers.

▨ Line the sides and bottom of the trench with large rocks. Build a good roaring wood fire along the bottom of the trench. Feed it and let it burn for at least 2 hours, or until the rocks are good and hot, and the beer is gone.

▨ Shovel the embers from the pit and immediately cover the hot stones with about 4 in (10 cm) of wet but not dripping seaweed.

▨ Cut three 2-ft (60-cm) squares from the piece of chicken wire. Wrap the clams, mussels and scallops separately in a bag made of the chicken wire. They should be tight enough to keep the shellfish from flopping around but loose enough to allow the shells to open. Wrap each fish in pieces of the remaining chicken wire.

▨ Begin layering the seafood in the pit, placing the salmon on the bottom layer because they take the longest to cook. Alternating with layers of seaweed go the rockfish, crabs, corn, clams, mussels and scallops. As you layer in the seafood, scatter the whole onions and all but 2 heads of the garlic. Finish with a layer of seaweed. Cover with the wet burlap bags.

▨ While the seafood steams, open the wine and pass it around. Begin shucking the oysters (see glossary). Divide the butter evenly between 2 medium pots. Separate and peel the cloves from the remaining 2 heads of garlic. Crush them and add them to one pot of the butter. Mince the parsley and add it to the pot with the garlic; add the juice of 3 of the lemons. Start eating the oysters. Into the other pot pour the raspberry vinegar. Put both pots in a warm place near the fire for the butter to melt.

▨ When the wine is half gone, or in about 3 hours, remove the seafood and corn from the trench. Use a gaff hook or long-handled rake to snag the wired packages. Wearing gloves and using wire cutters and pliers, open the packages and serve the fish and shellfish immediately, with paper cups of the butters for dipping, wedges of the remaining lemons, and oysters on the half shell if there are any left.

SERVES 16–24

Top to bottom: Baked Pacific Oysters with Bay Shrimp and Artichokes, Wasp Passage Oyster Stew

BAKED PACIFIC OYSTERS WITH BAY SHRIMP AND ARTICHOKES

Make these oysters up a day in advance and then roast them for a quick appetizer during barbecue season. A good dry Oregon Riesling is the perfect foil for these tangy palate teasers.

FILLING

2 cups (8 oz/250 g) diced ¼-in (6-mm) (canned, frozen or fresh) cooked artichoke hearts
½ cup (2 oz/60 g) freshly grated Parmesan cheese
½ cup (4 fl oz/125 ml) lemon juice
1 tablespoon minced garlic
½–1 teaspoon freshly ground black pepper
2 tablespoons chopped fresh mint
2 tablespoons chopped fresh parsley
1 lb (500 g) tiny peeled cooked bay shrimp
1 cup (4 oz/120 g) dry bread crumbs
1 tablespoon butter
salt and pepper to taste

2–2½ dozen shucked Umpqua oysters or other small fresh oysters, on the half shell (method on page 46)
½ cup (2 oz/60 g) freshly grated Parmesan cheese
2 tablespoons chopped fresh parsley

⊠ Preheat an oven to 425°F (220°C). Meanwhile, in a medium bowl, mix of all the filling ingredients, except the salt and pepper, until combined. Add salt and pepper.
⊠ Evenly divide the filling among the oysters. Sprinkle the cheese and parsley over the oysters, place on a large baking sheet, and bake in the preheated oven for 10–12 minutes, or until golden brown and bubbling.

MAKES 24–30 OYSTERS, SERVES 4–6

WASP PASSAGE OYSTER STEW

Wasp Passage, a narrow channel through the rocks between Shaw and Bell islands, was so named because it resembles the thin waist of the wasp. This classic oyster stew is made with real cream and fresh Pacific oysters, and is traditionally served on Christmas Eve.

1 onion, diced small
2 garlic cloves, minced
½ cup (4 oz/125 g) butter
½ cup (4 fl oz/125 ml) dry sherry or dry white wine
4 cups (32 fl oz/1 l) heavy (double) cream

4 cups (32 fl oz/1 l) shucked yearling oysters and their liquid
   (method on page 46)
1 teaspoon salt
½ teaspoon ground white pepper
2 tablespoons cooked chopped bacon (optional)
1 tablespoon minced green (spring) onion, green part only

▨ In a large saucepan, sauté the onion and garlic in 2 tablespoons of the butter over medium heat until translucent, about
5 minutes. Add the sherry or wine and bring to a boil for 1
minute. Lower the heat, add the cream, and stir until the liquid
begins to steam. Do not boil.
▨ Add the oysters and their liquid, and poach gently for 3
minutes or so until the oysters are just ruffled. Overcooking
will make them tough and rubbery. Season with the salt and
pepper. Stir in the bacon, if desired.
▨ Serve in warmed bowls, garnished with the green onions.
SERVES 6

Oregon

SMOKED SALMON RISOTTO WITH CHANTERELLES AND ROASTED GARLIC

*Enjoy this creamy risotto in the fall when the weather begins to chill
and chanterelles are abundant. Any cultivated or wild mushroom
can be substituted for chanterelles in this recipe. Savor your finished
risotto with an Oregon Pinot Gris.*

½ cup (4 fl oz/125 ml) olive oil
20 garlic cloves
1 onion, finely diced
1 lb (500 g) chanterelles or other fresh mushrooms, sliced
½ teaspoon saffron threads (optional)
¼ teaspoon dried red pepper flakes
1 teaspoon salt
1 tablespoon minced fresh rosemary
1½ cups (8 oz/250 g) Arborio *superfino* rice
6 cups (48 fl oz/1.5 l) chicken stock (see glossary)
1 cup (8 fl oz/250 ml) Pinot Gris or other dry white wine
½ cup (4 fl oz/125 ml) water (optional)
2 cups (8 oz/250 g) freshly shredded Parmesan cheese
pepper to taste
1 lb (500 g) cold-smoked salmon (lox), julienned, with 6
   whole slices reserved
6 fresh rosemary sprigs

▨ Heat the olive oil in a large, heavy saucepan and sauté the
garlic cloves over medium heat until they are nicely browned,
10–12 minutes; take care not to burn the garlic. Add the onions,
mushrooms, saffron, red pepper, salt and chopped rosemary to
the pan and sauté until the onions are translucent, 3–5 minutes.
Add the rice to the mixture and cook for 5–7 minutes longer,
stirring frequently, or until the rice is opaque.
▨ Add the chicken stock and wine to the risotto in 4 equal
increments, gently stirring to prevent the rice from sticking to
the pan. Wait until all the liquid has been fully absorbed each
time before your next addition; this will take about 5 minutes.
When all the liquid has been added, taste the risotto for
tenderness; if the grains are still too firm, add ½ cup (4 fl oz/125 ml)
water and continue cooking.
▨ The risotto is fully cooked when the grains are tender but
slightly chewy and the risotto has the texture of a thick
porridge. Remove from the heat and stir in 1 cup (4 oz/125 g)
of the cheese, and add salt and pepper. Gently fold in the
smoked salmon and divide the risotto among 6 plates. Pass the
remaining grated Parmesan and garnish with sprigs of rosemary and rosettes of smoked salmon.
SERVES 6

Oregon

FETTUCCINE WITH DUNGENESS CRAB AND ASPARAGUS

*This quick pasta is flavorful and light. The sweetness of fresh
Dungeness crab is especially good paired with crisp asparagus.*

1 lb (500 g) fresh fettuccine pasta
¼ cup (2 fl oz/60 ml) virgin olive oil
2–3 tablespoons minced garlic
½ teaspoon dried red pepper flakes
2 teaspoons grated lemon zest
2 cups (16 fl oz/500 ml) dry white wine
2 tablespoons fresh lemon juice
1 lb (500 g) fresh or frozen Dungeness crab leg and body
   meat
2 cups (8 oz/250 g) asparagus, cut in 2-in (5-cm) diagonal
   strips, lightly steamed
4 tablespoons mixed chopped fresh herbs such as chives,
   basil, thyme, marjoram, parsley and tarragon
salt and pepper to taste
1–1½ cups (4–6 oz/120–180 g) freshly shredded Parmesan
   cheese
lemon wedges and herb sprigs for garnish (optional)

▨ In a very large saucepan or stockpot, bring a large amount
of lightly salted water to a boil and cook the fettuccine until
al dente; drain.
▨ Meanwhile, in another large saucepan, heat the olive oil
over medium heat and cook the garlic, red pepper flakes
and lemon zest, stirring often, for about 3–4 minutes, or
until the garlic is translucent. Add the white wine and
lemon juice, bring to a low boil, and cook to reduce the
liquid volume by half.
▨ Add the drained cooked pasta, crab, asparagus, and
chopped fresh herbs to the pan. Cook, stirring gently, until
the ingredients are just heated through, about 3–4 minutes.
Add salt and pepper if necessary.
▨ Serve immediately, sprinkled with Parmesan and garnished with lemon wedges and herb sprigs, if desired.
SERVES 4

*Top to bottom: Fettuccine with Dungeness Crab and Asparagus,
Smoked Salmon Risotto with Chanterelles and Roasted Garlic*

PACIFIC NORTHWEST SEAFOOD STEW

A great dish to enjoy at the beach after a day of fishing, clamming and mussel gathering. Make the seafood stew base ahead and pack it in your ice chest. Take along a stew pot, add a good bottle of Northwest Chardonnay and a loaf of French bread to your picnic basket, and you're all set for a beach feast.

SEAFOOD STEW BASE

¼ cup (2 fl oz/60 ml) olive oil
1 tablespoon minced garlic
1 cup (8 oz/250 g) thinly sliced white onion
½ cup (4 oz/125 g) thinly sliced red bell pepper (capsicum)
½ cup (4 oz/125 g) thinly sliced green bell pepper (capsicum)
1 cup (4 oz/125 g) thinly sliced button (cultivated) mushrooms
1 cup (4 oz/125 g) thinly sliced fennel bulb (about 1 small bulb)
1½ teaspoons grated orange zest
½ cup (4 fl oz/125 ml) dry white vermouth or dry white wine
2 cups (16 fl oz/500 ml) clam juice
3 cups (24 oz/750 g) chopped ripe tomatoes or diced canned plum tomatoes with juice
1 teaspoon salt
dash of Tabasco (hot pepper) sauce
freshly cracked black pepper
¼ teaspoon crushed dried rosemary

Dungeness Crab and Bay Shrimp Cakes

1 teaspoon dried basil
¼ teaspoon dried thyme

¼ cup (2 fl oz/60 ml) olive oil
12 oz (375 g) littleneck clams in the shell
8 oz (250 g) mussels, scrubbed and debearded
8 oz (250 g) large shrimp, peeled and deveined, about 8 shrimp
4 oz (125 g) large scallops, sliced in half
8 oz (250 g) mixture of skinless firm-fleshed fish fillets, such as salmon, cod or halibut, cut into 1½-in (4-cm) pieces
4 small cooked red potatoes, cut in half
¼ cup (2 fl oz/60 ml) Pernod (optional)
fresh fennel fronds for garnish (optional)

◼ To make the seafood stew base: Pour the olive oil into a large stew pot or Dutch oven and heat over medium heat. Add the onion, peppers, garlic, mushrooms, fennel and orange zest. Cook, stirring often, for about 4–5 minutes, or until the onion is translucent.
◼ Add the vermouth or white wine, clam juice, tomatoes and seasonings. Turn the heat to high and bring the mixture to a low boil, then reduce the heat to low and simmer for 6–8 minutes. Remove from the heat and adjust the seasoning if necessary. If not using immediately, cool and refrigerate until needed.
◼ Pour the olive oil into a stew pot or Dutch oven and place over medium-high heat. When the oil is hot, add the clams, mussels, shrimp, scallops and fish. Sauté for 30 seconds. Add the potatoes and Pernod. Cook for 30 seconds more, then add the seafood stew base.
◼ Cover the pot and cook just until the clams and mussels open. Immediately remove from the heat and divide the fish and shellfish among individual large bowls. Ladle in the broth and vegetables.
◼ Garnish with fennel fronds. Serve immediately with warm French bread for dipping.

SERVES 4–6

British Columbia

DUNGENESS CRAB AND BAY SHRIMP CAKES

This is restaurateur John Bishop's version of crab cakes using our local bay shrimp. On a chilly winter's evening, Bishop serves these with a hot and spicy sauce; in the summer, these delicious cakes are wonderful accompanied with a chilled fruit salsa.

8 oz (250 g) fresh or frozen Dungeness crab meat
8 oz (250 g) tiny peeled cooked bay shrimp, coarsely chopped
1 cup (4 oz/125 g) fresh bread crumbs
2 tablespoons slivered onions
1 red bell pepper (capsicum), seeded and chopped
3 tablespoons mayonnaise
salt and freshly ground white pepper to taste
vegetable oil for cooking

◼ In a bowl, combine all the ingredients except the vegetable oil and mix well. Form the crab and shrimp mixture into 8 patties about ¾ in (2 cm) thick. The cakes may be prepared up to an hour ahead and refrigerated.
◼ Preheat an oven to 350°F (180°C). In a nonstick skillet brushed with a little vegetable oil, cook the patties over medium heat for 1–2 minutes on each side, or until golden brown.
◼ Place the cakes on a baking sheet and bake in the preheated oven until heated through, about 5 minutes. The cakes should be crisp on both sides.

MAKES 8 CRAB CAKES

Pacific Northwest Seafood Stew

Islands

SOOKE HARBOUR HOUSE SINGING SCALLOPS WITH CHIVE FLOWER SABAYON

Sooke Harbour House on British Columbia's Vancouver Island is an oasis for the culinary traveler. Singing scallops, called "swimming scallops" in Canada, appear often on the menu when they are in season. Their cool pink shells and bright orange roe are a visual treat.

2 lb (1 kg) fresh singing scallops in the shell
½ cup (4 fl oz/125 ml) fish stock (see glossary)
1½ cups (12 fl oz/375 ml) heavy (double) cream
2 large egg yolks
½ cup (4 fl oz/125 ml) dry white wine
2 tablespoons chopped fresh chives
single chive flowers snipped from one flower head

◼ Wash the scallops thoroughly to remove any grit and sand, scrubbing the shells well. In a large pot, combine the fish stock and heavy cream. Add the scallops, cover, and bring to a boil over high heat. Steam the scallops for 2–3 minutes, or until the shells open. Remove the pot from the heat and, with a slotted

Left to right: Spot Prawns with Lemon Pasta and Chives, Sooke Harbour House Singing Scallops with Chive Flower Sabayon

spoon, remove the scallops and set them aside in a warm place.

✣ Return the pot to the heat, bring the cream and stock mixture to a boil, and reduce for 8–10 minutes, or until the mixture reaches the consistency of heavy cream.

✣ Remove the pot from the heat. Whisk the egg yolks and wine together until frothy, then whisk this mixture into the reduced stock and cream. Stir in the chopped chives.

✣ To serve: Remove one half of each scallop shell and discard. Place the remaining shells with their scallop on individual plates. Ladle sabayon into each shell, then scatter with the chive flowers.

SERVES 4–6 AS AN APPETIZER

SPOT PRAWNS WITH LEMON PASTA AND CHIVES

The deep-cold-water spot prawns of Puget Sound are so called because of two small white round spots behind each "ear." Spot prawns are not to be confused with the smaller, less tasty, coonstriped shrimp, so called because of their raccoonlike stripes. The location of good shrimping holes is a closely guarded secret, handed down through generations of shrimpers and shrimp-lovers.

LEMON PASTA

3 cups (12 oz/375 g) semolina flour or unbleached all-purpose (plain) flour
3 eggs, beaten
1 tablespoon olive oil
2 teaspoons salt
¼ teaspoon ground white pepper
grated zest of 4 lemons, about 2 tablespoons
2 tablespoons minced fresh chives

2 tablespoons clarified butter (see glossary)
1 red (Spanish) onion, minced
4 garlic cloves, minced
30 large spot prawns or other large shrimp, peeled and deveined
½ cup (4 fl oz/125 ml) tarragon champagne vinegar or other white vinegar
½ cup (4 fl oz/125 ml) dry white wine
3 cups (24 fl oz/750 ml) heavy (double) cream
8 cups (64 fl oz/2 l) water
2 teaspoons salt, or to taste
1 tablespoon Dijon mustard
¼ cup (2 oz/60 g) diced red bell pepper (capsicum)
1 teaspoon ground white pepper
1 cup plus 2 tablespoons (1½ oz/45 g) chopped fresh chives
6 single chive flowers snipped from 3 flower heads

✣ To make the pasta: Mix the flour, eggs, oil, salt and pepper in a bowl or a food processor until blended but still crumbly. Place the dough on a lightly floured board. Sprinkle the dough with lemon zest and chives. Press the zest and chives into the dough, but do not overwork the dough. Divide the dough into 2 pieces, wrap in plastic, and refrigerate for 1 hour.

✣ Remove the dough from the refrigerator and let sit for 30 minutes. Flatten the dough into an oblong-shaped disk. Using a pasta machine, run the dough through the press several times, pressing it a little thinner each time. Cut the sheet into wide strips (¾ in/2 cm) for pappardelle, or thinner strips (¼ in/6 mm) for fettuccine. Keep the pasta on a plate covered with a slightly moist towel until time to cook.

✣ In a large skillet, place the butter, onion, garlic and prawns. Sauté over high heat until the prawns are pink and the onion is translucent, about 5 minutes. Remove the prawns with a slotted spoon and set aside.

✣ Add the vinegar to the onion and garlic in the pan and cook over high heat to reduce for 3 minutes, or until the pan is almost dry. Add the wine and cook to reduce by half. Add the cream and cook for about 5 minutes or until the bubbles are big and the cream is thickened; set aside.

✣ To cook the pasta, bring the water to a boil in a large stockpot. Add 1 teaspoon of the salt to the boiling water. Add the fresh pasta and cook for 1½ minutes or until the pasta is al dente. Drain the pasta and place in a warm serving bowl.

✣ While the pasta is cooking, stir the mustard, red pepper and cooled prawns into the cream mixture and heat through. Season with white pepper and the remaining teaspoon of salt, or to taste. Just before serving, add the fresh chives. Pour over the cooked pasta and toss. Serve at once, garnished with the remaining 2 tablespoons of chives and the chive flowers.

SERVES 6

PAN-FRIED CORNMEAL-DUSTED IDAHO TROUT

Trout are abundant in the cold clear streams of Idaho. The best "camper's breakfast," trout goes perfectly with eggs, bacon and clean fresh air.

2 fresh trout, 8 in (20 cm) long
½ cup (3 oz/90 g) cornmeal
salt and pepper to taste
4–6 tablespoons (2–3 oz/60–90 g) butter
lemon wedges

▣ Clean and wash the trout. Cut off the fins, leaving the heads and tails. Mix the cornmeal with salt and pepper to taste. Dredge the trout in the seasoned cornmeal.
▣ Melt the butter in skillet over medium-high heat. Fry the trout for 3–4 minutes on each side, or until firm and golden brown. Remove from the pan and serve at once with lemon wedges.

SERVES 4

NORTHWEST HANGTOWN FRY

Use yearling Pacific oysters for this very Northwest version of Hangtown Fry. Serve with crisp bacon, sour cream and a dollop of Yakima Beefsteak–Tomato Salsa (recipe on page 44). Add a green salad and garlic toast for a Sunday brunch or supper.

6 large eggs
3 tablespoons cream or milk
¾ teaspoon salt
pinch of dried tarragon
freshly ground black pepper to taste
12 freshly shucked small oysters (method on page 46)
flour seasoned with salt and pepper
3 tablespoons butter
¼ cup (2 oz/60 g) chopped red bell pepper (capsicum)
2 shallots, chopped
2 large mushrooms, sliced
1 cup (1½ oz/45 g) chopped fresh spinach leaves
¼ cup (1 oz/30 g) freshly grated Parmesan cheese
8 bacon strips, fried crisp
sour cream and fresh salsa for garnish (optional)

▣ Beat the eggs with the cream or milk and season with salt, pepper and tarragon. Set aside.
▣ Lightly dredge the oysters in the seasoned flour. Melt 2 tablespoons of butter in a 12-in (30-cm) skillet and quickly sauté the oysters over high heat. Set the oysters aside on a warm plate. Add the remaining tablespoon of butter to the pan and sauté the bell pepper, shallots and mushrooms for 2–3 minutes, or until the shallots are translucent.
▣ Return the oysters to the skillet. Sprinkle the spinach over them and pour the egg mixture over all. Cook over medium heat, as for an omelet, lifting the edges of the cooked eggs to let the uncooked eggs cook; be careful not to overcook. When the eggs begin to set, remove from the heat, sprinkle the top with Parmesan and place under a broiler (griller) or in a hot oven until the mixture is just set, lightly browned and puffed up.
▣ Serve with bacon, and sour cream and fresh salsa, if you like.

SERVES 3–4

GEODUCK AND GREEN ONION HASH

Geoducks, pronounced "gooey-ducks," are not migratory birds, but rather gargantuan clams common to the Pacific Northwest. Like most chowder clams, they tend to be tough, so it's important to pound them well and chop them fine. This hash is great for breakfast with poached eggs, and it's also good for an impromptu dinner.

1 cup (8 fl oz/250 ml) sour cream
¼ cup (4 fl oz/125 ml) Dijon mustard

Clockwise from top left: Northwest Hangtown Fry, Pan-Fried Cornmeal-Dusted Idaho Trout, and Geoduck and Green Onion Hash

½ teaspoon salt
½ teaspoon freshly ground black pepper
½ teaspoon grated lemon zest
1½ tablespoons chopped fresh thyme, or 1 teaspoon dried thyme
12 oz (375 g) chopped geoduck or fresh or canned clams
1 cup (6 oz/180 g) sliced green (spring) onions
½ cup (4 oz/125 g) diced red bell pepper (capsicum)
3 cups (1 lb/500 kg) coarsely grated peeled russet potatoes
3–4 tablespoons olive oil
minced green (spring) onions and lemon wedges for garnish

◩ In a large bowl, combine the sour cream, mustard, salt and pepper, lemon zest and thyme; mix until evenly combined. Add the clams, green onions, bell pepper and potatoes, and stir all ingredients until lightly coated with the sour cream mixture.

◩ Heat the olive oil in a large nonstick skillet. Add the hash to the pan, cover, and cook over medium heat for 7–10 minutes, or until the hash begins to brown on the bottom. Turn it over in one cake with a spatula and cook, uncovered, on the second side until browned on the bottom, 5–7 minutes.

◩ Turn the hash onto a serving platter and garnish with green onions and lemon wedges.

SERVES 4

91

Western Washington

TERIYAKI YELLOWEYE ROCKFISH WITH PINEAPPLE SALSA

Yelloweye are sometimes referred to as "yelloweye snapper," but actually they are a member of the rockfish family. Any type of rockfish can be substituted for the yelloweye. Salmon is also delicious marinated in teriyaki and then grilled. The marinade may be kept refrigerated for up to 2 weeks.

TERIYAKI MARINADE

2 tablespoons orange juice (optional)
2 tablespoons fresh lemon juice
½ cup (4 fl oz/125 ml) soy sauce
4 teaspoons minced fresh ginger
2 teaspoons minced garlic
¼ teaspoon dried red pepper flakes
¼ cup (2 fl oz/60 ml) honey
1½ teaspoons Asian (toasted) sesame oil
2 tablespoons sake or dry sherry
2 tablespoons brown sugar

2 lb (1 kg) skinned yelloweye or other rockfish fillets, cut into 6 pieces
about 2 tablespoons peanut (groundnut) oil for cooking
Pineapple Salsa (recipe follows)
fresh lime wedges for garnish
fresh cilantro (coriander) sprigs for garnish

☒ To make the marinade: In a saucepan, combine all the marinade ingredients. Bring to a slow boil over medium-high heat, then remove the pan from the heat. Chill thoroughly.
☒ Place the fish pieces in a nonaluminum baking dish and pour the chilled marinade over the fish. Cover and refrigerate for 1½–2 hours.
☒ Heat a large cast-iron skillet over medium-high heat. Add a little peanut oil. Remove the fish from the marinade and place in the hot pan; cook on each side for about 2–3 minutes, or until nicely seared on each side and the flesh is opaque throughout.

☒ Remove the fish to individual plates and top with pineapple salsa. Garnish with lime wedges and cilantro sprigs.

SERVES 6

PINEAPPLE SALSA

2 tablespoons finely diced red bell pepper (capsicum)
1 cup (6 oz/185 g) finely diced fresh pineapple
½ teaspoon finely grated orange zest
1 orange, peeled and diced into ¼-in (6-mm) pieces
2 tablespoons chopped fresh cilantro (coriander)
¼ teaspoon salt
2 tablespoons fresh lime juice
1 teaspoon granulated sugar
2 teaspoons brown sugar
1 teaspoon cider vinegar
1 tablespoon finely diced red (Spanish) onion
¼ teaspoon dried red pepper flakes
½ teaspoon minced fresh ginger

☒ In a medium nonaluminum bowl, mix all the salsa ingredients together well.

MAKES 2 CUPS

Western Washington

SAKE KASU COD

Served in Seattle for about the last 40 years, kasu cod uses a flavoring made from sake lees, or, as the word kasu means in Japanese, "remnants." Mixed with sugar and sake, kasu makes a marinade that flavors as well as preserves fish. A sweet rich fish such as black cod or sablefish, which is actually a member of the skilfish family, should be the fish of choice. Kasu is available at well-stocked Japanese groceries.

1½ cups (12 fl oz/375 ml) kasu (sake lees)
1 tablespoon granulated sugar
1 tablespoon brown sugar
3 tablespoons sake

Left to right: Sake Kasu Cod, Salmon Cakes with Ginger Aïoli and Sesame Vegetable Slaw

Teriyaki Yelloweye Rockfish with Pineapple Salsa

3 tablespoons mirin or dry sherry
1½ teaspoons salt
4 fillets black cod, 6 oz (185 g) each, skin on
2 tablespoons vegetable oil

◼ To make the marinade: In a bowl, mix together the kasu, sugars, sake, mirin or sherry and salt. Spread half of the marinade in the bottom of a nonaluminum baking dish. Lay the fish over it, then spread the remaining marinade over the fish. Cover with plastic wrap and refrigerate for 48–72 hours.
◼ Prepare a fire in a charcoal grill. Remove the fish from the refrigerator 30 minutes before grilling.
◼ Some cooks prefer to wipe all the marinade off prior to cooking, while others like to let some of it remain. It's your choice. Brush the fish pieces with oil and grill flesh-side down 5 in (13 cm) from medium-hot coals for 4–5 minutes, then turn and cook the skin side for about 2–3 minutes more. Both sides of the fish should be slightly charred and the flesh should be opaque throughout.

SERVES 4

Western Washington

Salmon Cakes with Ginger Aïoli and Sesame Vegetable Slaw

This updated twist on the canned salmon patties popular in the sixties uses lightly baked or poached salmon and is sparked with an Asian-flavored aïoli and vegetable slaw.

GINGER AÏOLI

1 egg yolk
2 teaspoons minced garlic
1 tablespoon minced fresh ginger
2 tablespoons fresh lemon juice
1 cup (8 fl oz/250 ml) peanut (groundnut) oil or canola oil
2 tablespoons Asian (toasted) sesame oil
2 teaspoons rice wine vinegar
½ teaspoon soy sauce
¼ teaspoon salt
⅛ teaspoon *sambal oeleck* (Asian chili paste), optional

SALMON CAKES

1 lb (500 g) baked or poached salmon, slightly undercooked
¼ cup (2 fl oz/60 ml) mayonnaise
1 tablespoon sour cream
1 tablespoon lightly beaten egg
1 teaspoon Worcestershire sauce
dash of Tabasco (hot pepper) sauce
¼ teaspoon dry mustard
¼ cup (1½ oz/45 g) minced celery
¼ cup (1½ oz/45 g) minced green (spring) onion
3 tablespoons minced red bell pepper (capsicum)
1½ teaspoons minced garlic
¼ cup (1 oz/30 g) bread crumbs
2½ teaspoons fresh lemon juice
½–1 teaspoon salt
¼ teaspoon freshly ground black pepper
1 tablespoon chopped fresh parsley

2–3 eggs beaten with 1 tablespoon water
about 3 cups (12 oz/375 g) bread crumbs
peanut (groundnut) oil for frying
Sesame Vegetable Slaw (recipe follows)
lemon slices for garnish
fresh cilantro (coriander) sprigs for garnish

◼ To make the ginger aïoli: Place the egg yolk, garlic, ginger and lemon juice in a food processor. With the motor running, slowly add the oils and vinegar until emulsified. Season with soy sauce, salt and *sambal oeleck*. The consistency of the aïoli should be like that of mayonnaise.
◼ Refrigerate until needed.
◼ To make the salmon cakes: In a large bowl, mix all the salmon cake ingredients together. Divide into 12 portions. Firmly form the portions into patties and dip into the egg wash, then in the bread crumbs, coating well.
◼ In a large skillet, pour peanut oil to a depth of 1½–2 in (4–5 cm). Heat until hot but not smoking, 350°–375°F (180°–190°C). Fry the crab cakes in batches until golden brown on each side, turning as needed. Drain on paper towels and keep warm in a very low oven while cooking all the crab cakes. Serve immediately with Sesame Vegetable Slaw and Ginger Aïoli, garnished with lemon slices and cilantro sprigs.

SERVES 6

SESAME VEGETABLE SLAW

1½ cups (5 oz/135 g) very finely sliced Savoy cabbage
½ cup (1½ oz/45 g) very finely sliced red cabbage
1 cup (8 oz/125 g) matchstick-cut carrots
½ zucchini (courgette), cut into matchsticks
½ English cucumber, seeded and cut into matchsticks
1 tablespoon minced red (Spanish) onion
½ red bell pepper (capsicum), cut into matchsticks
3 tablespoons rice wine vinegar
1 tablespoon cider vinegar
1 tablespoon fresh lemon juice
3 tablespoons sugar
3 tablespoons Ginger Aïoli (recipe above) or mayonnaise
   mixed with ½ teaspoon minced fresh ginger
¼ teaspoon freshly ground black pepper
1 teaspoon salt
2 tablespoons chopped fresh cilantro (coriander)
1 tablespoon toasted black sesame seeds (optional)
1 tablespoon toasted white sesame seeds
1 bunch fresh chives cut into ½-in (1.5-cm) lengths

◼ In a large bowl, combine the prepared vegetables. Chill until needed.
◼ In another bowl, whisk together the vinegars, lemon juice, sugar, aïoli, seasonings and cilantro. Pour this mixture over the prepared vegetables and toss well. The slaw can be refrigerated for up to 30 minutes before serving.
◼ Right before serving, toss in the sesame seeds and chives.

SERVES 6

Top to bottom: Vancouver Fried Rice, Tempura Prawns with Vietnamese Dipping Sauce, and Pacific Rim Stuffed Salmon

PACIFIC RIM STUFFED SALMON

One of the most significant influences on the Vancouver food scene is the Asian culture. And one of the most influential Japanese chefs in Vancouver is Hidekazu Tojo of Tojo's Restaurant. His philosophy of aestheticism and simplicity, along with his sense of improvisation and experimentation, is brought to play in Tojo's inventive food and presentations.

1 salmon fillet, about 2–3 lb (1–1.5 kg) skinned
2 cups (16 fl oz/500 ml) soy sauce
1 cup (8 fl oz/250 ml) sake
2 tablespoons minced fresh ginger
6 dried shiitake mushrooms
1 carrot
1 onion
2 large asparagus spears
1 lb (500 g) fresh or frozen Dungeness crab meat or surimi
¼ cup (2 fl oz/60 ml) teriyaki sauce
cooked asparagus for garnish
zest of 1 lemon or lime for garnish

▣ Place the salmon fillet on a cutting board and cut partway through the flesh down the center bone line; fold the flesh open on each side to make one flat piece 1½ times the original width. Combine the soy sauce, sake and fresh ginger in a large nonaluminum baking dish. Add the salmon, cover and place in the refrigerator for 4 hours.
▣ To make the stuffing: Place the dried mushrooms in a bowl of warm water and soak for 30 minutes. Meanwhile, cut the carrot, onion and asparagus into long matchstick strips. Pat the mushrooms dry and cut them into thin strips. Add the crab meat or surimi and toss well.
▣ Preheat an oven to 350°F (180°C). Place a large strip of plastic wrap on a flat surface and place the fillet, spread out, on the plastic, skinned side down. Spread the stuffing down the length of the fillet to form a long strip down the center. Using the plastic wrap as a guide, roll up the salmon and stuffing jelly-roll fashion, and twist the ends of the plastic wrap closed. Do not roll the plastic into the fish. Roll it around the fish like a casing, making sure the fish is rolled up tightly. Tuck the ends of the plastic underneath the roll. Wrap the salmon roll again with aluminum foil, making sure all the edges are sealed and the ends are tight. Place on a baking sheet and bake in the preheated oven for 35–40 minutes.
▣ Remove from the oven. Unwrap and discard the foil, but leave the plastic wrap on the salmon. Heat the teriyaki sauce and keep warm over low heat. Using a sharp knife, cut the plastic-wrapped salmon into 2-in (5-cm) slices.
▣ Remove the plastic from the salmon, place the slices on a serving dish, and garnish with asparagus spears. Pour teriyaki sauce over the salmon and sprinkle with zest.

SERVES 6–8

VANCOUVER FRIED RICE

Dynasty restaurant has brought the elegance of Chinese fine dining to Vancouver. Chef Kam Shing Lam delivers true Cantonese cooking of the kind found in the best Hong Kong hotels. This flavorful fried rice with crab, scallops, large prawns and cod is one of Dynasty's most popular dishes.

4 tablespoons (2 fl oz/60 ml) vegetable oil
4 oz (125 g) fresh or frozen Dungeness crab meat
4 oz (125 g) scallops, finely diced
4 oz (125 g) large prawns, peeled and deveined, finely diced
4 oz (125 g) rock cod fillet, finely diced
⅓ cup (3 oz /90 g) finely diced carrots
1 small onion, finely diced

⅓ cup (3 oz/90 g) finely diced Chinese broccoli stem
2 eggs, beaten
3½ cups (7 oz/210 g) cooked long-grain white rice (1 cup or 5 oz/155 g uncooked)
1 teaspoon soy sauce
salt and freshly ground pepper to taste

▣ Place a wok or heavy skillet over high heat for 30 seconds. Add 2 tablespoons of the oil and heat for 30 seconds. Add the crab meat, scallops, prawns, rock cod, carrots, onion and broccoli, and stir-fry for 2 minutes. Remove the seafood and vegetables from the wok with a slotted spoon and pour out the oil.
▣ Add the remaining 2 tablespoons of oil to the pan, heat 30 seconds, and pour in the eggs.
▣ Reduce the heat to medium-high and add the rice. Using a spoon, toss the rice to keep it loose and free of lumps. Add the seafood, vegetables and soy sauce, and stir-fry until heated through. Season to taste with salt and pepper. Serve hot.

SERVES 6

TEMPURA PRAWNS WITH VIETNAMESE DIPPING SAUCE

On the Pacific coast, the terms prawn and shrimp are often used interchangeably, but in commercial usage shrimp refers to the smaller species and prawns to the larger. From tiny shrimp to good-sized prawns varying in size from 2–8 inches (5–20 cm), they are harvested year round. Like all crustaceans, they change color from gray-green to bright pink or red when cooked. Fish sauce, or nuoc mam, *is as important an ingredient in Vietnamese cooking as soy sauce is in Chinese and Japanese cooking. In Vietnam, fish sauce is used as a table condiment and as flavoring in almost every dish.*

1 egg
1 cup (8 fl oz/250 ml) ice water
1 cup (4 oz/125 g) all-purpose (plain) flour
1½ teaspoons baking powder
½ teaspoon salt
12 large prawns, peeled and deveined with tails left on
1 teaspoon soy sauce
1 teaspoon sake
4 cups (32 fl oz/1 l) vegetable oil
½ cup (4 fl oz/125 ml) fish sauce
1 cup (8 fl oz/250 ml) rice wine vinegar
½ cup (4 oz/125 g) sugar
1 cup (8 fl oz/250 ml) water
¼ cup (2 oz/10 g) shredded carrots
¼ cup (1 oz/30 g) chopped peanuts

▣ To make the batter: Beat together the egg and ice water. Combine the flour, baking powder and salt and add to the egg and water mixture. Stir lightly until just blended. (Do not place the batter near heat or let it sit too long, or it will become gluey.)
▣ Rinse and pat the prawns dry with paper towels. To prevent the prawns from curling during deep-frying, make 4 or 5 slight cuts on the underside of each prawn.
▣ Sprinkle the prawns with soy sauce and sake and lightly toss.
▣ In a deep-fryer or large, heavy pot, preheat the oil to 350°F (180°C).
▣ Drop 3 prawns into the batter. With chopsticks, lift each one out of the batter, letting the excess drain back into the bowl. Gently slip the prawns into the hot oil and deep-fry for about 2–3 minutes, or until golden brown. Drain on paper towels. Repeat until all the prawns are cooked.
▣ To make the dipping sauce: Stir together the fish sauce, vinegar, sugar, water, carrots and peanuts.
▣ Serve the hot prawns with the dipping sauce.

SERVES 4

British Columbia

DEEP-FRIED SMELTS, CHINESE STYLE

Smelt is a small, delicate, troutlike fish found in the coastal waters of British Columbia and usually netted inshore. Often cooked whole, the edible bones of the fish provide a satisfying crunch, and the flesh is sweet.

4 cups (32 fl oz/1 l) plus 1 tablespoon vegetable oil
2 jalapeño (hot green) chilies, seeded and minced
4–6 garlic cloves, minced
1 tablespoon soy sauce
1 tablespoon water
2 lb (1 kg) smelts
1¾ cups (7 oz/215 g) all-purpose (plain) flour
¼ cup (1 oz/30 g) cornstarch (cornflour)
1½ teaspoons salt
lemon wedges
1 bunch, about 2 oz (60 g), fresh cilantro (coriander) for garnish

▨ To make the sauce: Add 1 tablespoon oil to a skillet and heat over medium heat. Add the chilies and garlic, and cook for about 30 seconds, or until just lightly browned. Remove from the heat, stir in the soy sauce and water, and set aside.
▨ In a deep-fryer or a large, heavy pot, preheat the oil to 375°F (190°C). Meanwhile, rinse the fish and drain on paper towels.
▨ In a large, shallow baking dish, combine the flour, cornstarch and salt. Dredge the fish in the flour to coat well.
▨ Place one-fourth of the fish in the basket of the deep-fryer or drop into the oil and cook for about 2 minutes, or until golden brown and crisp. Drain on paper towels and keep warm in a very low oven. Repeat with the remaining fish until all are cooked. Serve hot with the sauce poured over.
▨ Accompany with lemon wedges and garnish with cilantro.

SERVES 6–8

Islands

SCALLOP WONTONS WITH TOMATO-GINGER CHUTNEY

Since the first Chinese came to the Northwest to work on the railroads and in the mining camps, their cuisine has had a subtle but pervasive influence on the cooking of the region. Most early-day cooks in logging camps, restaurants and private homes were Chinese, and their light touch with seafood set the standard for Northwesterners. This healthful dish exemplifies the marriage between ancient and modern cuisines.

TOMATO-GINGER CHUTNEY

 tomatoes, peeled, seeded and diced
1 tablespoon minced fresh ginger
1 tablespoon minced shallot
2 garlic cloves, minced
2 tablespoons chopped fresh cilantro (coriander)
¾ cup (12 fl oz/375 ml) seasoned rice wine vinegar

SCALLOP WONTONS

1 cup (8 fl oz/250 ml) peanut (groundnut) oil
12 wonton wrappers
36 large fresh Alaskan weathervane or other sea scallops, about 3 lb (1.5 kg), muscle removed
1 lime, cut into 6 wedges

▨ To make the chutney: Place the tomatoes, ginger, shallot, garlic, cilantro and vinegar in a small nonaluminum container. Let sit at room temperature to allow flavors to blend. (This will keep in the refrigerator for 4 days.)

▨ To make the wontons: In a large skillet, heat the peanut oil to 350°F (180°C). Fry the wonton wrappers 3 at a time in the hot oil until golden. Drain on paper towels and place in a very low oven to keep warm. Repeat until all the wrappers have been fried.

*Left to right: Deep-Fried Smelts, Chinese Style, and
Scallop Wontons with Tomato-Ginger Chutney*

◨ Pour off the peanut oil, reserving it for another use. Using the same pan, sear the scallops quickly over high heat on each side until just firm and lightly browned, about 3 minutes. Remove the pan from the heat.

◨ To assemble the wontons: On each plate place 1 fried wonton, mound it with 6 scallops, and top each scallop with a generous tablespoon of the chutney. Top each serving with a second wonton. Garnish with lime wedges.

SERVES 6

Western Washington

MICROBREW BEER–BATTERED FISH

Fish and chips are a Pacific Northwest tradition. The batter is made with hearty local microbrews, and the fish is served with homemade tartar sauce and Idaho fries. The tartar sauce is used as a dip for both fish and chips.

BATTER

¾ cup (3 oz/60 g) all-purpose (plain) flour
¾ cup (3 oz/60 g) cornstarch (cornflour)
½ teaspoon baking soda (bicarbonate of soda)
1 tablespoon sifted powdered (icing) sugar
2 teaspoons salt
¼ teaspoon ground white pepper
½ teaspoon granulated garlic
¼ teaspoon paprika
¼ teaspoon dried dill
¼ teaspoon dried thyme
½ teaspoon grated lemon zest
½–¾ cup (4–6 fl oz/125–180 ml) microbrewed hearty ale (dark beer)
½ cup (4 fl oz/125 ml) plus 1–2 tablespoons water, if needed

peanut (groundnut) or vegetable oil for frying
1½ lb (750 g) fresh firm-fleshed white fish fillet such as ling cod or halibut, skinned and cut diagonally into 12 pieces
lemon wedges for garnish

◻ To make the batter: In a large bowl, mix together all the dry batter ingredients. Stir in the ale and ½ cup of the water to make a light batter that will coat the fish, adding 1–2 tablespoons of water as needed. The batter should have the same consistency as crepe batter.

◻ Pour 5 in (13 cm) of oil into a deep-fryer or large Dutch oven. Heat to 375°F (190°C). Dip the fish pieces one at a time into the batter, coating them well. Carefully drop a few pieces at a time into the hot oil and fry, turning if necessary; don't let the fish pieces stick together. Cook until golden, about 3½ minutes. Drain on paper towels and keep warm in a very low oven while cooking the remaining fish in batches. Serve immediately with lemon wedges.

SERVES 4–6

British Columbia

HOT CRAB MELT WITH TWO CHEESES

An old standby on the West Coast, Dungeness crab with cream cheese is perfect for a rainy-day lunch.

8 oz (250 g) fresh or frozen Dungeness crab meat
2 teaspoons fresh lemon juice
2 tablespoons minced fresh chives or minced green (spring) onion
2 tablespoons minced red bell pepper (capsicum)
2 tablespoons minced celery
4 oz (125 g) cream cheese at room temperature
½ teaspoon Dijon mustard
½ cup (2 oz/60 g) grated sharp Cheddar cheese
salt and freshly ground pepper to taste
2 French rolls, cut in half, or English muffins, split

◻ In a bowl, place the crab meat and sprinkle with the lemon juice.
◻ Add the chives or onion, bell pepper, celery, cream cheese, mustard, half the Cheddar, salt and pepper, and mix well.
◻ Divide the crab meat mixture among the rolls and top with the remaining Cheddar. Place under a broiler (griller) until heated through and cheese is bubbly.

SERVES 2

Left to right: Hot Crab Melt with Two Cheeses, Microbrew Beer–Battered Fish

Left to right: Black Cod with Six Onion Relish and Savory Vinaigrette,
Mussels with Leeks and Tarragon Cream

BLACK COD WITH SIX ONION RELISH AND SAVORY VINAIGRETTE

Black cod is also known as sablefish or butterfish, because it is so smooth and finely textured. The row of little bones that runs down the middle of each fillet can be easily removed after the fish is cooked.

SAVORY VINAIGRETTE

½ cup (4 fl oz/125 ml) extra-virgin olive oil
¼ cup (2 fl oz/60 ml) balsamic vinegar
1½ teaspoons chopped fresh basil, or ½ teaspoon dried basil
1½ teaspoons chopped fresh parsley
1½ teaspoons chopped fresh lemon thyme, or ½ teaspoon dried thyme
1½ teaspoons chopped fresh summer savory, or ½ teaspoon dried savory
½ teaspoon salt
¼ teaspoon freshly ground pepper
1 teaspoon grated lemon zest

1 tablespoon peanut (groundnut) oil
6 black cod fillets, 4–7 oz (125–220 g) each
1½ cups (12 fl oz/375 ml) Six Onion Relish (recipe on page 190)
1 lime, cut into 6 wedges
18 chives, tied into knots of 3

⊠ To make the vinaigrette: Whisk all the ingredients together in a small bowl and set aside.
⊠ In a large skillet, heat the peanut oil over medium-high heat for 3 minutes, or until a drop of water sizzles. Cook the fillets for about 2½–3 minutes on each side, or just until opaque throughout.
⊠ To serve, divide the onion relish among 6 warmed plates. Place a fillet on the onion relish on each plate and drizzle with 1 tablespoon of the vinaigrette. Garnish with a lime wedge and a chive knot. Pass the remaining vinaigrette.

SERVES 6

MUSSELS WITH LEEKS AND TARRAGON CREAM

The shimmery blue mussels that cling to the rocks and pilings of Puget Sound are both prolific and tasty. Like most shellfish, their flavor is best in the cool months.

5 leeks, white part only, cut into matchsticks
2 garlic cloves, minced
½ cup (4 fl oz/120 ml) rice vinegar
½ cup (4 oz/125 ml) Riesling or other fruity white wine
¼ cup (2 fl oz/60 ml) Pernod
1 cup (8 fl oz/250 ml) heavy (double) cream
2 lb (1 kg) mussels in the shell, scrubbed and debearded
4 tablespoons chopped fresh tarragon, or 1 tablespoon dried tarragon
¼ teaspoon salt
½–1 teaspoon freshly ground pepper
1 tablespoon chopped fresh parsley
1 tablespoon minced red bell pepper (capsicum)

⊠ In a medium stockpot, place the leeks, garlic and vinegar. Cook over medium heat until the vinegar is reduced to 1 tablespoon, about 10 minutes. Add the wine and cook to reduce by half. Add the Pernod and the cream; bring to a simmer. Raise the heat and, just as the cream begins to bubble, add the mussels and tarragon.
⊠ Cover and steam just until the mussels open, about 3 minutes; do not overcook. Season with salt and pepper.
⊠ Serve in warm large bowls, and sprinkle each serving with parsley and red pepper.

SERVES 6

Eastern Washington

PAN-FRIED WALLEYE WITH ROMESCO SAUCE

The walleye is a member of the perch family and is plentiful in the Columbia River. Its firm yet flaky texture is delicate and sweet in flavor, a perfect combination with spicy romesco sauce. Pan-frying

creates a deliciously crisp exterior, while the inside stays moist and tender. Serve the sauce on the side for dipping.

½ cup (2 oz/60 g) sliced almonds, toasted (see glossary)
2 slices bread, toasted
4 garlic cloves
1 red bell pepper (capsicum), seeded and coarsely chopped
2 tomatoes, coarsely chopped

¼–½ cup (1–2 oz/ 30–60 g) fine fresh bread crumbs
four 4–6 oz(125–185 g) walleye or perch fillets
2 tablespoons oil for frying
2 tablespoons butter
lemon wedges

◼ To make the sauce: In a blender or food processor, combine the almonds, bread and garlic, and purée until smooth. Add the bell pepper, tomatoes, lemon juice, cayenne pepper and pepper flakes. Purée until smooth. With the machine running, slowly add the vinegar, then the oil. The sauce should be smooth and thick. Let sit at room temperature until served.
◼ Mix together the flour, salt and pepper and bread crumbs. Dredge the fillets in this mixture, pressing the mixture lightly into the fish.
◼ Heat the oil and butter in heavy skillet over medium heat until the oil sizzles. Add the fillets and cook for 3–4 minutes on each side, or until they are golden brown on both sides and opaque throughout.
◼ Transfer to a serving plate and serve with romesco sauce and lemon wedges.

MAKES ABOUT 3 CUPS (24 FL OZ/750 ML) SAUCE; SERVES 4

Oregon

PAN-ROASTED STEELHEAD WITH APPLES, ONIONS AND SAGE

Steelhead are large trout that migrate to sea and return to fresh-water in the Pacific Northwest. They're a wonderful treat, but one available only to patient sportsmen and -women. Try salmon steaks or even boneless rainbow trout if you're not lucky enough to have some steelhead.

6 steelhead or salmon steaks, 8 oz (250 g) each
2 cups (16 fl oz/500 ml) natural unfiltered apple juice
1 Walla Walla Sweet onion or other sweet onion, cut into ½-in (1.5-cm) slices
2 cups (10 oz/315 g) peeled and diced tart green apples
6 crushed garlic cloves
2 tablespoons fresh lemon juice
2 tablespoons soy sauce
5 fresh sage sprigs
salt and pepper to taste
2 tablespoons olive oil
sage sprigs for garnish (optional)

◼ In a shallow nonaluminum pan, place the steelhead or salmon steaks, apple juice, onion, apples, garlic, lemon juice, soy sauce and sage. Cover and refrigerate for 6–8 hours, turning the fish several times during this period.
◼ Warm a large serving platter in a low oven. Remove the fish from the marinade and blot dry with a paper towel. Strain and reserve the marinade and the apples and onions, but discard the garlic and sage.
◼ Lightly season the fish steaks with salt and pepper. Heat a large nonstick skillet over medium heat, add the olive oil, and cook a few fish steaks at a time for 3–5 minutes on each side, or until dark golden brown on each side. Repeat, keeping the fish warm in a very low oven until all the fish is cooked.
◼ Quickly sauté the apple and onion mixture in the same skillet for 2–3 minutes. Add 1 cup (8 fl oz/250 ml) of the reserved marinade. Bring to a low boil and add salt and pepper.
◼ Arrange the onions and apples around the fish and pour the pan juices over. Garnish with fresh sage sprigs, if desired.

SERVES 6

Left to right: Pan-Fried Walleye with Romesco Sauce, Pan-Roasted Steelhead with Apples, Onions and Sage

2 teaspoons fresh lemon juice
1 teaspoon cayenne pepper
2 teaspoons dried red pepper flakes
½ cup (4 fl oz/125 ml) balsamic vinegar
1 cup (8 fl oz/250 ml) olive oil
¼ cup (1 oz/30 g) all-purpose (plain) flour
salt and pepper to taste

SMOKED SALMON BENEDICT WITH SOUR CREAM–CHIVE HOLLANDAISE

This makes for a special brunch, served with glasses of bubbly champagne and bowls of fresh strawberries. If fresh chives are not available, substitute thinly sliced green (spring) onions.

SOUR CREAM–CHIVE HOLLANDAISE

½ cup (4 fl oz/125 ml) dry white wine
1 tablespoon orange juice
1 teaspoon fresh lemon juice
1 teaspoon minced shallot
2 tablespoons sour cream
2 egg yolks
¼ teaspoon Tabasco (hot pepper) sauce
¾ cup (6 fl oz/180 ml) melted butter
1 tablespoon minced fresh chives
salt and freshly ground black pepper

6 oz (185 g) thinly sliced smoked salmon
4 Orange Scones, split crosswise (recipe follows)
1 teaspoon distilled white vinegar
8 eggs
fresh chives cut into 1-in (2.5-cm) lengths for garnish
salmon caviar for garnish (optional)

◾ To make the hollandaise: Reserve 2 tablespoons of the white wine. Pour the remaining white wine, orange juice, lemon juice and shallot into a small saucepan. Place over high heat and cook to reduce to 2 tablespoons. Remove from the heat and stir in the sour cream. Set aside.

◾ In a medium stainless steel bowl, whisk the egg yolks, 2 tablespoons reserved white wine and Tabasco. Place over, but not touching, simmering water in a double boiler and whisk constantly, scraping down the sides often. When the eggs begin to look frothy, remove the double boiler from the heat (overheated eggs will turn the sauce to scrambled eggs) and, while continuing to whisk, slowly drizzle in the melted butter. After all the butter has been incorporated, remove the bowl from the double boiler. Whisk in the sour cream mixture and chives. Season to taste with salt and pepper.

◾ Preheat an oven to 300°F (150°C). Lay smoked salmon slices on the scone halves and place on a baking sheet. Heat in the preheated oven until warmed through, 4–5 minutes.

◾ Meanwhile, fill a large skillet with water and add the vinegar. Place over medium-high heat and bring to a simmer. Crack the eggs into the simmering water and poach for about 2 minutes, or until just opaque and cooked to the desired doneness. Remove from the water with a slotted spoon, draining well.

◾ Place 2 warmed scones with salmon on each plate. Place an egg on each half and top with dollops of hollandaise. Garnish with chives and salmon caviar. Serve at once.

SERVES 4

Left to right: Smoked Salmon Benedict with Sour Cream–Chive Hollandaise, Spinach and Crab-Stuffed Baked Prawns

ORANGE SCONES

2¼ cups (9 oz/280 g) all-purpose (plain) flour
2 tablespoons sugar
1 teaspoon cream of tartar
¾ teaspoon baking soda (bicarbonate of soda)
½ teaspoon salt
¼ cup (2 oz/60 g) cold butter
¼ cup (2 oz/60 g) vegetable shortening (vegetable lard)
3 tablespoons fresh orange juice
2 tablespoons milk, plus 1–2 tablespoons more if needed
1 large egg
2 teaspoons finely grated orange zest
1 egg white mixed with ½ teaspoon water for glaze

◙ Preheat an oven to 375°F (190°C). Sift together the dry ingredients into a large bowl. Cut in the butter and shortening with a pastry cutter or 2 knives.
◙ In a separate bowl, mix together all the remaining ingredients except the egg white glaze. Make a well in the center of the dry ingredients and pour the liquid into it. Combine with a few swift strokes. Add 1–2 tablespoons additional milk if needed. Do not overmix. Place on a lightly floured board and pat into a ¾-in (2-cm)-thick circle.
◙ Place on a baking sheet and cut into 8 wedges. Brush lightly with the egg white glaze. Bake in the preheated oven for 18–22 minutes, or until golden.

MAKES 8 SCONES

SPINACH AND CRAB-STUFFED BAKED PRAWNS

These delicious stuffed prawns are great for a special dinner party. Prepare them in advance and pop them in the oven right before your guests sit down for dinner. Serve with a chilled Northwest Chardonnay.

STUFFING

3 tablespoons butter
3 tablespoons finely diced onion
3 tablespoons finely diced celery
1 teaspoon minced garlic
2 tablespoons all-purpose (plain) flour
2 tablespoons dry sherry
2 teaspoons fresh lemon juice
1 teaspoon Dijon mustard
dash of Tabasco (hot pepper) sauce
½ cup (4 fl oz/125 ml) half & half (half milk and half cream)
1 cup (1½ oz/45 g) coarsely chopped fresh spinach leaves, packed
½ teaspoon salt
pinch of white pepper
dash of Worcestershire sauce
2 teaspoons minced fresh parsley
tiny pinch of dried tarragon
3 tablespoons freshly shredded Parmesan cheese
1 tablespoon dry bread crumbs
4 oz (125 g) fresh or frozen Dungeness crab meat

20 large (16–20 per lb/500 g) prawns peeled and deveined with tails left on
2 tablespoons butter
Herbed Bread Crumbs (recipe follows)
½ cup (4 fl oz/125 ml) dry sherry
salt and freshly cracked pepper to taste

◙ To make the stuffing: In a large skillet over medium-high heat, melt the butter, add the onions and celery, and sauté for 1 minute; add the garlic and cook 30 seconds more. Whisk in the flour and cook for 1 minute, stirring constantly. Reduce the heat to medium and, while whisking, add all at once the sherry, lemon juice, mustard, Tabasco sauce and half & half. Cook for about 1–2 minutes, or until the sauce is thick.
◙ Add the spinach and seasonings, stirring well. Cook for about 1 minute, then add the remaining ingredients. Remove from heat and adjust the seasoning if necessary. Let cool until set.
◙ Preheat an oven to 475°F (240°C). To stuff and bake prawns: Butterfly the prawns by cutting them partially through on the inside of the curve; spread the 2 halves open flat. Divide the stuffing among the butterflied prawns, pressing it firmly onto the prawns. Dip the stuffing side into the Herbed Bread Crumbs. Place the prawns in a buttered 9-by-13-in (23-by-33-cm) baking pan, stuffing side up and tails against the sides of the pan. Drizzle the sherry around the prawns and season with salt and pepper as desired.
◙ Bake on the middle rack of the oven for 6–8 minutes, or until the bread crumbs are lightly golden and the prawns are pink. Serve immediately.

SERVES 4

HERBED BREAD CRUMBS

1½ cups torn fresh Italian or French bread, about 3 oz (90 g)
2 tablespoons soft butter
dash of Tabasco (hot pepper) sauce
¼ teaspoon salt
2 tablespoons chopped fresh parsley

◙ Place all the ingredients in a blender or food processor and process for about 30 seconds, until all ingredients are well combined and the bread crumbs are about pea size.

Oregon

SEARED SEA SCALLOPS WITH ROASTED PEPPERS AND POLENTA

Succulent scallops echo the sweetness of roasted peppers and creamy polenta. Try a crisp Pinot Gris with this summery dish.

1½ lb (750 g) sea scallops
¼ cup (2 fl oz/60 ml) olive oil

POLENTA

8 cups (64 fl oz/2 l) water
2 tablespoons extra-virgin olive oil
2 tablespoons butter
2 cups (10 oz/310 g) coarsely ground cornmeal (polenta)
1 cup (4 oz/125 g) freshly grated Parmesan cheese
1 teaspoon salt
pepper to taste

3 roasted and peeled red, green and yellow bell peppers
    (capsicums), cut into strips (see glossary), to make about 2
    cups (1 lb/500 g)
salt and pepper to taste
1 cup (8 fl oz/250 ml) crème fraîche
1 bunch fresh cilantro (coriander), stemmed

▧ In a medium bowl, toss the scallops in the olive oil.
▧ To make the polenta: Bring the water to a boil in a large, heavy saucepan; add the olive oil, butter and salt and reduce the heat to low. Gradually whisk in the polenta and stir constantly for 15–20 minutes, or until the mixture is smooth and has the texture of porridge. Stir in the Parmesan. Add pepper. Cover and remove from the heat; keep warm.
▧ Heat a large nonstick skillet over medium-high heat, add the oil, and cook the scallops in a single layer without stirring for 2–3 minutes, or until they are a rich golden brown. Carefully turn the scallops and brown on the other side for 1 minute. Remove the scallops from the pan. Add the peppers to the pan and stir briefly to warm them through. Add salt and pepper and set aside.
▧ To make the sauce: Place the crème fraîche in a blender or food processor, add the cilantro, and purée until smooth. Add salt and pepper.
▧ Divide the warm polenta among 6 warmed plates or wide-rimmed soup bowls and arrange the julienned peppers on top. Place the scallops on the peppers and drizzle with the cilantro crème fraîche. Serve at once.

SERVES 6   *Photograph on page 4*

Western Washington

HALIBUT WITH HAZELNUT CRUST AND LEMON THYME–APPLE VINAIGRETTE

This dish is excellent paired with wild seasonal greens tossed with a little of the vinaigrette. The hazelnuts in the crust mixture may be replaced with almonds, walnuts or pecans.

LEMON THYME–APPLE VINAIGRETTE

1 red apple
3 tablespoons hazelnut oil or olive oil
2 teaspoons minced shallot
2 teaspoons sugar
¼ cup (2 fl oz/60 ml) fresh lemon juice
2 teaspoons Dijon mustard
½ cup (4 fl oz/125 ml) vegetable oil
1½ teaspoons chopped fresh lemon thyme or thyme
¼ teaspoon salt
pinch of cayenne pepper
1 tablespoon water

HAZELNUT CRUST

1½ cups (8 oz/250 g) hazelnuts
1 pinch of dry mustard
1¼ teaspoons salt
¼ teaspoon cayenne pepper
1 tablespoon grated lemon zest
1 teaspoon dried thyme

1¼ lb (625 g) skinned halibut fillet
¼ cup (2 oz/60 g) butter, melted
3–4 tablespoons vegetable oil
fresh lemon thyme sprigs for garnish (optional)

▧ To make the vinaigrette: Cut the apple in half and core. Chop half of the apple and reserve the other half for garnish.
▧ In a small skillet, heat the hazelnut oil over medium-low heat and add the chopped apple. Cook for 1 minute, then add the shallots and sugar. Continue cooking the apple until tender, about 1 minute. Add the lemon juice and remove from the heat. Let cool, then purée in a blender until smooth.
▧ Pour the puréed mixture into a medium bowl. Add the Dijon, then slowly whisk in the oil. Add the lemon thyme and season with salt and cayenne pepper. Stir in the water. Cut the remaining apple half into ¼-in (6-mm) dice. Toss into the dressing. Refrigerate until needed.
▧ To make the crust: Toast and skin the hazelnuts (see glossary). Place all the crust ingredients in a blender or food processor and pulse until minced but not powdered. Place in a large, shallow dish. Set aside.
▧ Preheat an oven to 425°F (220°C). Cut the halibut fillet diagonally into 4 pieces about ½ in (1.5 cm) thick. Dip each piece in the melted butter, coating well. Immediately press each fish piece firmly into the nut crust mixture, turning and coating all sides well.
▧ Place the coated fish on a baking sheet and bake in the preheated oven for about 6 minutes, or until the coating is lightly brown and the fish opaque throughout.
▧ Carefully remove the fish to individual plates and drizzle the vinaigrette over it. Garnish with fresh lemon thyme sprigs, if you like. Pass extra vinaigrette.

SERVES 4

Islands

STEAMED HALIBUT WITH BLACKBERRY BUTTER

The cold waters of the Pacific Northwest are home to the halibut. At around 300 pounds, it is one of the largest market fish in the ocean. Caught on a long line, a traditional fishing method, the halibut are brought onto boats with a gaff. Halibut fishing requires skill, stamina, strength and, according to some fishermen, a well-honed sense of humor. Fresh halibut has shimmering, opalescent flesh, but when frozen it turns white and loses its sheen.

2 tablespoons minced shallot
1 garlic clove, minced
¼ cup (2 fl oz/60 ml) balsamic vinegar
1 cup (6 oz/185 g) blackberries
¼ cup (2 fl oz/60 ml) Semillon, Riesling or other fruity white
    wine
2 tablespoons port

Left to right: Steamed Halibut with Blackberry Butter, Halibut with Hazelnut Crust and Lemon Thyme–Apple Vinaigrette

1½ cups (11 oz/340 g) unsalted butter, cut into pieces
4 cups (32 fl oz/1 l) water
½ lemon, cut into wedges
1-in (2.5-cm) piece fresh ginger, cut into thin slices
1 small fir or pine twig, about 4 in (10 cm) long (optional)
6 halibut fillets, 6–8 oz (185–250 g) each
small bunch fresh chives
freshly ground black pepper (optional)

◼ To make the blackberry butter: In a medium saucepan, place the shallot, garlic, vinegar and berries. Over high heat, reduce the liquid to about 1 tablespoon, being careful not to let it scorch. Add the white wine and reduce again to about 1 tablespoon of liquid. Add the port and reduce for 2 minutes, or until the mixture is syrupy.

◼ Lower the heat and gradually begin whisking in the butter, a few chunks at a time. Before each few pieces are completely melted, add another few, whisking as each batch of butter is added. The sauce must be kept warm but not hot, or the butter will separate. Remove the blackberry butter from the heat as the last piece of butter is incorporated.

◼ Immediately strain the butter mixture into a small bowl. Season to taste with salt. Keep in a warm place until ready for use.

◼ Place the water, lemon, ginger and fir or pine twig in a large steamer with a tight-fitting lid. Bring the water to a boil with the lid on. Place the fillets on a steamer tray over the boiling water. Cover and steam for 10 minutes, or until the halibut is opaque and firm to the touch.

◼ Serve the fish immediately on warm plates surrounded by the blackberry butter. Garnish with fresh chives and a few grinds of fresh black pepper, if you like.

SERVES 6

British Columbia

PACIFIC NORTHWEST CRAB POT WITH DIPPING SAUCES

After a successful day of crabbing at the beach, Pacific Northwesterners enjoy their catch simply boiled and served with a variety of sauces for dipping and plenty of napkins. Fresh seawater is preferred for the ultimate beach crab pot boil.

6–8 live Dungeness crabs
salt (optional)
Herb Butter Sauce (recipe follows)
Cucumber-Yogurt Sauce (recipe follows)
Louis Dressing (recipe on page 60)

◙ In a large pot, bring to a boil enough seawater or fresh water to cover the crabs. Add ¼ cup (2 oz/60 g) of salt for each gallon of fresh water. Plunge the live crabs into the boiling water and cover.

◙ Return to a boil, reduce heat, and simmer for 10–20 minutes, depending on the size of the crabs.

◙ Remove the crabs and plunge them immediately into cold water. Pull off the top shells and either discard or scrub for use as serving containers. Lift off the gills on either side of the back of each crab and discard. Turn the crab on its back and break off the mouth parts and the tail or apron, and scrape out the entrails. Rinse thoroughly in cold water.

◙ Break the body shell in two and pick or shake out the meat. Break off the legs. Pull out the movable small claws or pincer claws and the sharp cartilage. Break the legs apart at the joints, using a nutcracker to gently crack the hard shell of each section, and remove the meat whole from each section.

◙ To serve the cracked crab, place the meat into the cleaned top shell and arrange the cracked legs attractively around it. Serve with one or more of the dipping sauces.

HERB BUTTER SAUCE

1½ cups (12 oz/375 g) unsalted butter
4–5 tablespoons minced fresh herbs such as dill, basil, cilantro (coriander), tarragon or chives
juice of 1 lemon or lime
grated zest of 1 lemon or lime
salt and freshly ground pepper to taste

◙ In a small saucepan, melt the butter. Add the herbs, juice and zest. Season with salt and pepper. Serve warm.

MAKES ABOUT 1½ CUPS (12 FL OZ/375 ML)

CUCUMBER-YOGURT SAUCE

1 cup (8 oz/250 g) grated and drained English cucumber
1 cup (8 fl oz/250 ml) yogurt
¼ cup (2 fl oz/60 ml) mayonnaise
1 tablespoon chopped green (spring) onion
1 tablespoon freshly grated Parmesan cheese
1 tablespoon fresh lime juice
1 teaspoon Dijon mustard
salt and freshly ground black pepper to taste

◙ Combine all the ingredients. Mix well and chill.

MAKES ABOUT 2 CUPS (16 FL OZ/500 ML)

Pacific Northwest Crab Pot with Dipping Sauces

HALIBUT WITH STRAWBERRY-MINT SALSA

John Bishop is the most consistent restaurateur in Vancouver. While he is always offering new and exciting ideas, it's the simplicity of his cooking that his loyal following prizes, as in this recipe for baked halibut with a bright fruit salsa.

2 cups diced strawberries, about 12 oz (375 g)
¼ cup (2 oz/60 g) chopped red (Spanish) onion
2 tablespoons fresh lime juice
¼ cup (2 fl oz/60 ml) puréed passion fruit, or 2 tablespoons orange juice
2 tablespoons chopped fresh mint

4 slices halibut fillet, 5 oz (155 g) each slice, skinned
olive oil for rubbing fish
salt and freshly ground pepper to taste
fresh mint sprigs for garnish

☒ To make the salsa: Combine the strawberries, onion, lime juice, passion fruit and mint in a nonaluminum bowl and marinate in the refrigerator for 1–2 hours.
☒ Preheat an oven to 400°F (200°C). Rub each piece of the halibut with olive oil and lightly season with salt and pepper. Place the halibut on a baking sheet and roast until the flesh is opaque when cut with a small knife, about 6 minutes.
☒ To serve, arrange the fish on plates. Spoon the salsa over the fish and garnish with mint sprigs.

SERVES 4

SAUTÉED STURGEON WITH PINOT NOIR AND GINGER GLAZE

Sturgeon is a meaty white freshwater fish abundant in the large rivers and lakes of Oregon. You can use pike or halibut with equal success in this recipe; just be careful not to overcook the fish.

6 sturgeon steaks, 8 oz (250 g) each
¼ cup (2 fl oz/125 ml) canola or other vegetable oil
½ cup (4 fl oz/125 ml) pink, sweetened pickled ginger with juice, chopped (*Beni Amasu Shoga*)
2 cups (16 fl oz/500 ml) Pinot Noir wine

Halibut with Strawberry-Mint Salsa

2–3 tablespoons sugar
1 tablespoon soy sauce or tamari
10 garlic cloves, crushed
1 tablespoon cornstarch (cornflour) mixed with 1 tablespoon water
salt and pepper to taste
4 tablespoons (2 oz/60 g) butter
½ cup (3 oz/90 g) julienned green (spring) onions

☒ Place the sturgeon in a shallow nonaluminum container. Combine 1 tablespoon of oil, half the ginger and its juice, the wine, sugar and soy sauce in a medium bowl and pour the mixture over the sturgeon. Add the garlic. Cover and marinate in the refrigerator for 8 hours, turning the steaks twice during this period.
☒ Drain the marinade into a small saucepan, removing the garlic cloves and ginger, and bring to a boil. Reduce the liquid to 1 cup (8 fl oz/250 ml). Blot the steaks dry on paper towels.
☒ Whisk together the cornstarch and water. Whisk this mixture into the simmering wine marinade to thicken it.
☒ Heat a large nonstick skillet over medium-high heat, add 1 tablespoon of the oil, and cook 2 sturgeon steaks for 3 minutes on each side. Keep warm in a very low oven while cooking the remaining steaks 2 at a time as above.
☒ Taste the simmering sauce and add salt and pepper. Whisk in the butter until completely emulsified. Pour the sauce over the fish and garnish with rosettes of the remaining ginger and a sprinkle of julienned green onions.

SERVES 6

COLUMBIA RIVER STURGEON WITH CHANTERELLES, SUN-DRIED TOMATOES AND BASIL

The sturgeon is one of the ugliest fish on earth, but also one of the tastiest. This prehistoric creature is prized for its firm white flesh and its caviar roe.

1 lb (500 g) sturgeon fillet
salt and freshly cracked black pepper to taste
flour for dusting
¼ cup (2 fl oz/60 ml) olive oil
1 tablespoon fresh lemon juice
2 teaspoons minced garlic
2 teaspoons minced shallot
1½ cups (6 oz/185 g) thinly sliced fresh chanterelles or other fresh mushrooms
2 tablespoons chopped sun-dried tomatoes
½ cup (4 fl oz/125 ml) dry white wine
¼ cup (1/3 oz/10 g) minced fresh basil
½ cup (4 fl oz/125 ml) heavy (double) cream
⅓ cup (2½ oz/75 g) fresh goat cheese (chèvre)
4 fresh basil sprigs

☒ Cut the fish on a diagonal into 4 pieces, season with salt and pepper, and dust with flour.
☒ In a large skillet, heat the oil over medium heat. Sauté the sturgeon until lightly browned on one side, 1½ minutes, then turn and cook 1½ minutes longer. Add the lemon juice, garlic, shallot, chanterelles and sun-dried tomatoes. Cook for another 1½ minutes, then pour in the white wine. Add the fresh basil and cream. Increase the heat a little and let the sauce cook for 1–2 minutes, or until it is slightly thickened.
☒ When the sauce is reduced and the fish is opaque throughout, remove the fish to a warm plate. Add the goat cheese to the sauce and blend it in. Adjust the seasoning if necessary and spoon the sauce over the fish.
☒ Garnish with basil sprigs.

SERVES 4

Left to right: Sautéed Sturgeon with Pinot Noir and Ginger Glaze, Columbia River Sturgeon with Chanterelles, Sun-Dried Tomatoes and Basil

Planked White King Salmon with Cranberry Relish

PLANKED WHITE KING SALMON WITH CRANBERRY RELISH

The albino king salmon has long been celebrated in Northwest Native American lore. Today their numbers seem to be increasing, and they can be caught around the mouth of the Fraser River during the fall run. Although this meat is pearly white, the flavor is the same as that of their salmon-colored brothers. For this version of the Native American method of plank cooking, you will need two 12-by-8-by-1-in (30-by-20-by-3-cm) untreated cedar planks.

½ cup (4 fl oz/125 ml) peanut (groundnut) oil or olive oil
6 white king or king salmon steaks, 6–8 oz (185–250 g) each
½ cup (4 fl oz/125 ml) melted butter
juice of 1 lemon
salt and freshly ground pepper (optional)
Cranberry Relish (recipe follows)

▨ Season two 12-by-8-by-1-in (30-by-20-by-3-cm) cedar planks by rubbing both sides with the oil and placing them in a 250°F (130°C) oven for 1½ hours.
▨ Preheat an oven to 450°F (230°C). Meanwhile, place 3 salmon steaks on each plank. Brush each steak with the melted butter, then squeeze a little lemon directly onto each steak. Season with salt and pepper if necessary.
▨ Place the planks in the preheated oven and roast the salmon for 7 minutes or until firm to the touch. Remove the planks from the oven and slip the blade of a large spatula between the fish and the plank. The steak will slide off smoothly.
▨ Serve immediately with the cranberry relish on the side.

SERVES 6

CRANBERRY RELISH

½ cup (4 fl oz/125 ml) orange juice
½ cup (4 fl oz/125 ml) raspberry or other fruit vinegar
1½ cups (12 oz/375 g) sugar
½ cup (4 fl oz/125 ml) honey
1 cup (8 oz/250 g) minced red (Spanish) onion
6 garlic cloves, finely minced
1 cup (8 oz/250 g) minced yellow or green bell pepper (capsicum)
1 tablespoon minced fresh ginger
6 whole cloves
1 tablespoon whole coriander seed, crushed
½ teaspoon dried red pepper flakes (optional)
4 cups (12 oz/375 g) fresh or frozen cranberries

▨ Bring the juice, vinegar, sugar, honey, onion and garlic to a simmer in a medium nonaluminum pot. Add the peppers, ginger and spices, and simmer for 5 minutes. Add the cranberries, bring to a slow boil, and cook gently for 10 minutes, or until the berries begin to pop, stirring occasionally with a wooden spoon. Let cool. The relish will keep, covered, in the refrigerator for 3 weeks.

MAKES 5 CUPS (42 FL OZ/1.2 L)

Islands

PAN-FRIED OYSTERS WITH ROCK ISLAND TARTAR

Oysters like three things: water that is a particular mixture of salt and fresh, water that is just the right temperature, and other oysters. These briny creatures also enjoy a complementary relationship with foods that are creamy, smooth and tart, like Meursault or champagne, butter with lemon, and a good homemade tartar sauce.

ROCK ISLAND TARTAR SAUCE

1 cup (8 fl oz/250 ml) good mayonnaise, preferably homemade
4 teaspoons minced sweet pickle
4 teaspoons small capers, drained and rinsed
1 teaspoon minced onion
1 tablespoon minced fresh parsley
1 teaspoon minced fresh tarragon, or ½ teaspoon dried tarragon
2–4 garlic cloves, minced
1 tablespoon tarragon vinegar or other white wine vinegar
2 drops Tabasco (hot pepper) sauce

2 eggs
½ cup (4 fl oz/125 ml) milk

½–1 teaspoon ground white pepper
1 cup (4 oz/125 g) all-purpose (plain) flour
½ cup (30 oz/90 g) cornmeal
1 tablespoon cornstarch (cornflour)
1 teaspoon salt
1 teaspoon paprika
4–6 oysters per person, shucked (method on page 46)
3 tablespoons melted butter
3 tablespoons peanut (groundnut) oil
2 tablespoons minced fresh parsley
1 lemon, cut into wedges

▨ To make the tartar sauce: Blend all the ingredients together in a bowl. Refrigerate for at least 4 hours to let the flavors blend.
▨ Whisk together the eggs, milk and white pepper in a small bowl. In another bowl, blend the flour, cornmeal, cornstarch, salt and paprika. Dip the oysters in the egg mixture one at a time, then dredge in the flour mixture.
▨ In a large skillet, heat the butter and oil over medium-high heat. Fry the oysters for 3–4 minutes, or until golden, turning as necessary.
▨ Drain on paper towels, dust with parsley, and serve immediately with the tartar sauce and lemon wedges.

SERVES 6

Pan-Fried Oysters with Rock Island Tarter

Western Washington

The map shows: San Juan Islands, Orcas I., Lopez I., Whidbey I., Camano I., Juan de Fuca Strait, OLYMPIC MTS, Hood Canal, Bremerton, Puget Sound, Everette, SEATTLE, TACOMA, Aberdeen, Grays Harbor, OLYMPIA, Willapa Bay, MT. RAINIER, Longview, MT. ST. HELENS, Vancouver, CASCADE RANGE, Lake Chelan, WENATCHEE MTS, Wenatchee, SADDLE MTS, Yakima, Toppenish, Columbia River

WESTERN WASHINGTON

Ridged and forested and dotted with lakes and salt-water inlets, western Washington packs a lot of geography into a relatively small space. Bounded on the east by the Cascade Range and on the west by the Pacific Ocean, it encompasses two mountain ranges, several major rivers, a sheltered inland sea so large that its first European explorers thought they might have found the mythical Northwest Passage and dozens of islands. Its mild climate and jumbled topography combine to provide an unparalleled selection of native foods.

Native provender ranges from the exquisite—the wild blackberries and strawberries of the mountains—to the weird, notably the geoduck (pronounced "gooey-duck"), a huge, unkempt clam found under the sand along Puget Sound. The best-known wild food is the salmon, but there are dozens of others.

From earliest written reports, descriptions of western Washington have focused on its beauty and its food. George Vancouver, leader of the first European expedition to explore Puget Sound, described the vista of mountains, forest and water as a "most grand picturesque effect," and his men dined happily on oysters (the es-

Previous pages: A tapestry of seasonal colors surrounds the aptly named Picture Lake at the foot of Mt. Shuksan in Washington's Cascade Range. Left: Seattle's bustling Fishermen's Terminal is home to a vast array of boats and one of the world's biggest fishing fleets.

115

teemed and now rare Olympias), clams, the spring shoots of salmonberries and salmon.

Peter Puget, the expedition officer for whom the Sound is named, commented that "the Natives either from Ignorance or Indolence prefer the Stony Beach to the more healthful and delightfull plains which distinguish this favored Land from the Rest of the Coast of America." But he was wrong on both counts. Most of the plains were unsuitable for agriculture, having a thin covering of leached out soil over yards of gravel or clay. Even today, the "stony beach" is a more reliable source of food. And where the fields were healthful, the Native Americans were already at work.

Along Puget Sound and on the ocean coast, tribes had a varied diet based primarily on seafood. To their staples of salmon and oolichan, the smelt they rendered for its oil, they added shellfish, herring roe, halibut and—among the Makah on the northern coast—whale. Native methods for cooking salmon—broiled over coals or preserved with alder smoke—are still popular today.

Seasonal food-gathering rounds also included trips to carefully tended prairies, where periodic burning and replanting kept camas fields and berry patches productive. Berries ripened from spring through late fall, starting with the neon orange salmonberry, named for its resemblance to salmon eggs, and moving on through thimbleberries, salal, native blackberry and blackcaps, huckleber-

ries and—on the southern ocean coast—wild cranberries. Berries were eaten fresh, pounded into pemmican mixtures or dried.

James Swan, who was one of the first whites to live on the Olympic Peninsula, recalled a meal served by the Clallam Tribe in 1859 that consisted of clams, broiled salmon, trout, mussels, oysters and barnacles. The menu is not so different from that of restaurant fare today.

The foraging instinct is still strong here, even though urbanites now far outnumber country dwellers. Respectable Seattleites sow their lawns with fairy ring mushroom spawn and pick blackberries in vacant lots. In spring, commuters check for roadside cottonwood leaves the size of a quarter, the signal that it's time to look for morels under last autumn's fallen leaves. In summer, attention turns to U-pick signs along the highway: strawberries, then raspberries (nearly half the nation's crop is grown in western Washington), then blueberries and sweet corn and then apples.

Shellfish-lovers wait out the summer fallow season, when poisonous red tide organisms thrive and oysters soften in their spawning transformation. With the first rains of fall, salmon and steelhead move upriver and chanterelles and boletes emerge in the foothills. Hunters go out after deer and elk. Tiny, intensely flavored huckleberries ripen in October and keep until Thanksgiving. The pies are unforgettable, worth the effort of hours of picking.

Long before Northwest cuisine became a culinary buzzword, good home cooks were gathering and using this seasonal abundance. Immigrant newcomers and De-

The broad straight flats of Grayland Beach State Park on the west coast of Washington, provide the perfect setting for clamming, beach combing or a quiet meditative stroll by the sea.

pression-pinched old-timers stretched their budgets with as much free food as they could find. The fact that it was also delicious was a welcome bonus, but often not the main concern. And while the "good restaurants" might confine their local selections to salmon steaks, cafés served up oyster burgers and salmon and chips. In the 1940s, a genial promoter and folksinger named Ivar Haglund began an empire built on clam chowder, clam nectar, fried clams and a number of clam ditties including the anthem of Ivar's House of Clams softball team: "Go Savage Clams, pound 'em into patties; Go Savage Clams, rip 'em into strips."

The Western Washington Fair is another storehouse of local food traditions. Begun in 1900 and held every September, the Puyallup Fair, as everyone calls it, is the place for Fisher scones, made with locally milled flour and slathered with jam from Puyallup Valley raspberries. Milkshakes and ice cream served up by Dairy Women chapters feature the production of local herds, and 4-H steers may give you a reproachful look as you walk by munching on an onion cheeseburger. In the exhibition halls, gardeners and farmers compete in the matter of the biggest squash, the greenest beans, the best apple pie.

Even the drawbacks of a cool, damp summer engender a perverse pride. One Seattle publisher printed an entire cookbook devoted to green tomatoes, a reflection of reality in the western Washington garden. Likewise, the sweet corn harvest, which in rainy summers may not arrive until Labor Day, provokes a fanaticism probably unknown in Iowa.

Western Washington has two different climates— one generally temperate and the other spectacularly wet. On the Olympic Peninsula and the ocean beaches to the south, westerlies push the soggy ocean air inland to dump up to two hundred inches of water a year on one of the planet's few temperate-zone rain forests. The climate and soil are perfect for growing immense firs and cedars but problematic for agriculture. Only the "rain shadow" along the Sequim and Dungeness valleys on the northern peninsula makes good farmland. Those prairies became the first dairy center in the state, although the pastures have now largely been filled with housing.

The peninsula was once so rich in clams that settlers harvested them with a horse and plow. Like the oysters that preceded them as a peninsula cash crop, fresh clams were sold primarily to restaurants in California. Hogs, on the other hand, went north to Victoria, B.C., where the meat was cured and sent to England. At first Indian canoes were used to transport the hogs. They carried a crew of six: four to paddle, one to splash water over the hogs to keep them from overheating, and one to bail the water back out.

The peninsula's bounty is no longer so free and easy. The salmon runs are a remnant of the former multitudes; the Olympia oysters are few; the razor clams are ailing. But the food is still there. Enterprising chefs have established destination restaurants featuring bold regional cooking: salmon and oysters and crab, of course, but also Columbia River sturgeon, local cranberries and wild mushrooms. These splendid meals have helped to swell the numbers of people who work to defend the region against further damage.

The Olympic Mountains snag most of the eastbound rain clouds, so the climate along Puget Sound is still mild, but much dryer. Although the glaciers that carved

Pike Place Farmers Market, offering fresh local produce and seafood daily, is one of Seattle's most popular and animated attractions. Here, discerning shoppers ponder in amazement the enormity of the day's catch.

the Sound and sculpted most of Puget Sound country left behind gravelly clay barely worthy of the name of soil, the flood-prone river valleys of the Puyallup, Snohomish, Skagit, Stillaguamish, Nooksack and others, contain fine agricultural land. Peas, green beans, cabbages, broccoli, strawberries, raspberries, blueberries, rhubarb, salad greens—anything that doesn't require constant sunshine—all thrive.

In the summer, daylight begins at 4:00 A.M., and sunset lingers until 10:00 P.M. The winters, though correspondingly dark, are seldom very cold. Apples grown under these conditions achieve a complexity of flavor that is hard to obtain in the hot summers east of the Cascades, and true strawberry lovers scorn sturdy California imports and wait for the ripening of the fragile, succulent local fruits.

Just south of the Canadian border, dairy farms dominate the Nooksack Valley lowlands, and berry crops line the roads along the hills. Most of the dairy families, and their cows, originated in the Holstein-Fresian region of

Mount Rainier National Park boasts over 300 miles of hiking trails with scenic wonders like this vista of Tipsoo Lake.

the Netherlands. Local delicatessens carry convenience packages for making Boerenkool, a kale and potato combination that is a sure sign of Dutch heritage.

The Skagit Valley drainage to the south is better known for peas, carrots and flowers—both ornamental and functional. The Skagit is a famous producer of tulips and daffodils and also grows immense quantities of cabbage and broccoli seed. Acres of yellow cabbage flowers, humming with bees, line the freeway in mid-spring.

Closer to the sprawl of Seattle and Tacoma, development has forced out most of the truck farms and dairies that used to serve the Puget Sound population. But increasing sophistication has meant more demand for fresh local food, as witnessed by the success of the farmers' markets that sprout up in nearly every town. The biggest, oldest and most famous is the Pike Place Market in Seattle, where locals, tourists and chefs have been rubbing elbows and sampling produce since 1906. "Highstall" vendors in their raised booths sell produce from around the world, while the lowstallers are local farmers. Together, their selections provide a snapshot of Seattle's culinary proclivities: edible flowers, flavored vinegars, new potatoes in colors from gold to purple, green peas, snowpeas, sugar snap peas, fresh herbs and dry herbal wreaths, lemongrass for Thai cooking and epazote for Mexican dishes. Pike Place is open daily and can provide a living, though a hard one, for an experienced farmer. Most of the other markets attract part-time farmers and ambitious gardeners, who may come for the camaraderie as much as the money.

South of Tacoma is the site of one of the first farms in western Washington, the Puget Sound Agricultural Com-

pany. As in most of the Northwest, the first practitioners of large-scale agriculture were employees of the Hudson's Bay Company. At Fort Vancouver on the Columbia River and later at Fort Nisqually, cattle, sheep, grain, apples and vegetables supplied the HBC employees and customers. Dr. John McLoughlin, Chief Factor at Fort Vancouver and de facto head of Northwest government for a generation, was known as much for his table as for his cultivated conversation and ferocious temper. Officers and guests dined on roast beef and pork, boiled mutton, baked salmon, beets, carrots and turnips, all homegrown.

Today, the market gardeners around Nisqually tend to concentrate on the lighter fare preferred by customers at the Olympia Farmers' Market, the second largest in the state. Eunice Farmilant, who has turned five acres of rock and mud in a rural subdivision into a productive vista of raised beds, greenhouses and nesting geese and ducks, works to keep on top of the latest food trends. One year she marketed organically grown artichokes and "purple crops" like violet-leaved anise hyssop. The next year it was yellow tomatoes and tomatillos. "People like something new," says Eunice. "You have to keep hustling."

Although the freeway corridor from Portland, Oregon, to Vancouver, B.C., is increasingly urbanized, Seattle is still the unchallenged metropolis of Western Washington. In the past twenty years it has completed the transition from a provincial center to a major city, a sophisticated player in the Pacific Rim economy. One sign of this change is in the prevailing attitude toward coffee. Because of its large Scandinavian population, Seattle has always been a heavily caffeinated town. Kitchens in the Ballard neighborhood, the city's Nordic center, came equipped with the eternal pot of simmering coffee, strong enough to keep a halibut crew on duty through a three-day blow. But nowadays the coffee action is on the street, at the espresso cart. What does a Seattleite say when she sees an espresso cart on every other corner? goes one joke. Answer: "Why isn't there one on every corner?" Debates on the best roast, best grind and best equipment can drown out all other social conversation.

A similar shift toward public consumption has taken place in food. Not so long ago the best meals by far were those served by inspired home cooks. "When I had moved from our home in the country and gone to Seattle I had left behind a very fine cuisine the like of which I could not find in the university community," recalled Angelo Pellegrini, who was raised first in a Tuscan village and then in the logging town of McCleary, near Olympia. "And no wonder! The entire state, the whole Northwest,

had not yet discovered garlic!" Pellegrini found his necessary garlic in the kitchens of Seattle's Little Italy. Italian market gardeners were the mainstay of the early Pike Place Market, joined later by Japanese and Filipino growers from the Green River Valley. In those households, often too poor or too unfamiliar with English to fully participate in the postwar rush out of the Victory Garden and into the supermarket, the virtues of fresh food, knowledgeably prepared, remained paramount. Restaurants might stick with prime rib and peas, but the Pellegrinis' guests got homegrown artichokes braised with rabbit and served with his own wine.

Dozens of Seattle restaurants today offer food based on that kind of sensibility: a peasant's grasp of the good life's essentials, expressed in a sophisticated cuisine.

"The beauty of the island was that we had all the food we could possibly eat or use," wrote Louise Ekenstam Ostling, who came as a child to Anderson Island in Puget Sound in 1879. The eleven Ekenstam children thrived on garden produce, the deer that came to eat the garden, salmon purchased from the Indians for a nickel apiece, and wild and orchard fruit. No matter how far life has come from that pastoral scene, some of its flavor is still found in western Washington cooking.

Westport, known as the salmon capital of the world, attracts tourists looking for a taste of fresh seafood or some musical entertainment on a sunny afternoon.

Meat, Poultry
and Game

A spit-roast barbecue is enjoyed in the wine country of Washington's Yakima Valley.

MEAT, POULTRY AND GAME

In early Northwest days, game meats were a life-sustaining necessity. Today the Pacific Northwest Venison Producers, a cooperative of game farmers, breeders and venison producers from Oregon, Washington and British Columbia, make venison available to the consumer at specialty butcher shops, but some still opt to hunt for the deliciously flavored meat.

In the late twenties, entrepreneurial young boys raised rabbits, feeding them with cuttings from mowing the neighbors' lawns, then selling the dressed rabbits on their paper routes for 25 cents each. Cooked like fried chicken, "rabbit fries" were the favorite dish, served up with mashed potatoes and rich rabbit gravy. Rabbits have always run wild on many of the islands. A strange rabbit tale is told by a man who grew up in the sixties in what was then called "Garlic Gulch," the Italian section of Seattle's Rainer Valley. His father used to take him and his brother on the ferry over to Lopez Island. They would then drive the car out into a field, and the boys would lie on the hood with their feet tied to the car so they wouldn't fall off. After the sun had gone down and the moon was casting its glow on the field, the father would drive slowly through the field with the headlights on. Any passing rabbits would be mesmerized by the car lights and the boys would reach down and pick up the dazed creatures by the ears. The rabbits were then taken home and braised in a robust stew of garlic, red wine and mushrooms. Some say this kind of rabbit hunting still goes on today.

Chicken has always been a favorite throughout the Northwest, enjoyed roasted, smoked, stir-fried with fresh vegetables or the very popular teriyaki style in a soy, brown sugar and ginger marinade. Chicken and dumplings was found on many Oregon and Washington menus in the

Roasted duck are a favorite among shoppers in Vancouver's Chinatown.

Previous pages, clockwise from top: Venison Sausage (page 142), Shepherd's Pie (page 134), Roast Chicken Stuffed with Autumn Fruits (page 135) and Roast Leg of Lamb with Merlot Marinade (page 150)

122

Venison, leaner than beef and often preferred, is a popular game meat in the Northwest.

early days. It still is at Tad's, a restaurant in Troutdale, Oregon. People have been lining up on Saturdays and Sundays here since the 1940s to get a home-style helping of slow-simmered chicken with fluffy dumplings. This Southern dish was brought to the Northwest by Southern migrants. Soon after they arrived, this dish started appearing at church potluck suppers and then on the menus of small diners and cafés.

Before the days of refrigeration, drying, smoking and salting were common methods of preserving meats. The Spaniards who came to North America following Columbus found the Native Americans drying meats into jerky. The meat was cut into thin long strips, sometimes seasoned with sugar and salt, then hung in trees or on the tops of huts and teepees to dry. Jerky has made a comeback as a popular snack item; it can be purchased in many grocery stores and taverns. Many hunters enjoy making their own jerky, often brining it in a soy sauce, pepper and brown sugar mixture, then either oven-drying it or smoking it dry over branches of apple wood.

The term *venison* today refers to the meat of antlered animals such as deer, elk, antelope, reindeer and moose; in earlier days it meant the meat of any game animal or bird. Most of the venison eaten now is deer, some of whom have an exceptional diet from browsing in backyards, eating new rosebuds and nipping off the tender young sprouts and leaves of fruit trees. Venison is similar to beef except that it is very lean. The tender cuts can be roasted, pan-fried or grilled; the less tender cuts are used for flavorful stews or soups, or ground for venison burgers or sausages. Venison mincemeat was put up by many hunters and still is by some. It's made into rich, holiday pies and topped with billows of fresh whipped cream.

Pheasant, quail and duck are found in the Northwest hunter's freezer. Even doves are hunted in eastern Washington for their delicate tiny breasts, which are quickly roasted and served, two or three to a person. Especially popular in B.C. is a holiday dish of plump, roasted Canadian goose stuffed with such goodies as blueberries, apples and huckleberries. Turkeys are stuffed with fresh oyster bread stuffing, a tradition as old as the first Christmas Eve oyster stews, when extra oysters were added to the turkey stuffing. Tourtière pie is a Christmas favorite that graces the tables of Canadians. Its flaky sour cream crust is filled with almost any savory meat mixture today, although it was originally made from turtle doves.

The British will put almost anything in a pie. To *pie* actually means "to jumble together," like the ingredients in shepherd's pie, a dish probably brought to the Northwest by some of the many New Englanders who colonized Oregon. This mixture of leftover cooked lamb, gravy and vegetables is placed in a casserole or deep pie dish, topped with whipped potatoes and baked till golden. Today the lamb is probably from Ellensberg, Washington, and the potatoes from Idaho.

Beef, pork and lamb dishes have long appeared on Northwest tables, from wintertime beef and root-vegetable stews and apple-stuffed pork chops, to spit-roasted Ellensberg spring lamb basted with a Merlot wine marinade. Hot sunny Northwest days are celebrated with backyard barbecues and picnics at the park. Thick, juicy steaks, sausages and hamburgers stuffed with Oregon blue cheese and grilled over hot coals are typical fare, while families and friends enjoy a game of volleyball or share stories over a microbrew or a glass of sun tea. As the sun sets and the Northwest evening air begins to cool, blankets and supplies are gathered up while Fido chews the long-awaited steak bone and the lone incinerated forgotten hamburger patty.

Western Washington

PENINSULA CRANBERRY POT ROAST

Cranberry bogs are abundant on the drizzly Long Beach Peninsula, and signs advertising cranberries are everywhere. Peninsula-inspired whole-berry cranberry sauce adds flavor to slow-simmered pot roast, making for a hearty home-style Sunday dinner. Serve with fluffy whipped potatoes.

½ cup (2 oz/60 g) all-purpose (plain) flour
2 teaspoons salt
¼ teaspoon ground black pepper
3½ lb (1.75 kg) boneless chuck roast
¼ cup (2 fl oz/60 ml) vegetable oil
2 celery stalks, diced
2 garlic cloves, minced
2 cups (16 fl oz/500 ml) dry red wine
3 cups (24 fl oz/750 ml) beef stock (see glossary)
1 tablespoon red wine vinegar
1 can (16 oz/500 g) whole-berry cranberry sauce
1 unpeeled orange, quartered
4 carrots, peeled and cut into 2-in (5-cm) pieces
2 onions, peeled and quartered
2 cloves
1 bay leaf
¼ teaspoon ground cinnamon
½ teaspoon dried thyme

GARLIC WHIPPED POTATOES

3–4 russet potatoes, peeled and cut in half, about 3 lb (1.5 kg)
1 teaspoon salt
10–12 garlic cloves
⅓ cup (3 oz/90 g) butter
¾ cup (6 fl oz/180 ml) heavy (double) cream or milk
salt and white pepper to taste
minced fresh parsley for garnish

GRAVY

¼ cup (2 oz/60 g) butter
¼ cup (1 oz/30 g) reserved seasoned flour (above)
4 cups (32 fl oz/1 l) reserved pot roast cooking liquid (above)
salt and freshly ground black pepper to taste

◪ Combine the flour, salt and pepper; rub into the surface of the meat, coating it well. (Reserve the leftover flour for the gravy.) Heat the oil in a large pot or Dutch oven over medium-high heat and brown the roast well on all sides, about 2 minutes per side, for a total cooking time of 6–7 minutes. Add the celery and garlic and sauté for 30 seconds or so. Pour in the wine and boil it while scraping up the cooked bits on the bottom of the pan. Add the remaining ingredients. Bring to a boil, cover, reduce heat to low, and simmer for 3–3½ hours, or until fork tender.

◪ To make the potatoes: About 25 minutes before the meat will be done, place the potatoes, salt and garlic in a medium saucepan with water to cover. Cover the saucepan, bring to a boil, and cook for 25 minutes, or until the potatoes and garlic are tender. While the potatoes are cooking, combine in a small pan over medium heat, the cream, white pepper and butter. Heat until the butter is melted and the milk is warm. Drain off the water from the potatoes and garlic and mash or whip in the pot while adding the hot cream mixture. Season with salt and pepper to taste.

◪ Remove the roast to a cutting board and cut it into thick slices, reserving the cooking liquid. Arrange the slices on a serving dish and keep them warm.

◪ To make the gravy: Melt the butter in a medium, heavy saucepan over medium heat. Whisk the reserved seasoned flour into the butter. Cook for 1 minute, then vigorously whisk in the reserved cooking liquid. Cook, whisking often, until thickened and free of lumps. Season with salt and pepper as desired.

◪ Arrange the carrots and onions around the slices of roast.

(Discard the orange pieces.) Pour some of the gravy over the slices and pass the rest in a sauceboat along with the whipped potatoes.

SERVES 6

Islands

BEEF SHORT RIBS WITH ROOT VEGETABLES

There is nothing so satisfying on a chill autumn day as the sound and smell of beef and garlic sizzling in the oven. The earthy flavors of winter vegetables are the perfect accompaniment.

Left to right: Beef Short Ribs with Root Vegetables, Peninsula Cranberry Pot Roast and Garlic Whipped Potatoes

2 tablespoons peanut (groundnut) oil or vegetable oil
6 lb (3 kg) beef short ribs
1 teaspoon salt
½ teaspoon freshly ground black pepper
½ cup (4 fl oz/125 ml) reduced beef stock (see glossary)
2 tablespoons red wine vinegar
2 tablespoons brown sugar, packed
1 tablespoon tomato paste (purée)
6 garlic cloves
1 cup (8 oz/250 g) chopped onion
2 teaspoons chopped fresh thyme, or 1 teaspoon dried thyme
2 carrots, halved and cut into 2-in (5-cm) pieces
2 rutabagas (yellow turnips), each cut into 6 wedges
2 parsnips, halved and cut into 2-in (5-cm) pieces

4 red potatoes cut in half
24 whole pearl onions

◪ Preheat an oven to 325°F (170°C). In a large, heavy pot or Dutch oven, heat the oil and brown the short ribs well on all sides; pour off the oil. Add the stock, vinegar, brown sugar, tomato paste, garlic and chopped onion to the pan. Cover tightly and braise in the preheated oven for 1½ hours.
◪ Add the vegetables, pearl onions and thyme; return to the oven and bake for 45 minutes longer, or until the vegetables and meat are tender.
◪ Heap the vegetables in the center of a large platter and surround with the short ribs and pan juices. Dust with the minced parsley and serve at once.

SERVES 6–8

Calves' Liver and Bacon with Orange-Leek Sauce

Eastern Washington

CALVES' LIVER AND BACON WITH ORANGE-LEEK SAUCE

Like trout fresh from the stream to the campfire frying pan, venison liver is a treat in the hunting camp because liver is always best fresh. Whenever possible, buy liver the day you plan to use it. Lamb, venison or baby beef liver may be used in place of calves' liver.

8 bacon slices
1 teaspoon butter
1 leek, white part only, sliced very thin
4 calves' liver slices, about 1 lb (500 g)
¼ cup (1 oz/30 g) all-purpose (plain) flour mixed with salt
  and pepper to taste
juice and grated zest of ½ orange, about ¼ cup
  (2 fl oz/60 ml) juice

In a large skillet, fry the bacon until crisp. Drain on paper towels and keep warm. Pour off all but 1 tablespoon of the bacon fat and set the skillet aside for sautéing the liver.

Melt the butter in another skillet over medium heat and add the sliced leek. Cover and cook slowly until tender. Set aside.

Dredge the liver in the seasoned flour and shake off the excess. Heat the reserved tablespoon of bacon fat in the skillet and sauté the liver over medium-high heat for 1–2 minutes on each side, or until done to your taste. Transfer to a serving plate and keep warm.

Add the orange juice and zest to the leeks over high heat and bring to a boil. Pour over the liver.

Arrange the bacon on the side. Serve with a green vegetable and fluffy mashed potatoes or Walla Walla Onion Rings (recipe on page 45).

SERVES 4

Oregon

CHICKEN WITH HERBED DUMPLINGS

Some things can't be improved on, such as apple pie, grandmothers and—oh yes—chicken and dumplings. A longtime favorite restaurant in Oregon is Tad's, on the Sandy River. Tad's is the "king" of chicken and dumplings. This recipe takes some time, but it's worth the effort if you can't get to Tad's.

1 roasting or stewing chicken, about 4½–5 lb (2.2–2.5 kg),
  cut into 6 pieces
1 onion, coarsely chopped
2 celery stalks
4 bay leaves
2 tablespoons black peppercorns
2 tablespoons chopped fresh thyme, or 1 tablespoon dried
  thyme
4 whole cloves
pinch of saffron (optional)
6 garlic cloves, crushed
1 cup (8 fl oz/250 ml) dry white wine
8 cups (64 fl oz/2 l) water
⅔ cup (5 oz/155 g) butter
1 cup (4 oz/125 g) all-purpose (plain) flour
1 cup (8 oz/50 g) fresh or thawed frozen pearl onions
2 carrots, peeled and cut into ¼-in (6-mm) rounds
4 cups (1 lb/500 g) shelled peas
salt and pepper to taste
chopped fresh parsley (optional)

HERBED DUMPLINGS

2 cups (8 oz/250 g) all-purpose (plain) flour
1 tablespoon baking powder
1 teaspoon sugar
½ teaspoon salt
¼ cup (2 oz/60 g) minced onion
½ teaspoon celery seeds
1 tablespoon chopped fresh sage, or 1 teaspoon dried sage
4 tablespoons chopped fresh parsley
1 cup (8 oz/250 ml) milk

Rinse the cut chicken pieces in cold water and drain. Place the chicken in a large pot with the chopped onion, celery, herbs, spices, garlic, wine and water. Cover, bring to a low simmer over medium heat, and cook until the chicken meat falls away from the bones, 2–2½ hours.

Remove from the heat and drain, reserving the stock. Let the chicken cool, then pull the meat from the bones, discarding the bones and skin.

Melt the butter in a large, heavy pot or Dutch oven over low heat. Gradually whisk in the flour until thoroughly blended and cook until golden, about 5–10 minutes, stirring frequently to avoid scorching. Remove the fat from the reserved chicken stock and whisk the stock into the flour-butter mixture, whisking between additions to avoid lumps. Cook at a low simmer until thickened, stirring frequently and skimming off any fat or foam that rises to the surfaces. Add the onions, carrots, peas and chicken. Reduce to a simmer and season with salt and pepper.

To make the dumplings: In a large bowl, mix the dumpling ingredients thoroughly to make a thick batter. If necessary, add water to the batter. Scoop the batter into large tablespoonfuls and drop into the simmering liquid. Cover and cook the dumplings for about 15–20 minutes, or until puffy and cooked through.

Serve in large bowls, garnished with chopped parsley, if you like.

SERVES 6–8

Chicken with Herbed Dumplings

RIB EYE STEAK WITH HA CHA CHA BARBECUE SAUCE AND FRIZZLED ONIONS

The Driftwood Ranch on Orcas Island is home to a prize herd of Charolais cattle. Cowboys in the islands may not always wear cowboy boots, but they do know what to do with a choice piece of beef.

BARBECUE SAUCE

1 tablespoon peanut (groundnut) oil
1 onion chopped
8 garlic cloves, crushed
2 cups (16 fl oz/500 ml) tomato sauce (puréed tomatoes)
⅓ cup (2½ fl oz/75 ml) dark molasses
½ cup (3 oz/90 g) brown sugar, packed
½ cup (4 fl oz/125 ml) red wine vinegar
1 dried ancho or poblano (mild) chili, ground
½ teaspoon ground cinnamon
¼ teaspoon ground cloves
1 teaspoon ground cumin
1 teaspoon ground black pepper
1 teaspoon paprika
½ teaspoon cayenne pepper
1 teaspoon salt
1 teaspoon liquid smoke (optional)

peanut (groundnut) oil, for frying
salt and freshly ground black pepper to taste
6 rib eye or spencer steaks (rib fillets), 1½ in (4 cm) thick
1 cup (4 oz/125 g) all-purpose (plain) flour
1 teaspoon salt
1 teaspoon cornstarch (cornflour)
2 red (Spanish) onions, peeled and sliced into ⅛-in (3-mm) rings

◙ To make the barbecue sauce: In a small saucepan, heat the oil and sauté the onion and garlic over low heat until translucent, about 5 minutes. Add all of the remaining ingredients and simmer over low heat for 30 minutes. Keep warm.

◙ In a large skillet, heat 1 tablespoon of the peanut oil over high heat. Salt and pepper both sides of the steaks and cook for 3 minutes on each side for medium rare, or until the meat springs back when touched. Baste with the barbecue sauce. The steaks may also be grilled over medium-hot coals. Set aside and keep warm.

◙ Heat 3–4 inches (7.5–10 cm) of peanut oil to 350°F (180°C) in a deep, heavy pan. Mix the flour, salt and cornstarch together in a medium bowl. Dredge the onion rings in the flour. Shaking off any excess flour, fry the onion rings until golden, about 5 minutes.

◙ Serve the steaks on big platters surrounded by the frizzled onions. Pass extra barbecue sauce on the side.

SERVES 6   *Photograph pages 10–11*

STOUT-BRAISED BEEF WITH ONIONS AND SOUR CREAM

Long, slow cooking produces an infusion of flavors that can't be equaled by any other method. This braised beef dish melds the malt and hop flavors of hearty stout with the sweetness of yellow onions and accents of mustard and allspice. Try making it a day or two ahead to reheat at your convenience. Serve with egg noodles or steamed new potatoes.

4 bacon strips cut into 1-in (2.5-cm) squares
1 cup (4 oz/125 g) flour
2 tablespoons salt

1 tablespoon ground white pepper
1 tablespoon ground allspice
3 lb (1.5 kg) beef sirloin tips or sirloin roast cut into 2½-by-½-by-½-in (6.5-by-1.5-by-1.5-cm) strips
2 large onions, cut into thin wedges
1 teaspoon sugar
1½ cups (12 fl oz/375 ml) stout
4 cups (32 fl oz/1 l) beef stock (see glossary)
¼ cup (2 fl oz/60 ml) Dijon mustard
1 cup (8 fl oz/250 ml) sour cream
1 cup (6 oz/180 g) finely sliced green (spring) onions for garnish

◙ In a large, heavy saucepan over medium heat, cook the bacon until lightly browned, 7–10 minutes.

◙ Meanwhile, combine the flour, salt, white pepper and allspice. Dredge the sirloin tips or roast in this mixture, shaking off any excess. Brown the beef in the bacon drippings for 12–15 minutes, stirring occasionally to prevent it from sticking and burning. Add the onions and sugar, and cook until they are translucent, about 5–7 minutes longer. Stir in the stout, beef stock and mustard and bring to a simmer. Reduce the heat to medium-low and skim the fat from the mixture, stirring occasionally to prevent scorching. Add salt and pepper. Cover and cook for 2–3 hours, or until the meat is fork tender. Serve topped with dollops of sour cream and garnished with green onions.

SERVES 6–8

BRAISED PHEASANT WITH YAKIMA VALLEY HARD CIDER AND APPLES

Yakima's Grant's Brewery makes a hard cider with approximately 6 percent alcohol. Pheasant braised in hard cider is tender and has the subtle, sweet flavor of apples.

1 pheasant, 1–1½ lb (500–750 g) dressed
3–4 tablespoons olive oil
½ cup (6 oz/180 g) coarsely chopped celery
½ cup (4 oz/125 g) coarsely chopped carrot
½ cup (4 oz/125 g) coarsely chopped yellow (brown) onion
2 cups (16 fl oz/500 ml) Yakima Valley or other hard apple cider
¼ cup (2 fl oz/60 ml) brandy or Calvados
1 tart green apple, peeled and sliced
2–3 tablespoons heavy (double) cream
salt and freshly ground pepper to taste

◙ Preheat an oven to 350°F (180°C). Meanwhile, cut the pheasant into quarters. Rinse well and pat dry. In a heavy ovenproof skillet, brown the pheasant pieces in 3 tablespoons of the olive oil over medium-high heat.

◙ Remove the pheasant and sauté the celery, onions and carrots for about 5 minutes, adding more oil as necessary.

◙ Return the pheasant to the skillet. Pour the cider over the pheasant and vegetables and bring to a boil. Cover and bake in the oven for about 50 minutes.

◙ Remove the pheasant from the skillet and keep warm. Strain the juices and return them to the skillet. Discard the vegetables. Add the brandy or Calvados to the juices and bring to a simmer. Return the pheasant to the pan, add the apple slices, cover, and return to the oven for about 20 minutes, or until the meat begins to come away from the bones.

◙ Place the pheasant on a serving platter, garnish with the apple slices, and keep warm.

◙ Cook the liquid in the skillet over high heat to reduce by half. Whisk in the cream, adjust the seasoning, and pour the sauce over the pheasant.

SERVES 2

Top to bottom: Stout-Braised Beef with Onions and Sour Cream, Braised Pheasant with Yakima Valley Hard Cider and Apples

SKAGIT VALLEY DUCK SAUSAGE

Skagit Valley abounds in reed marshlands and is a prime location for duck hunting. Duck sausages are excellent grilled and served with Crimson Cherry Chutney (recipe on page 201).

1 medium duck, about 4 lb (2 kg), or 1 lb (500 g) raw duck
   meat and 6 oz (185 g) skin
4 oz (125 g) boneless pork butt or shoulder, cut into cubes
¼ cup (2 oz/60 g) chopped white onion
2 garlic cloves, minced
2 teaspoons fresh thyme, or 1 teaspoon dried thyme

1 teaspoon chopped fresh rosemary, or ½ teaspoon
   dried rosemary
⅓ cup (3 fl oz/80 ml) dry red wine
1½ teaspoons chopped green peppercorns
1 bay leaf
¼ teaspoon ground black pepper
1 shallot minced
pinch of ground allspice
¼ teaspoon ground cardamom
pinch of dried red pepper flakes
2 teaspoons salt
2 tablespoons orange liqueur
medium hog casings (optional)

◼ Skin and bone the duck, reserving the meat and skin. You should have about 1 lb (500 g) meat and 6 oz (185 g) skin.

Western Washington

PAN-ROASTED SWEETBREADS WITH MOREL MUSHROOM CREAM

Fresh morels come into season about the second week in April in the Northwest, depending on the weather and the location, and the season lasts about 4–6 weeks. Serve these crisp pan-roasted sweetbreads with tender steamed spring asparagus and new red potatoes.

8 cups (64 fl oz/2 l) water
1 teaspoon salt
4 whole sweetbreads, about 1½–2 lb (750 g–1 kg) total
1 carrot, coarsely chopped
1 onion, coarsely chopped
2 celery stalks, coarsely chopped

MOREL MUSHROOM CREAM

1 tablespoon butter
1 shallot, minced
1 garlic clove, minced
½ cup (2 oz/60 g) chopped fresh morel mushrooms; or
    ¼ oz (5 g) dried morels, soaked in the white wine for 30
    minutes, strained, and chopped (reserve wine)
3 tablespoons brandy
½ cup (4 fl oz/125 ml) dry white wine
2 cups (16 fl oz/500 ml) heavy (double) cream
1 teaspoon fresh lemon juice
½ teaspoon salt
pinch of white pepper
salt and freshly ground pepper to taste
flour for dusting
3 tablespoons vegetable oil, clarified butter or a mixture of both
sautéed fresh morels (optional)

◼ Place the water and salt in a large pot and soak the sweetbreads for 3–4 hours.
◼ Drain the sweetbreads and return them to the pot. Add the carrot, onion and celery.
◼ Cover with fresh cold water and bring just to a boil over high heat. Remove immediately and drain. Run cold water over the sweetbreads to refresh them.
◼ Peel off most of the outer membrane, keeping the sweetbreads intact. Place the sweetbreads in a baking dish and cover with plastic wrap. Place another pan or dish on top and weight with a few heavy cans or jars. Refrigerate for 3 hours or overnight.
◼ To make the mushroom cream: Heat the butter in a heavy saucepan over medium heat. Add the shallot, garlic and mushrooms. Cook, stirring, for 1–2 minutes, or until the shallots are translucent. Add the brandy and white wine, and cook to reduce the liquid, about 5 minutes. Add the cream and let come to a simmer; reduce heat and slowly simmer, stirring often, for 20–30 minutes, or until the mixture is reduced to about 1½ cups (12 fl oz/375 ml) and slightly thickened. Stir in the lemon juice and season with salt and pepper.
◼ Remove the sauce to a blender and blend until smooth (in batches, if necessary) for about 30 seconds, using caution because the sauce is very hot. Keep the sauce warm.
◼ Preheat an oven to 450°F (230°C). Season the sweetbreads with salt and pepper and dust with flour. Heat the oil and/or butter in a large, heavy skillet over medium-high heat. Add the sweetbreads and cook on one side until golden brown, about 2–3 minutes. Turn and cook 2–3 minutes more, or until crispy brown. Place the skillet in the oven and bake the sweetbreads for about 6 minutes, or until just cooked through.
◼ Place ¼ cup (2 fl oz/60 ml) of sauce on each of 4 warm dinner plates. Place the sweetbreads on top of the sauce and spoon the remaining sauce over them. Serve with sautéed fresh morels on the side, if desired.

SERVES 4

Left to right: Pan-Roasted Sweetbreads with Morel Mushroom Cream, Skagit Valley Duck Sausage

◼ Place the reserved meat and skin and all the remaining ingredients, except for the salt, orange liqueur and hog casings, in a large nonaluminum bowl. Cover and marinate in the refrigerator for 2–2½ hours.
◼ Drain the marinated ingredients, reserving the marinade. Fit a meat grinder with a ⅛-in (3-mm) plate; grind all the drained ingredients and place in a bowl. Add the salt, orange liqueur and reserved marinade. Mix together well. Form into patties, or stuff into hog casings and tie into 4-in (10-cm) lengths.
◼ Poach the sausage lightly, then fry, grill, or smoke them. Smoked sausages will keep for 1 week; uncooked sausages will keep 3 days in the refrigerator and up to 2 months in the freezer.

MAKES ABOUT 8–10 SAUSAGES

British Columbia

ROAST PORK TENDERLOIN WITH RED CURRANT SAUCE

A hard-to-beat combination of juicy pork tenderloin and red currant sauce perfect for special guests.

4 pork tenderloins (whole fillets), about 2–3 lb (1–1.5 kg)

MARINADE

2 onions, cut in half and thinly sliced
1 teaspoon minced fresh ginger
½ teaspoon ground cardamom
1 teaspoon ground cinnamon
½ teaspoon ground coriander
1½ teaspoons dried oregano
2 garlic cloves, minced
juice of 2 oranges
juice of 2 lemons
salt and freshly ground pepper to taste

2 tablespoons butter
1 teaspoon olive oil

Top to bottom: Spanish Lamb Stew, Roast Pork Tenderloin with Red Currant Sauce

2 tablespoons minced shallot
1½ cups (12 fl oz/375 ml) chicken stock (see glossary)
½ cup (4 fl oz/125 ml) good red currant jelly
2 tablespoons soft butter blended with 2 tablespoons flour
salt and freshly ground pepper to taste
lemon juice to taste (optional)
fresh chives and fresh red currants for garnish (optional)

◩ Place the tenderloins in a nonaluminum baking pan. Combine all of the marinade ingredients and pour over the pork. Cover and refrigerate for 6 hours, turning the meat 3–4 times during this period. Remove from the refrigerator 30 minutes before roasting.
◩ Preheat oven to 375°F (190°C). Remove the pork from the marinade and pat dry. Strain the marinade and reserve.
◩ Roast the tenderloins in the preheated oven for 25 minutes, or until the meat is pale pink when cut into, or an instant-read thermometer inserted in to the center of a tenderloin reads 140°–145°F (60°–63°C).
◩ Meanwhile, prepare the sauce: In a heavy skillet, heat the butter and oil over medium-high heat. Add the shallots and cook for 1 minute. Add the reserved marinade and cook to reduce to 3 tablespoons. Add the stock and reduce to 1 cup (8 fl oz/250 ml). Whisk in the currant jelly until melted. Crumble bits of the blended butter and flour into the hot sauce, stirring constantly until the ingredients are well blended and the sauce thickens.
◩ Taste and correct the seasoning, adding drops of lemon juice to taste, if desired. Cover and keep warm.
◩ When the pork is done, transfer it to a carving board. Cut the pork into ½-in (1.5-cm) slices. Place the slices down the center of each dinner plate, spoon sauce around one side, and garnish with fresh chives and red currants, if desired.
◩ Serve at once with the remaining sauce on the side.

SERVES 4–6

Eastern Washington

SPANISH LAMB STEW

Now an "official" ghost town, Shaniko, Oregon, was once the wool capital of the world. In the early 1900s, tens of thousands of sheep from throughout the rangelands of central Oregon, Idaho and Nevada were driven to Shaniko each year at shearing time by skilled Basque herders. Many a pot of lamb shanks and beans simmered in the caravans that were home to the herders, and many a weary sheepdog probably enjoyed the leftovers.

3 lamb shanks, cut into 2–3 pieces
¼ cup (1 oz/30 g) all-purpose (plain) flour, seasoned with salt and pepper to taste
¼ cup (2 fl oz/60 ml) olive oil
1 medium onion, coarsely chopped
1 carrot, peeled and split lengthwise
1 garlic clove, minced
2½ cups (20 fl oz/600 ml) beef stock (see glossary)
1½ cups (12 fl oz/375 ml) water
1 cup (8 fl oz/250 ml) dry red wine
1 tablespoon tomato paste (purée)
1 fresh rosemary sprig, or 1 teaspoon dried rosemary
2 cups (12 oz/370 g) canned white beans, or presoaked and parboiled dried white beans
6–8 small boiling onions, peeled
2 large carrots, sliced diagonally ¾ in (2 cm) thick
grated lemon zest and chopped fresh parsley and rosemary for garnish

◩ Preheat an oven to 325°F (165°C). Meanwhile, dredge the shanks in the seasoned flour. Heat the oil in a heavy skillet over medium-high heat and brown the shanks well, turning frequently. Remove the shanks to a large ovenproof casserole.
◩ Drain the excess fat from the skillet and add the chopped

Minted Lamb with Pear Relish

onion, split carrot and minced garlic. Sauté the vegetables for 2–3 minutes. Stir in the stock, water, wine, tomato paste and rosemary. Bring to a boil and pour over the meat in the casserole.
▓ Cover the casserole and bake in the preheated oven for 2 hours, or until tender. Remove the shanks from the oven, leaving the oven on. Remove the shanks from the casserole with a slotted spoon. Strain and degrease the liquid. Add salt and pepper as necessary.
▓ Remove the fat and gristle from the shanks, keeping the meat on the bones, and return the shanks to the casserole. Add the white beans, small onions and sliced carrots. Pour the sauce over, cover, and bake for about 1 hour, or until the vegetables are tender.
▓ Garnish with lemon zest, parsley and fresh rosemary, and serve with green salad and lots of crusty bread.

SERVES 6–8

Western Washington

MINTED LAMB WITH PEAR RELISH

Be sure to purchase a good Gewürztraminer wine, preferably from a Northwest winery, for this recipe and drink the remainder with dinner. You will be pleasantly surprised at how well Gewürztraminer complements the grilled lamb, pears and mint.

MARINADE

¼ cup (2 fl oz/60 ml) olive oil
¼ cup (2 fl oz/60 ml) Gewürztraminer wine
1 garlic clove, minced
1 teaspoon minced fresh ginger
¼ teaspoon dried red pepper flakes
1 tablespoon chopped fresh mint

6 thick lamb chops
salt and freshly cracked black pepper to taste

Pear Relish (recipe follows)
fresh mint sprigs for garnish (optional)

▓ Stir together all the marinade ingredients and pour into a nonaluminum baking dish. Add the lamb chops and marinate at room temperature for at least 1 hour, turning once.
▓ Meanwhile, prepare a fire in a charcoal grill. Remove the chops from the marinade and season with salt and pepper.
▓ Grill the chops over medium-hot coals for about 2–3 minutes per side for medium-rare, or until done to your taste. Serve immediately with pear relish, garnished with mint sprigs.

SERVES 6

PEAR RELISH

2 tablespoons olive or vegetable oil
1 red (Spanish) onion, thinly sliced
3 pears, cored and diced
¼ cup finely diced red bell pepper (capsicum)
1 garlic clove, minced
1 teaspoon minced fresh ginger
3 whole star anise
¼ teaspoon ground cinnamon
pinch of dried red pepper flakes
3 tablespoons sugar
2 tablespoons distilled white vinegar
¼ cup (2 fl oz/60 ml) Gewürztraminer wine
2 tablespoons fresh lemon juice
grated zest of 1 lemon
1½ teaspoons salt
⅓ cup minced fresh mint

▓ In a heavy saucepan, heat the oil, add the onion, and sauté for about 1 minute. Add all remaining relish ingredients except the mint and bring to a boil. Turn the heat down to a simmer and cook, stirring occasionally, until thickened and syrupy, about 35–45 minutes.
▓ Let cool, then stir in the mint. Serve at room temperature. Pear relish will keep, tightly covered and refrigerated, for up to 1 week.

MAKES ABOUT 2 CUPS (16 FL OZ/500 ML)

133

Eastern Washington

SHEPHERD'S PIE

An all-American interpretation of a very British standby, perhaps brought over the Oregon Trail from New England. To pie (as all old printer's devils know) is to make a jumble of things. Shepherd's pie in Scotland or England is likely to be just that: lamb and a combination of vegetables "jumbled" together and baked in a crust. This version is made from cubed cooked Northwest lamb, and mashed potatoes form the pie "shell." It's the perfect midweek encore for the Sunday roast.

2 tablespoons butter
2 tablespoons minced shallots
1 cup (6 oz/180 g) minced celery
1 large garlic clove, minced
3 cups (24 fl oz/750 ml) lamb or beef gravy
beef or lamb stock as needed (see glossary)
3 cups (1 lb/500 g) leftover roast lamb or beef, cut into
   fine cubes
½ cup (¾ oz/20 g) chopped fresh parsley

1 teaspoon chopped fresh thyme, or ¼ teaspoon dried thyme
2 teaspoons grated lemon zest
3 egg yolks, beaten
3 cups (24 fl oz/750 ml) mashed potatoes
paprika for garnish

▨ Preheat an oven to 350°F (180°C). Meanwhile, in a large skillet, melt the butter and sauté the shallots, celery and garlic over medium heat until the shallots are translucent. Add the gravy and, if necessary, thin with stock to the consistency of heavy cream. Add the diced meat and heat through. Stir in the parsley, thyme and lemon zest. Taste carefully for seasoning.
▨ Add the egg yolks to the mashed potatoes. Mix well and taste for seasoning.
▨ Line the sides of a 10–12-cup (2.5–3-l) ovenproof casserole with half of the mashed potatoes. Pour the lamb mixture into the center. Spoon or pipe in the remainder of the potatoes around the edges of the casserole on top of the meat mixture, leaving the center open. Sprinkle paprika on the potatoes as a garnish.
▨ Bake in the oven until the lamb is bubbling and the potatoes are browned, about 30 minutes.

SERVES 6   *Photograph pages 120-121*

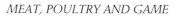

4 garlic cloves
2 cups (16 fl oz/500 ml) fresh-pressed apple cider
fresh sage sprigs for garnish (optional)

❖ Preheat an oven to 325°F (170°C). Season the duck well inside and out with the salt and pepper. Mix the fruit and sage together in a medium bowl. Add the garlic. Stuff the duck with the fruit mixture and place on a rack in a roasting pan. Mix the cider and dried sage together to use as a basting liquid.
❖ Roast the duck uncovered in the preheated oven, basting it with the cider every 10 minutes or so, for 20 minutes per pound (500 g), or until a meat thermometer inserted on the inside of a thigh reads 140°–145°F (60°–63°C).
❖ Allow the duck to sit for 10 minutes before carving. Drain off the fat.
❖ Serve with the pan juices and garnish with sage sprigs, if you like.

SERVES 4

Roast Duckling with Pressed Cider and Sage

Islands

ROAST DUCKLING WITH PRESSED CIDER AND SAGE

Early in this century the San Juan Islands were the largest fruit-growing region in the state. Today, old orchards abound in the islands, poking up in the middle of overgrown forests. The venerable apple and pear trees continue to produce year after year, providing islanders with a continuing supply. Cider-pressing parties are a favorite activity in the fall when the leaves turn gold and the light mellows.

1 duck, about 5–6 lb (2.5–3 kg)
1 teaspoon salt
½ teaspoon freshly ground black pepper
1 cup (6 oz/185 g) chopped apple
1 cup (8 oz/250 g) chopped pear
½ cup (3 oz/90 g) golden raisins
2 tablespoons minced fresh sage, or 2 teaspoons dried sage
1 tablespoon dried sage

Eastern Washington

ROAST CHICKEN STUFFED WITH AUTUMN FRUITS

The stuffing for this roast chicken is accented with dried fruits, making this a perfect dish for dinner on a cool autumn evening. Bake extra stuffing in a baking pan and serve with French-cut green beans.

3–4 lb (1.5–2 kg) roasting chicken
salt and ground black pepper
¾ cup (6 fl oz/180 ml) dry white wine
1 cup (5 oz/155 g) coarsely chopped mixed dried fruit such as apples, pears, apricots and prunes
½ cup (3 oz/90 g) diced celery
1 cup (8 oz/250 g) diced yellow (brown) onion
¼ cup (2 oz/60 g) butter
3 cups (6 oz/180 g) dried bread cut into 1-in (2.5-cm) cubes
¾–1 cup (6–8 fl oz/180–250 ml) chicken stock (see glossary)
1 tablespoon chopped fresh thyme, or 1 teaspoon dried thyme
2 tablespoons olive oil

❖ Rinse the chicken well, drain and pat dry. Season the cavity of the chicken with salt and pepper. Set aside. Preheat an oven to 425°F (220°C).
❖ Meanwhile, to make the stuffing: Pour the white wine over the dried fruit and let it sit for 20 minutes.
❖ In a skillet, sauté the celery and onion in butter over moderate heat for about 5 minutes, or until the onion is translucent.
❖ Pour the celery and onions over the bread crumbs, and add the wine and fruits. Mix gently to combine. Add ¾ cup (6 fl oz/180 ml) of the stock, thyme and salt and pepper. If the stuffing appears too dry, add more stock. Mix to combine thoroughly.
❖ Fill the cavity of the chicken loosely with the stuffing. Close the opening with skewers or a large needle and cotton string. Brush the chicken with olive oil and rub with salt and pepper.
❖ Put the chicken on a rack in a shallow pan. Roast in the preheated oven for 20 minutes, basting several times with the pan juices. Lower the heat to 350°F (180°C) and roast the chicken until golden brown, about 45 minutes–1 hour, basting several times, or until a meat thermometer inserted into a thigh reads 160°F (71°C). Remove from the oven and let sit for 15 minutes.
❖ Transfer the stuffing from the chicken to a serving bowl and carve the chicken as desired.

SERVES 4–6 *Photograph pages 120–121*

British Columbia

MARKET POT AU FEU

From Chartwell Restaurant in the Four Seasons Hotel, this pot au feu is a good example of the blending of ethnic and regional cuisines in the Pacific Northwest. Serve with steamed jasmine rice.

6 tablespoons (½ oz/10 g) minced fresh cilantro (coriander)
4 tablespoons minced fresh thyme
4 chicken thighs, skinned, boned and cut in half
1 lb (500 g) boneless veal shoulder, cut into 2-in (5-cm) chunks
2 ducks, 3–4 lb (1.5–2 kg) each, cut into serving pieces
3 tablespoons vegetable oil
½ cup (4 oz/125 g) butter
1 red (Spanish) onion, sliced
3 garlic cloves, crushed
8 whole green (spring) onions
½ red bell pepper (capsicum), diced
½ yellow bell pepper (capsicum), diced
8 cups (64 fl oz/2 l) chicken stock (see glossary)

Cornish Game Hens with Lemongrass served with chopped fruit and wild rice

1 zucchini (courgette), cut diagonally into ½-in (1.5-cm) slices
1 pattypan squash, cut diagonally into ½-in (1.5-cm) slices
8 baby corn-on-the-cobs
salt and freshly ground black pepper to taste
4 tablespoons chopped fresh garlic chives or chives
8 oz (250 g) fresh shiitake mushrooms, sliced

◪ Combine 3 tablespoons of the cilantro with the thyme in a small bowl. Place the chicken, veal and ducks in a nonaluminum baking dish, pat the herbs all over them, and cover with plastic wrap. Refrigerate overnight.
◪ Preheat an oven to 350°F (180°C). In a heavy skillet over high heat, heat the oil and sear the chicken, veal and duck in batches, browning all sides. Remove from the pan and set aside.
◪ Clean the skillet and place over medium heat. Melt half of the butter in the pan. Add the red onion, garlic and green onions. Sauté until the onions are translucent but not browned. Add the peppers and chicken stock. Bring to a boil, reduce heat, and simmer until the liquid is reduced by half.
◪ In a large ovenproof casserole, alternate layers of chicken, veal and duck with the vegetables, seasoning each layer with salt, black pepper, chopped garlic chives and the remaining cilantro. Pour the onion-stock mixture over all, then add the shiitake mushrooms and remaining ¼ cup (2 oz/60 g) butter.
◪ Cover and bake in the preheated oven for 1 hour, or until the meat and vegetables are tender, skimming foam and fat as necessary.

SERVES 8

British Columbia

CORNISH GAME HENS WITH LEMONGRASS

Southeast Asian cuisine adds a touch of the exotic to the cooking of Vancouver. Serve this dish with rice and a green salad.

3 Cornish game hens, split in half

MARINADE

2 tablespoons soy sauce
3 garlic cloves, minced
3 tablespoons chopped fresh ginger
¼ cup (2 fl oz/60 ml) fish sauce
4 fresh lemongrass stalks, thinly sliced (remove coarse outer leaves and use white portion at base of stalk)
juice of 2 lemons
3 tablespoons sugar
1 teaspoon chili paste with garlic
½ teaspoon salt
½ teaspoon freshly ground pepper
6 tablespoons (3 fl oz/80 ml) vegetable oil

✣ Remove any giblets from the hens and reserve for another use. Rinse the hens under cold running water; drain well and pat dry. Place the hens in a nonaluminum baking dish.
✣ Combine all of the ingredients for the marinade and pour it over the hens, spreading it evenly to make sure the hens are completely coated. Let stand at room temperature for at least 30 minutes, or up to 2 hours.
✣ Preheat an oven to 350°F (180°C). Remove the hens from the marinade, reserving the marinade. In a heavy skillet over medium-high heat, heat the oil and sauté the hens until brown on both sides. (If necessary, brown the hens in 2 batches or use 2 skillets.) Place skin side up in a baking dish and bake, basting the hens with the reserved marinade, for 30 minutes, or until the juice runs clear when the hens are pierced with a knife.

SERVES 6

Left to right: Braised Sausage with lentils, Venison Stew with Prunes

Eastern Washington

VENISON STEW WITH PRUNES

An ideal way to enjoy the rich, full flavor of venison. Serve this savory stew over soft polenta (recipe on page 104).

2 lb (1 kg) boneless venison rump or shoulder
1 tablespoon juniper berries, crushed
1 tablespoon black peppercorns
2 garlic cloves, coarsely chopped
1½ cups (12 fl oz/375 ml) dry red wine
2–3 tablespoons olive oil
2 cups (12 oz/360 g) celery, cut into 1-in (2.5-cm) diagonals
6–8 peeled small boiling onions
8 oz (250 g) dried pitted prunes
¾–1 cup (6–8 fl oz/180–250 ml) beef stock (see glossary)
salt and pepper to taste

◼ Preheat an oven to 350°F (180°C). Meanwhile, remove all connective tissue and/or fat from the venison and cut the meat into 1-in (2.5-cm) cubes.
◼ In a nonaluminum bowl, combine the venison, juniper berries, peppercorns and garlic. Add 1 cup (8 fl oz/250 ml) of the red wine. Cover and marinate in the refrigerator for 2–3 hours, or overnight.
◼ Drain off the marinade and discard. Heat the olive oil in a heavy skillet over high heat and brown the venison. Then add the celery, onions and prunes. Add the remaining ½ cup (4 fl oz/125 ml) red wine and ¾ cup (6 fl oz/180 ml) of the beef stock. Cover and bake in the preheated oven for 45 minutes, or until tender, adding the remaining beef stock during baking if necessary.
◼ Remove from the oven. Season with salt and pepper and serve over soft polenta.

SERVES 4–6

Eastern Washington

BRAISED SAUSAGE
AND LENTILS

Use a flavorful sausage such as Skagit Valley Duck Sausage (recipe on page 130), Venison Sausage (recipe on page 142) or a spicy Italian-style large link sausage. Nutritious Washington-grown lentils make this hearty, satisfying dish a winter favorite.

¼ cup (2 oz/60 g) butter
1 celery stalk, finely diced
1 onion, finely diced
1 carrot, finely diced
2 garlic cloves, minced
1 cup (6 oz/185 g) dried lentils
2½–3 cups (20–24 fl oz/625–750 ml) chicken stock (see glossary)
salt and pepper to taste
2 tablespoons vegetable oil
1½–2 lb (750 g–1 kg) sausage
2 tablespoons chopped fresh parsley

◼ Preheat an oven to 350°F (180°C). Heat the butter in a large ovenproof casserole over low heat. Add the celery, onion, carrot and garlic, and cook until the onion is translucent, about 5 minutes. Add the lentils and 2½ cups (20 fl oz/625 ml) of the chicken stock. Season with salt and pepper.
◼ Cover and bake in the preheated oven for 15 minutes. Meanwhile, heat the oil in a heavy skillet and brown the sausage over medium-high heat for about 3–5 minutes on each side.
◼ Remove the lentils from the oven and add the sausage and more stock, if necessary. Bake for 25 minutes longer, or until the lentils are tender and the sausage is just cooked through.
◼ Add the chopped parsley and adjust the seasoning. Do not overcook the sausage or it will become dry and tough.

SERVES 4

British Columbia

DUCK BREAST WITH WILD BLACKBERRIES AND GINGER

A winning duo from Bishop's Restaurant in Vancouver: tender rosy duck breasts and plump blackberries. Blueberries may be substituted.

4 boned duck breast halves
salt and freshly ground pepper to taste
1 clove or 1 teaspoon coarsely chopped garlic
3 tablespoons chopped fresh ginger
1 tablespoon fresh thyme, or 1 teaspoon dried thyme
¼ cup (2 fl oz/60 ml) balsamic vinegar
1 cup (6 oz/185 g) wild or cultivated blackberries or blueberries
½ cup (4 fl oz/125 ml) chicken stock (see glossary)

❖ Preheat an oven to 425°F (220°C). Prick the skin of the duck breasts all over with a fork and season with salt and pepper.
❖ In a skillet over high heat, place the duck skin side down and cook for 2 minutes. Turn and cook for 1 minute.
❖ Place the duck skin side up on a baking sheet and roast in the oven for 10 minutes (for medium-rare). Remove from the oven and set aside.
❖ Meanwhile, add the garlic, ginger and thyme to the skillet and sauté in the duck fat over medium heat until lightly browned. Add the vinegar and cook to reduce to 1 tablespoon of liquid. Add the berries and chicken stock and cook to reduce by half.
❖ Season with salt and pepper.
❖ To serve, slice the duck breasts on the diagonal and spoon the sauce over the skin.

SERVES 4

Duck Breast with Wild Blackberries and Ginger

Coppa-Cured Pork Tenderloin with Pickled Peaches

COPPA-CURED PORK TENDERLOIN WITH PICKLED PEACHES

The dry-curing of meats requires patience and, of course, time. The rewards are evident in the intense flavor developed by this method. Coppacola curing renders a spicy tanginess in pork that embellishes many dishes from antipasto to sautés and soups. Use the meat from this recipe as you would prosciutto.

1 cup (8 oz/250 g) kosher salt
¼ cup (1½ oz/45 g) brown sugar, packed
3 lb (1.5 kg) pork tenderloins (whole fillets), trimmed of all
    fat and silverskin, 3–4 tenderloins
½ cup (4 oz/125 g) paprika
½ tablespoon cayenne pepper
2 tablespoons ground coriander
Pepper-Pickled Peaches (recipe on page 187), optional

▨ Mix the salt and brown sugar together. Place the meat in a nonaluminum container and sprinkle with all of the salt and sugar mixture. Cover and refrigerate for 2 days, turning the meat at least twice during that period.

▨ Rinse off the mixture and pat the meat dry with a towel. Mix the paprika, cayenne and coriander together and rub the meat generously with them.

▨ Roll each tenderloin up in a 1-foot (30-cm) square of cheesecloth (muslin). Tie each end with cotton twine and tie the roll once or twice around the middle. Tie the bundled "coppas" to a rack in a corner of the refrigerator so that they are not touching each other or any other object. Allow to cure until firm to the touch, about 2 weeks.

▨ Slice the meat paper thin and serve with the pickled peaches as an antipasto, or use in pastas and sauté dishes.

▨ The cured meat will keep in the refrigerator, loosely wrapped in waxed paper, for up to 1 month.

MAKES ABOUT 2 LB (1 KG)

Oregon

ROAST QUAIL WITH APRICOT AND GREEN PEPPERCORN RELISH

Oregon Pinot Noir and oven-roasted quail are a superb match. The spiciness of green peppercorns lends a complexity to the rich fruitiness of the relish. Use an equal number of dried apricots if fresh are not available; plump them by simmering in water for 20–30 minutes before making the relish.

1 large yellow (brown) onion, peeled and finely diced
2 tablespoons minced garlic
¼ cup (2 fl oz/60 ml) plus 2 tablespoons olive oil
1 cup (8 fl oz/250 ml) dry white wine
1 red bell pepper (capsicum), cored, seeded and finely diced
¼ cup (2 fl oz/60 ml) white wine vinegar
2 tablespoons green peppercorns, drained and lightly crushed
2 tablespoons sugar
1 teaspoon salt
12 fresh apricots, peeled, pitted and chopped, about 3–4 cups
12 boned quail (leg and wing bones remaining)
salt and pepper to taste
5 cups (1¾ lb/875 g) cooked wild rice (see glossary)

❖ In a large, heavy saucepan over medium heat, brown the onion and garlic in 2 tablespoons of olive oil for 2–3 minutes. Add the wine, bell pepper, vinegar, green peppercorns, sugar and salt, and cook to reduce the liquid by two-thirds, or until syrupy, about 12–15 minutes. Add the apricots and simmer for another 5 minutes. Add more salt, if needed. Remove from the heat.
❖ Preheat an oven to 450°F (230°C). Season the quail inside and out with salt and pepper. Combine the wild rice with 1½ cups (12 fl oz/375 ml) of the relish and mix thoroughly. Fill each quail with a handful of the rice mixture and close the cavity with a toothpick.
❖ In a large skillet, heat the remaining olive oil and quickly brown the quail on all sides. Transfer them to a roasting pan and roast in the preheated oven for about 10 minutes, or until the juices run pink when the quail are pierced with a knife.
❖ Arrange on a warmed serving platter and serve with additional rice and apricot relish. Any leftover relish will keep for 2 weeks in the refrigerator or 2 months in the freezer.

SERVES 6

Oregon

WALNUT-CRUSTED CHICKEN BREAST WITH RHUBARB-ONION CHUTNEY

The tart, crisp rhubarb of early spring lends a tang to this chutney, while the crisp, nutty breading keeps the chicken moist and tender.

6 boned chicken breast halves, skinned and pounded
   ½ in (1.5 cm) thick
salt and pepper to taste
1 cup (4 oz/125 g) all-purpose (plain) flour
3 eggs
½ cup (4 fl oz/125 ml) water
2 cups (9 oz/280 g) coarsely ground walnuts
½ cup (4 fl oz/125 ml) vegetable oil
fresh mint sprigs for garnish (optional)
Rhubarb-Onion Chutney (recipe follows)

❖ Season the chicken breasts with salt and pepper and dredge them in the flour, shaking off the excess. Beat the eggs with the water until well combined. Dip the chicken breasts in the egg mixture, then dredge them in the ground walnuts, taking care to coat them evenly.
❖ In a large heavy skillet, heat half of the vegetable oil over medium heat. Place 3 of the chicken breasts in the pan, and cook for about 5–7 minutes per side, or until golden brown. Transfer to a very low oven and repeat to cook the remaining breasts.
❖ Serve with the rhubarb chutney and garnish with mint sprigs, if desired.

SERVES 6

RHUBARB-ONION CHUTNEY

1 large yellow (brown) onion, finely diced
4 cups (20 oz/625 g) diced fresh rhubarb
¼ cup (2 fl oz/60 ml) white wine vinegar
¼ cup (2 oz/60 g) sugar
¼ cup (1 oz/30 g) raisins
2 tablespoons minced fresh ginger
2 tablespoons minced garlic
2 tablespoons Madras curry powder
½ teaspoon salt
3 tablespoons chopped fresh mint

❖ In a medium nonaluminum saucepan, combine all of the chutney ingredients except the mint and bring to a low boil over medium heat. Reduce the heat and cook until the onions and rhubarb are tender and the chutney has thickened, about 30 minutes; stir frequently to avoid scorching. Remove from the heat and let cool, then add the fresh mint. Pack in three 1-cup (8-fl oz/250-ml) sterilized glass canning jars (see glossary) and refrigerate for up to 3 weeks, or freeze for up to 2 months.

MAKES ABOUT 3 CUPS (24 FL OZ/750 M)

Islands

VENISON SAUSAGE

The islands are alive with deer and other game, and while there is very little hunting, occasionally a deer eats the prize roses one too many times. In the Native American tradition of honoring the animal, all the meat is put to good use.

2 lb (1 kg) fresh pork fat
5 lb (2.5 kg) boneless fresh venison trimmings
2 large onions, chopped
4 garlic cloves
2 bay leaves
2 teaspoons salt, or to taste
2 teaspoons freshly ground black pepper
½ teaspoon dried red pepper flakes
1 teaspoon paprika
1 teaspoon ground allspice
3 tablespoons minced fresh parsley
1 tablespoon chopped fresh thyme
sheep casings, about 3 yards (3 m)

❖ Put the pork fat and venison through a sausage grinder twice. Grind the onions, garlic and bay leaves and mix with the ground meat in a large bowl. Sprinkle with the remaining seasonings and mix well. Pan-fry a small patty of the sausage mixture to test for seasoning and adjust as needed.
❖ Cut the sausage casings into 3-foot (1-m) lengths and wash by hooking one end to the kitchen faucet and flushing with cold water. Fill the casings with the sausage mixture, using the small tube on the sausage stuffer; to make links, twist the casings every 4 in (10 cm). Tie at each end and refrigerate overnight to let the flavors blend.
❖ The sausage may be smoked in a home smoker according to the manufacturer's instructions, or roasted whole in a 350°F (180°C) oven for 20–30 minutes. Cooked sausage freezes well.

MAKES 30 SAUSAGES   *Photograph pages 120–121*

Top to bottom: Roast Quail with Apricot and Green Peppercorn Relish,
Walnut-Crusted Chicken Breast with Rhubarb-Onion Chutney

Lamb Chops, Basque Style

LAMB CHOPS, BASQUE STYLE

Fresh Oregon lamb is moist, tender and flavorful. This dish is a variation on a rustic lamb stew cooked by Basque shepherds while tending flocks in eastern Oregon.

12 lamb chops, about 3 lb (1.5 kg)
salt and pepper to taste
¼ cup (2 fl oz/60 ml) olive oil
3 tablespoons minced garlic

2 tablespoons fresh chopped marjoram, or 1 tablespoon dried marjoram
¾ teaspoon ground cumin
1 red bell pepper (capsicum), cored, seeded and cut into thin strips
1 green bell pepper (capsicum), cored, seeded, and cut into thin strips
1 large yellow (brown) onion, finely diced
1 cup (8 fl oz/250 ml) dry red wine such as Cabernet Sauvignon or Pinot Noir
6 cups (3 lb/1.5 kg) peeled, seeded and chopped fresh, or diced canned tomatoes, drained

▨ Season the lamb chops with salt and pepper. Heat a large, heavy skillet or saucepan over medium-high heat, add the olive oil, and sear a few chops at a time for about 2–3 minutes per side, or until lightly browned. Repeat until all the chops are seared.

▨ Reduce the heat to medium and add the garlic, marjoram and cumin to the pan. Sauté until the garlic is golden, about 2–3 minutes, being careful not to burn it.

▨ Add the peppers and onion and sauté until the onion is translucent, 2–3 minutes. Add the red wine and tomatoes and simmer to reduce the liquid, about 10–12 minutes. Add salt and pepper to taste.

▨ Place the lamb chops in the sauce, cover, and simmer 3–5 minutes longer to heat the lamb chops through.

▨ Serve in the pan, accompanied with rice and a rustic loaf of bread.

SERVES 6

British Columbia
ROASTED MUSTARD RABBIT WITH SPICED APPLE RINGS

Rabbit has a special affinity for mustard. The combination of mustards in this zesty marinade lose their sharp character when cooked and mellow into a rich flavor. Serve with fresh pasta. Chicken can be substituted for rabbit.

MARINADE

⅓ cup (2.5 fl oz/75 ml) Dijon mustard
⅓ cup (2.5 fl oz/75 ml) prepared whole-grain mustard
3 tablespoons distilled white vinegar
3 tablespoons olive oil

½ cup (4 fl oz/125 ml) unsweetened apple juice
juice of ½ lemon
1 large shallot, minced
salt and freshly ground pepper to taste

1 rabbit, about 5 lb (2.5 kg), cut into 6 serving pieces
salt and freshly ground pepper to taste
2 tablespoons olive oil
3 tablespoons butter
3 unpeeled red apples, cored and cut crosswise into ½-in (1.5-cm) rings
Chinese five-spices mix to taste
2 tablespoons balsamic vinegar or cider vinegar

▨ Combine the mustards, vinegar, oil, apple juice, lemon juice, shallot, and salt and pepper in a nonaluminum baking dish. Season the rabbit with salt and pepper and place in the marinade, turning to coat well. Cover and marinate for 4 hours or overnight in the refrigerator.

▨ Remove the rabbit pieces from the marinade and reserve the marinade.

▨ Preheat an oven to 350°F (180°C). Heat the oil in a skillet over medium-high heat. Add the rabbit pieces and cook, turning once, until golden brown, about 4 minutes on each side.

▨ Transfer the rabbit pieces (skin side up) to a 9-by-13-in (23-by-32.5-cm) baking dish.

▨ Roast the rabbit in the oven for 30 minutes, basting with the reserved marinade every 10 minutes.

▨ Meanwhile, add the butter to a skillet and sauté the apples until lightly browned, about 4 minutes. Sprinkle with five-spices and add the vinegar to the skillet. Turn the apples once, then remove from the heat and set aside.

▨ To serve, place the rabbit on warm plates and garnish with the apple rings.

SERVES 4

Left to right: Roasted Mustard Rabbit with Spiced Apple Rings, Mt. Bachelor Duck Confit (Page 146)

Oregon

MT. BACHELOR DUCK CONFIT

Confit is an age-old method of cooking, tenderizing and preserving meats. It works wonderfully on tougher cuts of game meats, especially legs of ducks or geese, transforming them into flavorful, fork-tender morsels. Aromas from the high desert region of eastern Oregon waft from this duck confit with nuances of sage, juniper and rosemary.

SALT CURE

1 cup (8 oz/250 g) kosher salt
1 tablespoon ground coriander
1 tablespoon ground ginger
1 tablespoon ground white pepper
1 tablespoon ground allspice

8 duck legs with thighs, about 3 lb (1.5 kg) total
12 garlic cloves
2 tablespoons black peppercorns
2 tablespoons dried juniper berries
12 bay leaves
4 large fresh sage sprigs
4 large fresh rosemary sprigs
4 cups (32 fl oz/1 l) canola or safflower oil
4 cups (32 fl oz/1 l) olive oil

▦ Combine all the ingredients for the salt cure. Dredge the duck legs evenly in the salt cure mixture. Place the duck in a nonaluminum container, cover, and refrigerate for at least 10 hours.
▦ Preheat an oven to 275°F (135°C). Meanwhile, rinse the duck legs gently in cold water to remove the salt mixture and pat dry.
▦ Place the legs in an ovenproof casserole or Dutch oven. Top with the garlic, peppercorns, juniper berries, herbs and oils.
▦ Place the duck legs in the preheated oven and cook, stirring gently once every hour, until the joints loosen and the meat is fork tender, about 3½–4½ hours.
▦ Let the duck legs cool in the cooking oil. Place the duck and the cooking oil in airtight containers in the refrigerator. The confit will keep for 2 weeks. Use the tender meat as you would chicken breast, to enhance salads, appetizers, pastas or soups.

MAKES ABOUT 2½ LB (1.2 KG)   *Photograph page 145*

Western Washington

THAI-FLAVORED CHICKEN SKEWERS

This recipe is excellent prepared with large prawns or pieces of pork tenderloin in place of the chicken breast, adjusting the cooking times as necessary. It's fun at an outdoor party to let everyone grill his or her own skewer.

MARINADE

2 tablespoons minced fresh lemongrass (optional)
2 tablespoons minced fresh ginger
2 teaspoons minced fresh garlic
1½ tablespoons soy sauce
2 tablespoons Thai fish sauce
½ cup (4 fl oz/125 ml) fresh lime juice
1 tablespoon Asian (toasted) sesame oil
1¾ cups (14 fl oz/425 ml) unsweetened coconut milk
½–1 teaspoon dried red chili flakes
½ teaspoon salt
3 tablespoons sugar

2 lb (1 kg) boneless chicken breast, skinned and cut into 48 equal pieces
12 green (spring) onions, root end cut into two 2-in (5-cm) pieces
2 red bell peppers (capsicums), about 8 oz (250 g) each, seeded and cut into twenty-four 1-in (2.5-cm) triangles
1 bunch fresh cilantro (coriander), stemmed and minced
black sesame seeds for garnish

▦ To make the marinade: In a small saucepan over medium-high heat, bring all the marinade ingredients to a slow boil

146

Thai-Flavored Chicken Skewers

and cook for 1 minute. Remove from the heat and let cool to room temperature.

▨ Soak 24 wooden skewers, about 6 in (15 cm) long, in water for 1 hour. Thread the skewers by alternating pieces of chicken, green onion, chicken and bell pepper. Repeat to use all the pieces.

▨ Place the skewers in a nonaluminum baking dish. Pour the cooled marinade and chopped cilantro over the skewers. Cover and refrigerate for at least 1½ hours or overnight, turning the skewers several times during this period.

▨ Prepare a charcoal fire in a grill. Remove the skewers from the refrigerator 30 minutes before grilling.

▨ Brush the cooking rack with a little oil. Grill the skewers a few at a time over medium-hot coals for about 1½–2 minutes per side, or until the chicken is lightly charred on the outside and opaque throughout. Spoon a little marinade over each skewer before serving and sprinkle with a few black sesame seeds.

MAKES 24 SKEWERS

BARBECUED RIBS WITH APRICOT GLAZE

This simple recipe makes tender, succulent ribs with a rich, dark glaze that combines sweet, hot and sour tastes. The baby back ribs are parboiled first to remove some of the fat and prevent flare-ups on the grill.

5 cups (40 fl oz/1.25 l) apple cider
1 tablespoon black peppercorns
1 teaspoon or more dried red pepper flakes
5 lb (2.5 kg) baby back ribs
1 jar apricot preserves, about 1¼ cups (10 oz/315 g)
1 tablespoon balsamic or cider vinegar
½ teaspoon salt

▨ Prepare a fire in a charcoal grill.
▨ While the coals are heating, combine the cider, peppercorns and 1 teaspoon of the red pepper flakes in a large saucepan or stockpot. Add the ribs and bring to a boil over medium heat. Reduce the heat to a simmer and cover the pan. Cook for 15–20 minutes. Transfer the ribs to a platter and let cool.
▨ Meanwhile, skim the cider thoroughly and cook over medium heat to reduce to ½ cup (4 fl oz/125 ml) liquid. Set aside.
▨ In a small saucepan, warm the preserves over low heat until melted. Strain the reduced cider and add to the preserves. Add the vinegar and salt and simmer for 5 minutes, or until smooth and glossy. Remove from the heat. For a spicy sauce, add more red pepper flakes, if desired. Let cool until thickened.
▨ Brush the ribs with the apricot glaze and cook over medium-hot coals for about 15–20 minutes, turning and basting often. Remove from the grill and cut into serving-size pieces.

SERVES 4

Grilled Picnic Burgers

GRILLED PICNIC BURGERS

Hamburgers are the all-time favorite grill food. This recipe uses caramelized onions to flavor the meat and keep it moist. Use ground chuck for grilling, as its high fat content binds the meat and makes a superb hamburger.

2 tablespoons butter
1 tablespoon olive oil
1 large yellow (brown) onion, chopped
1½ lb (750 g) ground beef chuck
salt and black pepper to taste
butter for rolls
4 French rolls

▨ Light a fire in a charcoal grill. While the coals are heating, heat the butter and oil in a skillet and sauté the onions over medium heat until the onions are golden. Remove from the pan with a slotted spoon.
▨ Season the ground chuck with salt and pepper, add the caramelized onions, and mix gently to combine. Divide the beef into 4 portions. Gently shape each portion to a 5-by-3-in (13-by-7.5-cm) patty about ¾ in (2 cm) thick.
▨ Grill the burgers over medium-hot coals for about 4 minutes on each side for medium-rare.
▨ Place buttered French rolls cut-side down on the grill for 1–2 minutes, or until lightly browned. Place each burger on a toasted bun and serve with your favorite condiments.

SERVES 4

LAMB BURGERS ON ROSEMARY-GARLIC BUNS

Grill lamb burgers over medium-hot coals and flavor them with smoke from chips of fruit woods such as apple, cherry or pear, if you like. Nutty-tasting arugula adds great flavor and crunch to these burgers.

ROASTED RED PEPPER MAYONNAISE

1 roasted red bell pepper (capsicum) (see glossary), or
    3 tablespoons diced purchased roasted red bell pepper
¼ cup (2 fl oz/60 ml) mayonnaise

LAMB BURGERS

1 lb (500 g) ground lamb
½ teaspoon freshly ground black pepper
2 tablespoons Dijon mustard
1 teaspoon minced fresh rosemary
1 tablespoon minced onion
1 teaspoon minced garlic
2 teaspoons balsamic vinegar
1 egg
salt to taste

whole-grain mustard
thinly sliced red (Spanish) or Walla Walla Sweet onions
arugula or lettuce leaves, washed and dried
4 Rosemary-Garlic Buns, (recipe follows) or other fresh, split buns (spread plain buns with garlic-rosemary butter after toasting)

▨ Prepare a fire in a charcoal grill. Peel and seed the roasted red peppers. Chop coarsely and place in a blender or food processor with the mayonnaise. Process until smooth and refrigerate until needed.
▨ To make the burgers: Mix the burger ingredients together in a medium bowl. Divide the meat into 4 portions and shape into patties ½ in (1.5 cm) thick. Grill over medium-hot coals for 2½–3 minutes per side for medium doneness.

Barbecued Ribs with Apricot Glaze, Lamb Burgers on Rosemary-Garlic Buns

▨ Toast the buns lightly on the grill, place the burgers on the buns, and serve with whole-grain mustard, roasted red pepper mayonnaise, thinly sliced onions and arugula or lettuce.

MAKES 4 BURGERS

ROSEMARY-GARLIC BUNS

½ cup (4 fl oz/125 ml) milk
1 tablespoon butter
2 tablespoons sugar
½ teaspoon salt
1 package active dried yeast
⅓ cup (3 fl oz/80 ml) warm water (110°F/43°C)
2 eggs
2½–3 cups (10–12 oz/310–375 g) all-purpose (plain) flour, as needed
2 teaspoons minced fresh rosemary
2 garlic cloves, minced
2 tablespoons freshly grated Parmesan cheese
1 tablespoon water
2 teaspoons poppy seeds

▨ In a small saucepan, bring the milk just to a simmer, remove from heat, and stir in the butter, sugar and salt. Stir to dissolve the ingredients and let cool to lukewarm.

▨ Pour the milk mixture into a large bowl. Dissolve the yeast in the warm water, then add to the milk mixture. Whisk in 1 egg, then mix in the rosemary, garlic and 1 tablespoon of the Parmesan cheese. Stir in as much flour as needed to make a smooth, moist dough. Place on a lightly floured surface and knead until smooth. Place in a large greased bowl, turn to coat on all sides, cover with a towel, and let rise in a warm place until doubled, about 1½ hours.

▨ Punch down the dough and place it on a lightly floured surface. Divide the dough into 6 pieces. Roll into balls and let rest for 10 minutes, covered with a towel. With a well-floured rolling pin, roll the balls into 3½–4-in (9–10-cm) rounds. Place on a greased baking sheet. Cover lightly with a towel and let rise until almost doubled in size.

▨ Preheat an oven to 350°F (180°C). In a small bowl, whisk the remaining egg with the tablespoon of water. Brush the tops of the buns lightly with the egg wash and place in the preheated oven. After about 10 minutes, when light browning begins to take place, remove the buns from the oven and very quickly repeat the egg wash, then sprinkle the buns with the poppy seeds and the remaining Parmesan cheese. Quickly return the buns to the oven. Bake 7–10 minutes longer, or until golden brown, a total cooking time of about 17–20 minutes. Let cool on wire racks.

▨ Extra buns may be cooled, wrapped, and frozen for later use.

MAKES 6 BUNS

Oregon

PEPPERED FLANK STEAK WITH OREGON BLUE CHEESE SAUCE

A London broil with a Northwest twist, this flank steak is a nice change from the usual barbecue fare. Serve it with crusty sourdough bread, a salad and a lush Pinot Noir.

3 lb (1.5 kg) flank steak
¼ cup (1 oz/30 g) cracked black pepper
¼ cup (1 oz/ 30 g) chopped garlic
6 bay leaves
1 tablespoon fresh chopped rosemary
¾ cup (6 fl oz/180 ml) Oregon or other good Pinot Noir
2 tablespoons olive oil
1 tablespoon red wine vinegar
1 cup (8 fl oz/250 ml) beef stock (see glossary)
¼ cup (1 oz/30 g) cornstarch (cornflour)
¼ cup (2 fl oz/60 ml) water
salt and freshly ground black pepper to taste
8 oz (375 g) Oregon blue cheese or other mild blue cheese, crumbled, about 2 cups, loosely piled
fresh watercress for garnish (optional)

◾ Rub the flank steak with the cracked black pepper and garlic and place in a nonaluminum container. Add the bay leaves, rosemary, Pinot Noir , olive oil and vinegar. Cover and refrigerate for 24 hours, turning the meat 2–3 times during this period.
◾ Prepare a fire in a charcoal grill. Remove the meat from the refrigerator 30 minutes before grilling.
◾ Remove the meat from the marinade and dry with a towel. Strain the marinade into a medium nonaluminum saucepan, discarding the herbs and spices, and boil over medium heat until it has reduced by half.
◾ Add the beef stock to the simmering wine mixture. Mix the cornstarch with the water and whisk it into the simmering stock.
◾ Reduce the heat to medium-low and allow the sauce to simmer and thicken for 5–7 minutes.
◾ Season the flank steak generously with pepper and salt and broil over medium-hot coals for 3 minutes on each side, then turn and cook 3 minutes again on each side for a total cooking time of 12 minutes for medium-rare. Cook 2 minutes longer on each side, for a total of 20 minutes, for medium.
◾ Transfer the meat to a warmed serving platter and let sit in a warm place.
◾ Remove the sauce from the heat and whisk in 1½ cups (6 oz/185 g) of the crumbled blue cheese, stirring until smooth. Add salt and pepper if necessary. Cut the broiled steaks into ¼-in (6-mm) thick diagonal slices.
◾ Serve topped with sauce and garnished with the remaining crumbled blue cheese and watercress, if you like.

SERVES 6–8

Islands

ROAST LEG OF LAMB WITH MERLOT MARINADE

Lopez Island farmers raise lamb in the European manner, feeding it on the tasty grasses that grow windward to the Strait of Juan de Fuca. This meat is a great match with the world-class Merlots of Washington state. Be sure to have an extra bottle or two on hand to drink with dinner.

1 boneless lamb leg, 4–6 lb (2–3 kg)
1 tablespoon freshly ground black pepper
8 garlic cloves, minced
4 fresh rosemary sprigs, or 1 tablespoon dried rosemary
¼ cup (2 fl oz/60 ml) olive oil
2 cups (16 fl oz/500 ml) good Washington Merlot, such as Chinook, Columbia or Latah Creek, or other full-bodied red wine
2 teaspoons salt

Peppered Flank Steak with Oregon Blue Cheese Sauce

◧ Coat the outside of the lamb with the ground pepper. Rub the garlic and pepper into the lamb. Chop half of the rosemary and rub it onto the lamb.

◧ Place the lamb, olive oil and Merlot in a nonaluminum container. Turn the lamb in the marinade and cover with the remaining rosemary. Cover and marinate in the refrigerator overnight, turning the lamb occasionally.

◧ Preheat an oven to 350°F (180°C). Remove the lamb from the marinade and wipe the rosemary and garlic off the surface. Place the lamb on a rack in a shallow roasting pan and salt it well.

◧ Roast the lamb in the preheated oven for 20 minutes per pound (500 g) or until the internal temperature reaches 145°–150°F (63°–66°C) for medium rare.

SERVES 8–12   *Photograph pages 120-121*

151

Clockwise from top: Tourtière Christmas Pie, Roast Prime Rib
of Beef with Herbed Popovers, Roast Turkey with Oyster-Corn
Bread Stuffing and Wild Turkey Gravy

ROAST TURKEY WITH OYSTER-CORN BREAD STUFFING AND WILD TURKEY GRAVY

*The ferries fill with visitors and homecoming islanders alike every
Thanksgiving weekend. The island kitchens are bursting with kids,
house guests and food. Wild turkeys are a protected species on the
islands, but they are great inspiration for a fearless turkey gravy.*

OYSTER-CORN BREAD STUFFING

1 cup (8 oz/250 g) chopped onion
1 cup (6 oz/180 g) chopped celery
1 cup (8 oz/250g) unsalted butter
6 cups (10 oz/315 g) diced corn bread
2½ cups (20 fl oz/625 ml) shucked yearling oysters
1 bay leaf, crushed
½ teaspoon ground white pepper
½ teaspoon ground nutmeg
1 teaspoon dried thyme
1 teaspoon dried ground sage
1 teaspoon dried basil
1 teaspoon paprika
1 teaspoon dried summer savory
½ cup chopped fresh parsley
1 teaspoon salt
¼ cup (2 fl oz/60 ml) Wild Turkey or other bourbon
1 egg, beaten

1 roasting turkey, 12–15 lb (6–7.5 kg)
3 tablespoons fresh lemon juice

GRAVY

reserved turkey giblets (above)
1 bay leaf
3 cups (24 fl oz/750 ml) water or more
½ cup (4 fl oz/125 ml) white wine
1–1½ cups (8½–12 fl oz/250–375 ml) reserved pan drippings
   from turkey (above)
½ cup (4 fl oz/125 ml) balsamic vinegar
½ cup (4 fl oz/125 ml) Wild Turkey or other bourbon
½ cup (2 oz/125 ml) flour
½ cup (4 fl oz/125 ml) milk
1 cup (8 fl oz/250 ml) heavy (double) cream
1 teaspoon salt
1 teaspoon freshly ground black pepper

▓ To make the stuffing: In a heavy skillet, sauté the onion and
celery in the butter until tender, about 5 minutes.

▓ In a large bowl, combine the corn bread, oysters, seasonings,
bourbon and egg. Gently toss with the onion, celery and butter
to mix all the ingredients. Refrigerate until ready for use.

▓ Remove the giblets from the turkey and reserve them. Wipe
out both cavities of the turkey with a clean towel moistened
with the lemon juice. Stuff the turkey loosely with the corn
bread mixture. Extra stuffing may be cooked in a covered
casserole for 1 hour at 350°F (180°C).

▓ Roast the turkey for 15 minutes per lb (500 g), or until a
meat thermometer inserted on the inside of the thigh reads
160°F (71°C) and the juices run clear when the turkey is
pierced with a knife.

▓ Allow the turkey to sit for 30 minutes before carving. Cover
with a clean dish towel to keep it warm.

▓ Meanwhile, to make the gravy: While the turkey is roasting,
place the giblets in a medium saucepan with the bay leaf, water
and wine; simmer over low heat for 3 hours. Add more water

to the giblets as needed, but never more than 3 cups at a time.
◪ Strain the giblets, reserving both the stock and the meat. Remove the meat from the bones and chop fine.
◪ After the turkey has been cooked and removed from the roasting pan, add the stock to the roasting pan, scraping the bottom and sides to remove the drippings. Transfer the stock and scrapings to a large saucepan, bring to a boil, cook to reduce by half, and set aside.
◪ In a medium saucepan, cook the vinegar to reduce it to 1 tablespoon, add the bourbon, and burn off the alcohol by boiling for 1 minute.
◪ In a small bowl, mix the flour and the milk together, whisking well to remove any lumps. Whisk the flour mixture into the bourbon over high heat for 2 minutes, or until the flour begins to turn golden. Gradually whisk in the stock while the gravy thickens. Stir in the heavy cream, chopped giblets, and salt and pepper. Keep warm.
◪ Carve the turkey and remove the stuffing from the carcass. Serve the turkey and stuffing on warm plates and pass the gravy separately.

SERVES 12–14

British Columbia

ROAST PRIME RIB OF BEEF WITH HERBED POPOVERS

Beef is king in the Cariboo area of British Columbia. Since early pioneer days, the cattlemen and ranchers of Cariboo have provided the rest of the province with award-winning beef. Ask your butcher for the end cut of a prime rib roast (the most tender section) for this recipe.

1 rib roast of beef (3–4 ribs, about 7 lb/3.5 kg)
seasoned salt to taste (recipe follows)
coarsely ground black pepper to taste
Herbed Popovers (recipe follows)

◪ Sprinkle the roast generously with seasoned salt and coarsely ground pepper and let stand at room temperature for 30 minutes.
◪ Preheat an oven to 325°F (165°C).
◪ Place the meat, rib side down, in a roasting pan and cook for 15–20 minutes per pound (500 g) for rare meat, or until a meat thermometer registers 130°F (54°C). For medium-rare doneness, cook the roast to 140°F (60°C), or about 20–25 minutes per pound.
◪ Remove the roast from the oven and let sit for 20 minutes. It will continue to cook and the juices will settle. Transfer the roast to a warm platter, reserving the pan juices to serve with the roast.

SERVES 12

SEASONED SALT

3 tablespoons onion powder
1 tablespoon garlic salt
1 tablespoon dried sweet basil
1 tablespoon dried marjoram
1 tablespoon dried mint leaves
1 teaspoon curry powder
¾ cup (6 oz/185 g) kosher salt

◪ Place all the ingredients except the kosher salt in a blender or electric coffee mill and grind to a powder. Add the salt and mix well.
MAKES 1 CUP (8 OZ/250 G)

HERBED POPOVERS

Herbs add a special touch to these popovers, which can be served for lunch or dinner. To serve for brunch, omit the herbs, add orange zest, chopped pecans and nutmeg, and serve with a fresh fruit butter or maple syrup.

4 eggs
1½ cups (12 fl oz/375 ml) milk
1½ cups (6 oz/185 g) all-purpose (plain) flour
½ teaspoon salt
1 tablespoon chopped fresh thyme
1 tablespoon chopped fresh parsley
1 tablespoon chopped fresh basil
about 3½ tablespoons butter for pans

◪ Preheat an oven to 400°F (200°C). In a food processor, process eggs, milk, flour, salt and herbs until smooth.
◪ Place 1 teaspoon of butter in each of 10 muffin pans, popover pans or glass custard cups about 2½ in (6.5 cm) in diameter, and place in the preheated oven for 1–2 minutes, or until the butter is melted. Fill each container half full with batter and bake for about 30 minutes, or until popovers are puffed and brown.
◪ Serve immediately.
MAKES 10 POPOVERS

British Columbia

TOURTIÈRE CHRISTMAS PIE

This traditional French Canadian meat pie is always served at Christmas. No one really seems to know its origin, but Pierre and Janet Berton, in their book The Centennial Food Guide, *describe how tourtes, a type of passenger pigeon, arrived in Quebec in great flocks each fall during the early eighteenth century. Today tourtière is made with almost any meat.*

SOUR CREAM PASTRY

2 cups (8 oz/250 g) all-purpose (plain) flour
1 cup (8 oz/250 g) butter, divided into 4 equal portions
½ cup (4 fl oz/125 ml) sour cream
1 egg yolk

FILLING

2 tablespoons butter
1 onion, chopped
2 garlic cloves, minced
1 celery stalk, diced
1 lb (500 g) ground pork
8 oz (250 g) ground veal
¾ cup (6 fl oz/180 ml) hot water
¼ teaspoon ground pepper, or to taste
½ teaspoon ground cinnamon
¼ teaspoon ground cloves
½ teaspoon dried savory

◪ To make the pastry: Place the flour in a food processor and distribute the butter evenly over the flour. Process until well blended. In a small bowl, mix the sour cream and egg yolk and add to the flour-butter mixture. Process until well blended. To make by hand, place the flour in a large mixing bowl. Cut in the butter with a pastry blender or 2 knives until the mixture resembles course meal. In a small bowl, combine the sour cream and egg yolk, and stir in to the flour-butter mixture until well blended.
◪ Transfer the mixture to a lightly floured board and shape into a flat disc. Cover with plastic wrap and chill for 1 hour, or until the pastry is firm enough to roll out.
◪ To make the filling: In a large skillet over medium-high heat, melt the butter. Add the onion, garlic and celery, and sauté until tender. Add the meat and water and simmer for 30 minutes. Add the seasonings, stir well, and simmer for 5 minutes. Let cool.
◪ Preheat an oven to 450°F (230°C). Roll out half of the pastry dough and line a 10-in (25-cm) pie pan. Spoon the filling into the bottom crust.
◪ Roll out the remaining dough for the top crust. Place over the filling and press all around the outer edges to seal. Cut slits in the pastry to allow steam to escape.
◪ Bake until the crust is golden, 15–20 minutes. Reduce the heat to 325°F (165°C) and bake for 30 minutes, or until the pastry is golden brown.
◪ Remove from the oven and let cool for 20 minutes, then cut into wedges and serve.

SERVES 6–8

BAKED HAM OMELET

This simple, quick recipe is so useful for brunch, lunch or dinner that it belongs in everyone's recipe file. You can cut the recipe in half and bake the omelet in an 8-by-8-in (20-by-20-cm) baking dish. Variations: Instead of the ham, use one or a combination of crab meat, sliced mushrooms, marinated artichoke hearts and shrimp.

½ cup (2 oz/60 g) all-purpose (plain) flour
1 teaspoon baking powder
12 eggs
½ teaspoon Tabasco (hot pepper) sauce
2 cups (6 oz/185 g) diced cooked ham
1 lb (500 g) Monterey Jack (mild white) cheese, shredded
2 cups (16 fl oz/500 ml) creamed cottage cheese
4 tablespoons (2 oz/60 g) butter, melted
salt and freshly ground white pepper

◪ Preheat an oven to 400°F (200°C). Butter a 9-by-13-in (23-by-32.5-cm) baking dish. In a small bowl, sift the flour with the baking powder.
Into a large bowl, beat the eggs, add the Tabasco, and stir in the flour, ham, cheeses and melted butter. Season with salt and white pepper to taste.
◪ Pour into a baking dish and bake in the preheated oven for 15 minutes. Reduce the heat to 350°F (180°C) and bake for 15 minutes longer, or until the omelet is puffed and light golden brown.
◪ Cut into 12 portions and serve at once.

SERVES 12

Top to bottom: Wild Turkey Hash, Baked Ham Omelet

WILD TURKEY HASH

Ben Franklin would no doubt be pleased to know that his candidate for "national bird" now thrives in all the contiguous states. Introduced to the Pacific Northwest in the 1960s, wild turkeys adapted well to the pine and oak forests of Klickitat County, Washington, on the eastern slopes of the Cascade Mountains. Spring and fall hunting seasons each year afford a few sportsmen and -women the thrill of a turkey hunt. The more readily available domestic turkey could be called our "national food," at least at holiday time. Turkey hash is a perfect way to use up holiday leftovers, or it can be made from cooked turkey breast.

4 tablespoons (2 oz/60 g) butter
½ cup (4 oz/125 g) chopped green bell pepper (capsicum)
½ cup (4 oz/125 g) chopped onion
2 tablespoons flour
½ cup (4 fl oz/125 ml) heavy (double) cream
2 cups (12 oz/340 g) diced cooked turkey
1 cup (2 oz/60 g) small French or Italian bread cubes
2 tablespoons chopped fresh parsley
½ teaspoon ground sage
½ teaspoon salt
freshly ground black pepper to taste

◪ Melt 2 tablespoons of the butter in a large saucepan over low heat. Add the onion and pepper and cook slowly until the onion is translucent. Blend in the flour. Add the cream and stir until thickened. Remove from the heat and stir in the diced turkey, bread cubes, herbs and seasonings. Mix well.
◪ Melt the remaining 2 tablespoons of butter in a heavy skillet, add the turkey mixture, and cook over medium heat, turning frequently until browned and heated through. If desired, brown under the broiler (griller) before serving.

SERVES 4

GRILLED CHICKEN WITH PICO DE GALLO

When fresh peppers and tomatoes are ripe and plentiful it seems natural to enjoy them in their simplest form. Pico de gallo is a fresh salsa that complements crisp grilled chicken. Serve with black beans and rice.

1 cup (8 oz/250 g) finely diced red (Spanish) onion
1 cup (8 oz/250 g) finely diced red bell pepper (capsicum)
1 cup (8 oz/250 g) finely diced green bell pepper (capsicum)
2 jalapeño (hot green) chilies, finely diced
2 large tomatoes, chopped
2 garlic cloves, minced
½ cup (¾ oz/20 g) chopped fresh cilantro (coriander)
2–3 tablespoons red wine vinegar
salt and freshly ground black pepper to taste
2 chickens, about 3–3½ lb (1.5–1.75 kg)
olive oil for brushing
lime wedges for garnish

◪ Prepare a fire in a charcoal grill. While the coals are heating, prepare the pico de gallo: In a medium bowl, combine the onion, peppers, chilies, tomatoes, garlic, cilantro and vinegar. Add salt and pepper. If necessary add more vinegar. Set aside.
◪ Rinse the chicken well, pat dry, and quarter. Brush the pieces with olive oil and season with salt and pepper.
◪ Grill the chicken over medium-hot coals, turning 3 or 4 times and brushing with olive oil each time, until lightly charred, crisp, and cooked through, about 30 minutes. Cook the dark

Eastern Washington

PORTUGUESE PORK CHOPS

Sweet red peppers and local white wine are as much a part of the cuisine of the lower Yakima Valley as that of the Iberian peninsula. These Old World flavors still thrive in the farming areas of the West.

4 pork loin chops, ¾ in (2 cm) thick
4 teaspoons paprika (preferably sweet Hungarian)
2 large garlic cloves, crushed
salt and freshly ground black pepper to taste
1½ cups (12 fl oz/375 ml) dry white wine such as Sauvignon Blanc
2 tablespoons olive oil

1 tablespoon lard (optional)
2 red bell peppers (capsicums), roasted, peeled and julienned (see glossary)
1 cup (8 fl oz/250 ml) chicken stock (see glossary)

◙ Place the chops in a shallow nonaluminum dish just large enough to hold them. Combine the paprika, garlic and salt and pepper and rub the chops well on both sides with this mixture. Pour the wine over the chops. Cover and refrigerate for 24 hours, turning the chops 3–4 times during this period.

◙ Remove the chops from the marinade and pat dry. Heat the oil and lard in a heavy skillet large enough to hold the chops in 1 layer. Add the chops and brown for 4–5 minutes, then turn and brown for 4–5 minutes on the second side.

◙ Meanwhile, place the marinade in a saucepan and cook to reduce by half. Add the stock and return to a boil. Add salt and pepper.

◙ Drain the excess fat from the chops. Add the liquid marinade to the chops, cover, and cook over low heat for 15–20 minutes. Add the bell peppers at the last minute and heat them through.

◙ Serve with rice.

SERVES 4

Left to right: Grilled Chicken with Pico de Gallo, Portuguese Pork Chops

meat 2–3 minutes longer than the white meat.

◙ Transfer to a serving platter, mound the pico de gallo alongside, and garnish with wedges of lime.

SERVES 6

EASTERN WASHINGTON AND OREGON, AND IDAHO

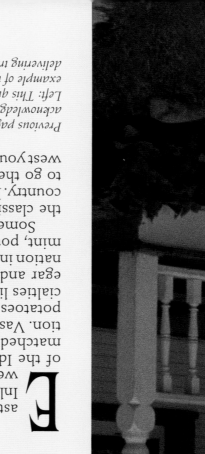

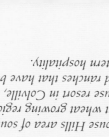

EASTERN WASHINGTON AND OREGON, AND IDAHO

E ast of the Cascades and west of the Rockies is the Inland Empire, the agricultural heart of the Northwest. Eastern Washington and Oregon, and parts of the Idaho panhandle, make up a region that is unmatched in the scale and diversity of its food production. Vast acreages are given to staple crops like wheat, potatoes and apples, while small producers make specialties like wild huckleberry jam, shallot-flavored vinegar and even lentil candy bars. The region leads the nation in the production of apples, pears, cherries, hops, mint, potatoes and carrots.

Some foods, such as the Walla Walla Sweet onion and the classic Delicious apple, are familiar throughout the country. But to taste the real flavor of the region, you have to go there. Driving through the Yakima Valley, to the west you can see the volcanic cones of Mount Adams and

Previous pages: The Palouse Hills area of southeastern Washington is acknowledged as the best wheat growing region in the United States. Left: This quaint roadhouse resort in Colville, Washington, is a charming example of the farms and ranches that have been restored as inns delivering true Northwestern hospitality.

Mount Rainier, whose ancient eruptions laid down much of the valley's mineral-rich soil, and the oblique ragged summit of Mount St. Helens, whose catastrophic eruption in 1980 coated eastern Washington with its latest layer of ash. The backdrop of pine-forested mountains frames a patchwork of orchards and row crops that provide an amazing array of food. If you're a tourist starting down the valley at Naches, you can pick your own snacking apples from an orchard of heirloom varieties and get some fresh cider for the road. The cider will cool you off after an hour spent picking among the sixty varieties of hot and sweet peppers raised at Krueger Pepper Gardens in Wapato. Then it's time for lunch and a rest, possibly in nearby Zillah, where a Mexican market sells burritos and taquitos, pan dulce and other baked goods, fresh tortillas by the ton and fresh masa to make your own, menudo and carne asada to go, herbal remedies, votive candles and other products for the valley's large and growing Hispanic population. Or you could visit the Yakima Nation Cultural Center in Toppenish, whose handsome building houses a restaurant serving Native American specialties including smoked salmon and puffy fry bread.

In Sunnyside, a few miles to the southeast, you can sample the authentic aged Goudas at the Yakima Valley Cheese Company, which uses the milk and cream from local dairies. Then on to Prosser, where one specialty farm sells twenty-three varieties of basil, and the Chukar Cherry outlet offers samples of dried Bing cherries encased in bittersweet chocolate, blueberries with white chocolate and other combinations of valley produce and gourmet imagination.

This culinary afternoon is crowded, but it leaves out more than it includes: more than twenty wineries just in the Yakima Valley; fresh locally made ales and stouts; U-pick asparagus, peaches and pears; and restaurants ranging from serious French to Polynesian to neighborhood Mexican cafés. And such a tour gives only a glimpse of the complexities of the region.

Wheat fields in the Columbia Basin stretch from horizon to horizon, their value determined as much by world politics as by the farmer's skill. Other growers have small pockets of land and an intensely local orientation. The catalog for Filaree Farms, a garlic-growing operation near Okanogan, Washington, provides its own perspective on Northwest history: Spanish Roja, a full-flavored variety that is its best seller, originally came to the Northwest with Greek immigrants to Portland, Oregon. German Red is from German-American farmers in Idaho, while Russian Red is a legacy of the Doukhobors, religious communalists in British Columbia.

The landscape of eastern Washington and Oregon and the Idaho panhandle is as diverse as its farms. Parts are beautiful but forbidding. The layered basalt cliffs of the channeled scablands in Washington and the red and green striped spires of the John Day region of Oregon are the result of a tumultuous series of geologic events: volcanic eruptions, Ice Age glaciers and the resulting Missoula Floods, cataracts of biblical proportions that scoured away soil and softer rock. The inviting rounded hills of the Palouse and the Blue Mountains, on the other hand, were built up by accumulations of the windblown soil called loess. Over the dramatic results of all this activity arches the huge sky of open country. At night starlight blazes through the dry air with an intensity forgotten by city dwellers.

Perhaps partly in response to these humbling vistas, humans have modified the region to an astonishing degree, damming some of the West's mightiest rivers into a series of lakes, pumping the water onto more than a million acres of cropland and replacing the deep-rooted natural grasses with more fragile plants.

Irrigation is the key to most farming here. One of its first practitioners, in 1842, was Kamiakin, a leader of the Yakima tribe. With the encouragement of Catholic missionaries, he raised potatoes, wheat and melons until 1855, when he went to war against whites who were encroaching on treaty land. The Yakimas' eventual defeat and confinement to their reservation was a precursor to the large-scale irrigation of the valley.

In the first years, it seemed that anything short of pineapples would grow around Yakima so long as there

Winchester Lake State Park is the picturesque remnant of the old logging days in Idaho when this reservoir was built to hold lumber.

Northwest wines have by now lost their parvenu status and are setting national standards for those grapes that respond best to mineral-rich volcanic soil, long hot summer days and cool nights. Gewürztraminers and Rieslings grown around Yakima and in the Columbia Basin are dryer than their California counterparts, and the wines retain the fragrance and fruitiness of the varieties without being too sweet. Merlots and Cabernets are representative reds.

In the Palouse and the Walla Walla Valley, and across the Columbia on the tablelands of central and eastern Oregon, dry-land wheat farming predominates. The soft white varieties of wheat best suited to Northwest conditions are not the choice for North American breads and pastas; they are grown almost exclusively for export. Their markets are in Asia, where they are used in a variety of noodles. Northwest wheat shows up in stores primarily in specialty oddities such as packaged wheatberries.

Lentil farmers, centered on both sides of the Washington-Idaho border near Spokane, are likewise dependent on exports, but a group of them have banded together to make their flavorful legume a household staple in their own country. In the small town of Fairfield, a group of family farmers packages and markets lentil products ranging from subtly spiced casseroles to a lentil-studded peanut-butter candy. They have developed a washing technique that shortens the cooking time to meet the requirements of a rushed age, and their legumes include green and yellow varieties and flavors bred for different cuisines. They hope eventually to develop a large enough domestic market to stabilize the wildly fluctuating price for their crop.

Northwest of Spokane toward the British Columbia border, the hills and forests of the Okanogan attract homesteaders more than large-scale farmers. Determined to make a living in one of the most remote and beautiful

was water. Even tobacco had a brief boom; a series of mild winters in the early 1880s seduced farmers into thinking they could make their fortunes on Fleur de Yakima cigars. The hard winter of 1886–87 killed that dream, along with tens of thousands of head of livestock throughout the West, and tobacco fields were replanted with hardier grapes and hops. Washington alone grows nearly three-quarters of the U.S. hop crop, and it uses some of them for the region's growing population of microbreweries. On an August day in the Columbia Basin, when the horizon wavers in the heat and even the sky looks sun-bleached, a mug of local ale is a blessing beyond expectation.

Building on early success, irrigation projects eventually became more and more ambitious, culminating in a string of massive dams, fourteen across the main channel of the Columbia. Striking agricultural juxtapositions—tender-flowered espaliered orchards next to tumbleweed-tangled cattle fences—are one result. The land that is watered grows tomatoes, melons, pears, apples, cherries, garlic, row crops, alfalfa for dairy herds, potatoes for billions of fast-food fries, grapes for wine and grape juice, asparagus and specialty salad greens. Outside of the Walla Walla Valley, the Palouse and a few other favored niches, unirrigated land might grow wheat (if a farmer is skilled and lucky) or sparse grass. Rainfall around the Tri-Cities in the Columbia Basin averages less than ten inches a year, a true desert in the Evergreen State. But irrigated Columbia Basin vineyards, many of them bordered by double rows of poplars to protect the vines from scouring winds, supply some of the Northwest's best-known wineries.

A replica of a sixteenth-century château, the Spokane Courthouse was designed in the 1890s by a young man who received his architectural training from a correspondence course.

Yakima Valley, located in south-central Washington, is one of the richest and most productive agricultural regions in the United States.

areas in the Northwest, they have developed an imaginative array of specialty products, from organic U-pick apples to French country goat cheese. At the Kitchen at China Bend, a small processing facility on Lake Roosevelt near the Canadian border, Bart Israel Alexander talks about his canned organic produce the way vintners discuss wines: "The purity of our process and the simplicity of our recipes allow the ingredients to express themselves in subtle vintage-like variations from batch to batch."

This may seem an unrealistic ambition for a jar of canned tomatoes, but a taste of the homegrown product is persuasive.

"People are surprised when our cheese tastes different from one batch to the next," says Laura Lee Misterly, who makes French country goat cheeses on her family's hillside farm near Kettle Falls and sells them to gourmet restaurants in Seattle. "But that's not a mistake. It's one of the benefits of a true seasonal diet."

The seasonal diet of the Alexanders and Misterlys' predecessors along the Columbia River was based upon one of the greatest natural food sources known to any culture, the immense annual salmon runs. Inland tribes rated their salmon species carefully, and their stories explain why tribes in some areas were favored with huge runs of fat Chinooks, which the white settlers called "June hogs," while other communities had to barter for their winter supply of dried fish. Coyote, the ubiquitous trickster-demigod of the Northwest tribes, had parceled out the largess of salmon according to the generosity ac-

corded him when he went in search of a wife. The people on the upper Columbia where the Misterlys and Alexanders now live gave him a handsome maiden, so he created Kettle Falls, one of the great fishing spots of the free-flowing Columbia.

The Kettle Falls salmon are now lost to the dams and irrigation that made the fruit and wine possible. No fish can get past the colossus of Grand Coulee Dam. But the area around Grand Coulee still draws fishermen. In an ironic twist that is lost on most Native Americans, the dams and irrigation diversions have raised the water table, creating lakes and marshes that support many species of sport fish and wildlife. Hunters and anglers come by the thousands for the trout fishing and duck hunting here.

Another casualty of the development of the inland Northwest was the old ranching kingdoms. The legendary cattle barons around Pendleton, Oregon, and Ellensburg, Washington, at first had the freedom of land no one else wanted. Cattlemen like Henry Miller in Oregon and Ben Snipes in Washington were emblems of the Wild West. But the arrival of the railroads, which made it possible to ship wool and produce, and of farmers, who built fences, meant the end of their domination. Sheep in turn lost ground to irrigated agriculture, although not before generations of Basque herders in Oregon and Idaho brought another cuisine—featuring salt cod and pigs' feet as well as all manner of lamb and mutton—to the Northwest cultural mix.

The fruit industry, with smaller acreage and premium prices, attracted would-be gentlemen farmers to the Hood River and Yakima valleys, as well as riverfront parcels in the valleys of the Okanogan and around Spokane. Retired businessmen and military officers joined young college graduates to grow apples and pears on scenic mountainsides. The brutal work of replacing native trees with fruit scions was performed by Japanese and Chinese laborers, one of whom, a field manager named Bing, lives on in the eponymous cherry. Today the seasonal labor is done primarily by Hispanic workers, who also have established the tortilla factories, Mexican bakeries, restaurants and food shops that now enrich the Yakima Valley.

Apples soon became the Northwest's best-known ambassadors. Even provincial Easterners who thought Seattleites lived in igloos were able to recognize a Washington Red Delicious. Although the Delicious, both red and yellow, is still the staple of the export trade, a parallel market in more flavorful varieties has grown up to satisfy gourmet tastes. Spartan and Fuji apples, Asian Nijisseiki pears and dozens of other varieties of fruits new and old appeal to the palate as well as the eye. What hasn't changed is the chancy nature of orcharding. "Las Vegas is more fun than raising cherries," says one former farmer. "And it's exactly the same deal."

Wallowa Lake in Oregon provides a cool respite from the hot summer sun and is said to be the home of the legendary Wallowa Lake Monster, apparently sighted as early as two centuries ago by Native Americans.

The problem is the weather. Apples, cherries, peaches and other tree fruits respond well to the dormancy period induced by a cold winter, but once the trees have bloomed a hard freeze can mean disaster. In the foothills orchard community of Naches, all conversation stops when a restaurant sound system broadcasts the local temperatures in a sibilant murmur. Low readings during blossom time will clear the tables as farmers head home to warm their trees.

Orchardists in vulnerable areas have an arsenal of frost-fighting tools. John Thompson, a fourth-generation Naches farmer, maintains an informal museum of old smudge pots and heaters. The oldest—no longer used—are squat little barrels that gave off oily, pitch-black smoke. Modern versions have afterburners to improve fuel efficiency and reduce pollution. Thompson says proudly that their smoke is nearly invisible. Another of his curios is a diesel-powered flamethrower that would warm four acres if it didn't set the trees on fire first.

Orchardists use computerized thermometers to compare the ground temperature with that twenty feet in the air. During temperature inversions, when a lid of warmer air traps frigid air around the trees, a wind machine works better than a heater. These giant fans stand storklike above rows of dwarf trees. Each one can stir twelve acres of air. Using a computerized thermometer to grow an heirloom apple may be the blend of innovation and tradition that will keep family farmers on the land of the Inland Empire.

VEGETABLES, FRUIT AND PRESERVES

The Northwest is known for its abundance of berries, both wild and cultivated .

VEGETABLES, FRUIT AND PRESERVES

Preserving has always been a way of life in the Northwest. The bounty of the season's harvest is captured at its peak of freshness by drying, pickling, canning or freezing. For many Northwesterners, a jar of canned fruit conjures up childhood memories of picking bushels of fruits and vegetables in the hot summer sun, then lugging them home where the real work began. It started with sterilizing jars, then went on to blanching, peeling and pitting such pickings as juicy freestone or Elberta peaches or rosy Tilton apricots.

Foods from asparagus to cherries to dilled pearl onions and beets were pickled. Big crocks of sauerkraut and dill pickles curing on kitchen counters were a summertime standard. Rows and rows of colorful jars in brilliant hues of purple, red, orange and green and filled with such delicacies as pepper pickled peaches, green minted pears, vegetable chow chow, bread and butter pickles, Marionberry preserves and brandied Bing cherries lined the pantry and cellars of Northwest homes. More common now are quickly made preserves that can be stored in the refrigerator for a few months without having to haul out the canner. In the days before refrigeration, Northwesterners wintered boxes of apples in the cool spaces under their beds.

European agricultural products such as the fruit trees planted in Washington at least fifty years before it became the forty-second state in 1889, were found to be highly adaptable to the Pacific Northwest. In 1893 the San Juan Islands were a favorite fruit-growing area, but it was soon found that transportation costs were too high from these remote islands. Some of those original trees still are producing heirloom apples such as the Yellow Winter Banana, the Wax Pippin and the Winter King. In the

The cornucopia of fruits readily available to Northwesterners has inspired a renaissance in home preserving.

Previous pages, left to right: Marionberry Vinegar (page 193), Mint-Pickled Melons (page 180) and Pepper–Pickled Peaches (page 187)

Even the most exotic palate can be satisfied with the growing number of specialty food and ethnic produce markets in the Northwest.

1920s, the ever-popular red Delicious apple was introduced as a relative newcomer to a state with one hundred years of apple-growing history; today it makes up 68 percent of Washington's total apple crop.

The Northwest has several other famous vegetables and fruits. Walla Walla onions are celebrated for their sweetness, which some claim comes from the rich soil, climate and pure water. The first seeds, of Italian origin, were planted in Walla Walla around 1900 by a Frenchman, producing an early onion so sweet that some say it can be eaten like an apple.

Idaho is the United States' potato capital, producing one-third of the national fall crop. This versatile vegetable is enjoyed traditionally baked and topped with butter, sour cream and chives and in such innovative preparations as whipped potatoes with roasted garlic and chopped fresh herbs. A Northwest potato oddity is to serve French fries with tartar sauce for dipping instead of ketchup. In September the little town of Shelley celebrates with the ™Idaho Potato Harvest Festival, paying tribute to the vegetable that made Idaho famous, with such activities as the world potato-peeling championship and the mashed potato tug-of-war.

Pike Place Market, the heartbeat of Seattle, was established in 1907 and has been bringing farmers' goods directly to their customers ever since. The oldest continuously operated market in the country, it abounds with local honeys, dairy products, vegetables, grains, meats, fish and fruits. Some farmers are on the road for as many as five hours to bring their fresh produce here.

Today the overcooked "army-green" beans and mushy carrots of the past are gone, replaced by lightly sautéed or steamed vegetables still brimming with just-picked flavor. Since 1982, Southeast Asian refugee farmers have been trained in commercial truck farming in the Northwest by the Indochinese Farm Project. These projects have brought new variety to our tables with Asian vegetables such as snow peas, baby bok choy, and gai lan (Chinese broccoli).

There probably isn't a vegetable that won't grow somewhere in the Northwest, but at summer's end green tomatoes are usually abundant in the home gardens of cooler climates. Picked before the first frost, they are thickly sliced, dipped in cornmeal or cracker crumbs and pan-fried, or put up as green tomato mincemeat to enjoy in a holiday Thanksgiving pie. Root vegetable dishes, such as mashed parsnips and carrots with butter and cream, have been popular from the early days. The Scandinavian settlers brought us the bean pot, slowly simmering overnight in the oven and brimming with beans, ham hocks, molasses, tomato, onions and brown sugar.

Then, of course, there are the wild vegetables and mushrooms coveted so dearly by gourmet foragers, from prickly stinging nettles to tender young shoots of cattails and crisp sea beans. Members of mycological associations comb the Northwest forests in search of chanterelles, boletes, matsutakis and numerous other edible wild mushrooms. Many take camp stoves, butter, garlic and fresh herbs with them so they can enjoy a quick sauté after an exhilarating day of mushroom hunting.

Most of the predominantly winter wheat grown in the Northwest is shipped to Asia for noodle making. This soft wheat is planted in the fall and harvested in the early spring. Sourdough starter made with wheat flour, water and wild yeast has long been a western tradition, but in the sixties and seventies its popularity grew with the natural foods movement, making for some tart and tasty breads and pancakes. Sometimes you hear tales of folks with starters that date back many years, but quite a few starters have been forgotten over time—in the back of the refrigerator.

Eastern Washington

SCALLOPED POTATOES WITH CARROTS

A countrified version of a French classic, made with milk in place of heavy cream. Always use Idaho bakers, of course, and a good Swiss cheese such as Jarlsberg or Emmenthaler.

5 tablespoons (2½ oz/80 g) butter
2 cups (1 lb/500 g) thinly sliced carrots
1 shallot minced
¾ cup (6 fl oz/180 ml) water
1¼ teaspoons salt
2–3 large Idaho russet potatoes, peeled and thinly sliced,
    about 6–7 cups (2–2¼ lb/1–1.1 kg)
freshly ground black pepper to taste
1 cup (4 oz/125 g) grated Swiss cheese
1 cup (8 fl oz/250 ml) milk, scalded

◼ Preheat an oven to 300°F (150°C). Meanwhile, in a medium, heavy saucepan, melt 1 tablespoon of the butter over medium-low heat. Stir in the carrots and shallot. Add the water and ¼ teaspoon of the salt. Cover and simmer for 15–20 minutes, or until the liquid has evaporated and the carrots are just tender.
◼ Butter a large ovenproof casserole 2 in (5 cm) deep. Arrange layers of potatoes and carrots in the casserole, seasoning each layer with salt, pepper, cheese and dots of butter.
◼ Pour the scalded milk over the potatoes and carrots. Top with a layer of cheese dotted with butter. Bake in the oven for about 1 hour, or until the milk is absorbed, the vegetables are tender, and the casserole is browned on top.

SERVES 6

Islands

SPICY SESAME SNAP PEAS

Snap peas bear early and long in Northwest gardens. Their beautiful green is a welcome addition to any salad, and they also beckon to be eaten right off the vine.

1 tablespoon peanut (groundnut) oil
3 shallots, minced
3 garlic cloves, minced
2 tablespoons Asian (toasted) sesame oil
1½ lb (750 g) sugar snap peas
1 small dried hot red chili pepper, crushed (optional)
½–1 teaspoon salt
2 teaspoons sesame seeds, toasted (optional)

◼ In a large skillet, heat the peanut oil and cook the shallots and garlic for about 3 minutes, or until translucent. Increase the heat to medium-high and add the sesame oil. Add the snap peas and toss in the pan for 2 minutes, or just until the peas turn bright green and are heated through.
◼ Sprinkle with the red pepper, salt and sesame seeds (if you like). Toss again and serve.

SERVES 6

Scalloped Potatoes with Carrots

Spicy Sesame Snap Peas

STEAMED BROCCOLI AND CHEDDAR RAREBIT

This ale-based sauce is perfect for broccoli. Make the rarebit quickly and serve it immediately; never boil it or the sauce will

break. *Tillamook Cheddar originates in a valley of the same name on the Oregon coast. If you can't get Tillamook, substitute your favorite sharp Cheddar.*

1 lb (500 g) grated sharp Tillamook Cheddar
2 tablespoons butter
2 tablespoons Dijon mustard
2 garlic cloves, bruised

cheese. Stir frequently until thickened and smooth, 7–10 minutes. Keep warm.

◩ Cook the broccoli in lightly salted boiling water in a large saucepan until it is bright green and tender, about 3 minutes. Serve the rarebit in a bowl or crock surrounded by the broccoli, or pour it over the broccoli.

SERVE 6–8

Steamed Broccoli and Cheddar Rarebit

1 teaspoon Tabasco (hot pepper) sauce
2 eggs
1 cup (8 fl oz/250 ml) pale ale
3 lb (1.5 kg) broccoli, cut into long spears

◩ In a double boiler over simmering water, melt the cheese, butter, mustard, garlic, and Tabasco, stirring frequently. Beat the eggs with the ale and gradually whisk into the melted

Eastern Washington

BASQUE ONIONS IN SOUR CREAM

Use mild, sweet onions for this easy dish. Serve with a grilled steak or chops.

2 tablespoons butter
3–4 Walla Walla Sweet onions or other mild white onions, cut into wedges
1 cup (8 fl oz/250 ml) chicken stock (see glossary)
1 bay leaf
1 cup (8 fl oz/250 ml) sour cream
salt to taste
paprika for garnish

◩ Preheat oven to 325°F (180°C). Meanwhile, in a large saucepan, melt the butter and cook the onions over medium heat for 1–2 minutes. Add the stock and bay leaf, cover, and cook slowly until the onions are tender and the liquid is almost evaporated. Remove the bay leaf and stir in the sour cream. Add salt as necessary.

◩ Pour the mixture into a shallow ovenproof casserole, sprinkle with paprika, and bake in the preheated oven until bubbly, 10–15 minutes.

SERVES 6

Basque Onions in Sour Cream

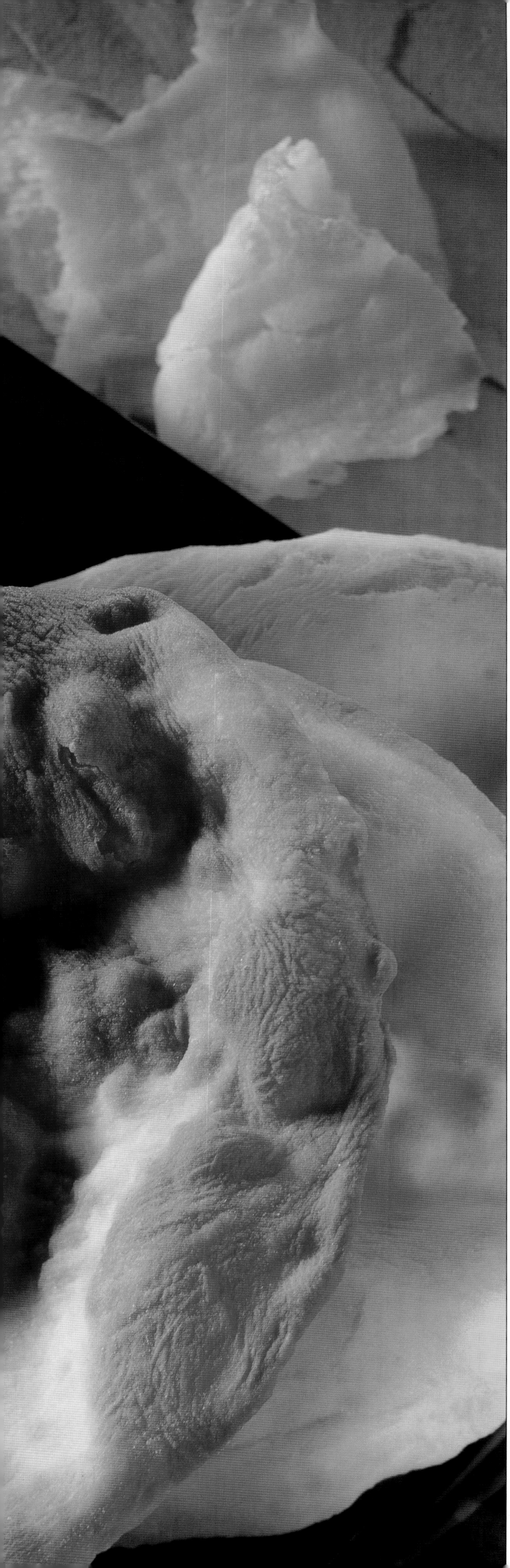

Eastern Washington

RED PEPPER JELLY

An ever-increasing variety of peppers thrive in the sunshine of the Yakima Valley. When you buy unfamiliar chili peppers, be sure to ask how hot they are. Choose a medium-hot variety for this jelly, and take care to remove the fiery seeds. Serve this jelly as a colorful accompaniment to roast chicken or pork, or with cream cheese and crackers as an appetizer.

3 large red bell peppers (capsicums), cored and seeded
3 fresh serrano (small hot red) chili peppers, cored and seeded
¾ cup (6 fl oz/180 ml) distilled white vinegar
3 oz (90 g) liquid pectin
3½ cups (1¾ lb/875 g) sugar

Cut the peppers and chilies into rough chunks and purée in a blender or food processor; you should have about 2 cups (16 fl oz/500 ml) of purée.

Mix the peppers, chilies and vinegar together in a large nonaluminum stockpot. Add the pectin and bring to a boil. Add the sugar and boil hard, stirring constantly, for 10 minutes.

Pour into five 1-cup (8-fl oz/250-ml) sterilized glass canning jars (see glossary) and seal. This jelly will keep several months in the refrigerator.

MAKES 5 CUPS (40 FL OZ/ 1.2 L)

Eastern Washington

INDIAN FRY BREAD

Indian fry bread is a part of many Native American celebrations. The Yakima Nation Cultural Center in Toppenish, Washington, serves fry bread in its popular restaurant. Try it with butter and huckleberry jam.

2 cups (8 oz/250 g) all-purpose (plain) flour
1 teaspoon salt
2 teaspoons baking powder
about 1–1¼ cups (8–10 fl oz/250–300 ml) water or milk
oil for frying

Combine the dry ingredients in a bowl, make a well in the center, and add 1 cup (8 fl oz/250 ml) of the liquid. Mix until it forms a soft dough; a little more liquid may be needed. Knead the dough on a lightly floured board until smooth and firm. The dough will remain soft. Cover and let sit for 10 minutes.

Pinch off pieces of dough about the size of an egg. Flatten each one evenly to about 5 in (13 cm) in diameter.

In a heavy skillet, heat 1½ in (4 cm) of oil to about 350°F (180°C). Fry 2 or 3 pieces of dough at a time until golden brown, about 5–7 minutes, turning them once. Drain on paper towels and keep warm in a very low oven. Repeat until all the remaining dough pieces are cooked.

Serve warm.

MAKES 8–10 BREADS

Top to bottom: Red Pepper Jelly, Indian Fry Bread

Eastern Washington

SHEEPHERDER'S BREAD

Everything always tastes better around the campfire, and bread is no exception. This is a dressed-up version of a back-country favorite. It takes some practice over a campfire, but it's well worth the effort! Try it first at home in a conventional oven or in a covered grill for a colorful addition to an informal meal.

2 cups (16 fl oz/500 ml) warm (110°F/43°C) water
¼ cup (2 fl oz/60 ml) melted butter, cooled to lukewarm
¼ cup (2 oz/60 g) sugar
1¼ teaspoons salt
2 packages active dried yeast
about 5 cups (20 oz/625 g) unbleached all-purpose (plain) flour
1 tablespoon chopped fresh rosemary, or 1 teaspoon dried
     rosemary
olive oil
fresh herb sprigs for garnish
coarse salt for garnish

Pour the hot water into a large bowl. Add the melted butter, sugar and salt. Stir in the yeast and let sit for 10 minutes, or until bubbly.

Add half of the flour to the yeast mixture and beat until very smooth. Cover with a cloth and let sit for 10–15 minutes. Stir in the rosemary and remaining flour until the dough holds some shape and begins to pull away from the sides of the bowl. The dough should not be too stiff.

Turn the dough out onto a lightly floured board and knead for 1–2 minutes, or until the dough is smooth and elastic. Cover with a clean, damp towel and let rise until almost doubled, about 1 hour.

Punch the dough down and knead it again. Brush the inside of a medium Dutch oven and the inside of the lid with olive oil. Form the dough into a ball and place it in the pot. Garnish the top of the loaf with herb sprigs and sprinkle coarse salt over the top. Cover with a damp towel and let rise until nearly doubled.

To bake in a conventional oven: Preheat the oven to 350°F (180°C). Put the lid on the pot and bake the bread for 20 minutes, then remove the lid and bake for 15–20 minutes longer, or until the bread is browned and hollow-sounding when tapped.

To bake over an open fire: Put the lid on the pot and hang the pot over the coals of an open fire, or place the pot on the cooking rack of a grill over hot coals. Bake until the loaf is browned and hollow-sounding when tapped, about 40 minutes.

Serve warm from the pot.

MAKES 1 LOAF

Islands

HIMALAYA BLACKBERRY PRESERVES

Island blackberries are plump and tender, and this preserve retains their natural color and flavor. Himalaya blackberries are a formerly cultivated berry that has escaped to the wild.

6 cups (2¼ lb/1.1 kg) large, firm ripe wild or cultivated
     blackberries (include a few underripe ones if possible)
4 cups (2 lb/1 kg) sugar
½ cup (4 fl oz/125 ml) fresh lemon juice
½ cup (4 fl oz/125 ml) water

Clean, wash and drain the berries carefully to avoid crushing them. In a large pot, bring the sugar, lemon juice, water and 1 cup (6 oz/185 g) of the berries gradually to a boil. Cook for 6 minutes, stirring constantly. Add the remaining berries to the syrup and cook for 2 minutes.

Seal tightly in six 1-cup (8-oz/250-g) sterilized glass canning jars (see glossary) and refrigerate for up to 2 months.

MAKES 6 CUPS (48 FL OZ/1.5 L)

Top to bottom: Sheepherder's Bread, Himalaya Blackberry Preserves

Oregon

WALNUT-STOUT BREAD

A hearty, honest loaf that keeps well. Cheese, smoked meats and rich, dark ales are complemented by this robust rye bread.

½ cup (4 fl oz/125 ml) warm (110°F/43°C) water
1 package active dried yeast
2 tablespoons sugar
2 cups stout (16 fl oz/500 ml) or other dark ale (dark beer) at room temperature
2 tablespoons olive oil
2 tablespoons unsweetened cocoa
1 tablespoon ground coriander
1 teaspoon ground aniseed
1 tablespoon salt
3 cups (12 oz/375 g) bread flour or all-purpose (plain) flour
3 cups (12 oz/375 g) medium rye flour
1 cup (4 oz/125 g) chopped walnuts
cornmeal for dusting
1 egg beaten with 1 tablespoon water

◻ In a very large bowl, whisk the warm water, yeast and sugar together; let stand for 10–15 minutes, or until foamy. Stir in the stout, olive oil, cocoa, spices and salt until combined.
◻ Sift together the 2 flours and gradually beat them into the mixture. When most of the flour has been added, add the walnuts and turn the dough out onto a lightly floured board. Knead steadily until smooth and elastic, 10–15 minutes.
◻ Clean the bowl and oil it lightly. Place the dough in the bowl and turn it to coat it lightly with oil. Drape a clean damp towel over the bowl and place it in a warm place until doubled, 1½ hours. Punch the dough down, turn it out on the board, and divide it into 2 pieces. Shape each piece into an even round and place on an oiled baking sheet that has been dusted with cornmeal.
◻ Allow the loaves to rise until doubled in bulk, 45 minutes–1 hour. Preheat an oven to 375°F (190°C). Brush the loaves with the egg-water mixture. Using a razor blade or a sharp knife, cut decorative slashes on the loaves. Bake until the crusts are firm and the loaf is hollow-sounding when tapped, 35–40 minutes.

MAKES 2 LOAVES

Oregon

BLUE LAKE GREEN BEANS WITH COUNTRY ALMOND BUTTER

A perfect green bean should be crisp and tender at the same time. Young Blue Lake beans are especially good embellished with this sweet-spicy almond butter.

2 lb (1 kg) Blue Lake green beans, trimmed
⅓ cup (3 oz/90 g) butter
1 cup (4 oz/125 g) slivered almonds, toasted (see glossary)
1 tablespoon whole-grain mustard
1 tablespoon honey
1 tablespoon fresh lemon juice
1 tablespoon grated lemon zest
2 tablespoons minced shallots or red (Spanish) onion
1 teaspoon minced garlic
salt and pepper to taste

◻ Blanch the green beans in lightly salted boiling water just until tender and bright green, 3–4 minutes. Plunge them into cold water, drain when cool, and set aside.
◻ Melt the butter in a large, heavy skillet over medium heat. Add the almonds, mustard, honey, lemon juice, lemon zest, shallots and garlic, and sauté gently for 2–3 minutes. Add the beans and continue cooking until they're heated through, 3–5 minutes. Add salt and pepper and serve immediately.

SERVES 6–8   *Photograph page 179*

Walnut–Stout Bread

Wild Mushroom Ragout

WILD MUSHROOM RAGOUT

For a richer flavor, soak a few dried wild mushrooms such as morels or porcini (cèpes) in brandy or sherry for 30 minutes, then add to the simmering ragout. Serve the ragout in a big cast-iron skillet with toasted country bread.

¼ cup (2 oz/60 g) butter
1 cup (8 oz/250 g) thinly sliced white onions
2 lb (1 kg) fresh mushrooms, preferably local wild
  mushrooms, quartered or sliced
1 tablespoon minced garlic
2 teaspoons chopped fresh thyme
1½ teaspoons minced fresh rosemary
about ¼ cup (2 fl oz/60 ml) chicken, mushroom,
  or vegetable stock (see glossary)

3 tablespoons dry sherry
1 cup (8 fl oz/250 ml) heavy (double) cream
2 tablespoons brandy (optional)
2–3 teaspoons fresh lemon juice
½ teaspoon salt
⅛ teaspoon freshly ground black pepper
2 tablespoons chopped fresh parsley

◩ In a large, heavy skillet, melt the butter over medium-high heat and sauté the onions, mushrooms and garlic until the mushrooms and onions are tender, about 3–4 minutes. Add the herbs, stock and sherry. Cook to reduce until only a little liquid remains, about 5 minutes.

◩ Add the whipping cream and cook until the mixture is lightly thickened, about 3 minutes. Add the brandy and lemon juice and cook 2 more minutes. Add the salt, pepper and parsley.

SERVES 6

Oregon

WILD RICE CAKES

These crisp rice griddlecakes are an excellent accompaniment to roasted meats and poultry. They may be varied with the addition of other herbs, nuts or vegetables to highlight a main course. As an appetizer, they're wonderful with sautéed wild mushrooms.

3 eggs, lightly beaten
2 tablespoons Dijon mustard
½ cup (2 oz/60 g) all-purpose (plain) flour
1 teaspoon salt
½ teaspoon ground white pepper
1 teaspoon ground coriander
1 cup (6 oz/180 g) minced green (spring) onions
3 cups (12 oz/375 g) cooked and chilled wild rice (see glossary)
2 tablespoons olive oil

◼ In a large bowl, whisk the eggs, mustard, flour, salt, pepper and coriander together until smooth. Add the green onions and wild rice, and stir until combined. The mixture should hold together when scooped; if necessary, add a bit of water.
◼ Heat a large skillet over medium heat and brush it with olive oil. Cook a few rounded spoonfuls of the wild rice mixture at a time until crisp and brown on one side (3–5 minutes), then turn to brown the other side (2–3 minutes).
◼ Keep warm in a very low oven while repeating to cook the remaining mixture.
◼ Serve warm.

SERVES 6

Left to right: Wild Rice Cakes, Blue Lake Green Beans with Country Almond Butter (page 176)

British Columbia

YAM FRIES

Serve these deep-orange fries with a colorful combination of sauces and dips such as soy and mustard sauce, guacamole, or sour cream and horseradish.

4 yams, peeled and cut into ½-in (1.5-cm) slices
peanut (groundnut) oil for deep-frying
salt to taste

▦ Cut the sliced yams into long thin strips and pat thoroughly dry with paper towels.
▦ Pour the peanut oil into a large, heavy skillet to a depth of 1½–2 in (4–5 cm) and heat the oil to 375°F (190°C). Add the yams and cook until crisp, about 4–5 minutes.
▦ Remove with a slotted spoon and drain well on paper towels.
▦ Place on a baking sheet, season with salt, and keep warm in a 300°F (150°C) oven until ready to serve.

SERVES 4

Idaho

IDAHO OVEN FRIES

The famous Idaho russet potato is ideal for baking whole or in wedges. Oven fries are simple to prepare, low in calories, and perfect to serve with a rib eye or salmon steak.

4 peeled Idaho russet potatoes, about 1½ lb (750 g)
¼ cup (2 fl oz/60 ml) olive oil
¼ cup (2 fl oz/60 ml) melted butter
2 tablespoons chopped fresh thyme
salt and freshly ground black pepper to taste

▦ Preheat an oven to 400°F (200°C). Meanwhile, cut the potatoes in half lengthwise, then cut each half into thirds to form wedges. Put the potatoes in a large nonaluminum bowl, drizzle the oil and butter over them, and sprinkle with the thyme, salt and pepper. Toss to coat the potatoes evenly.
▦ Arrange the potatoes on a baking sheet. Bake in the preheated oven for 20 minutes, then reduce the heat to 350°F (180°C) and bake 20–25 minutes longer, or until the potatoes are soft inside and brown and crisp on the outside. Serve immediately.

SERVES 4–6

Eastern Washington

MINT-PICKLED MELONS

These colorful pickles are ideal with grilled lamb or poultry and make an interesting addition to a relish tray. Be sure to select melons that are quite firm.

6 cups (10 oz/315 g) mixed melon balls such as honeydew,
    casaba and cantaloupe
2 tablespoons chopped fresh mint
1 teaspoon dried red pepper flakes
2 cups (16 fl oz/500 ml) water
2 cups (1 lb/500 g) sugar
½ cup (4 fl oz/125 ml) distilled white vinegar
1 tablespoon salt

▦ Fill a glass jar or ceramic crock with the melon balls. Add the fresh mint and pepper flakes.
▦ In a nonaluminum saucepan, bring all of the remaining ingredients to a boil. Simmer gently until clear and syrupy. Remove from the heat and let cool to room temperature. Pour over the melon to cover the fruit completely.
▦ Refrigerate for at least 24 hours before serving. Pickled melon may be kept in the refrigerator for up to 2 weeks.

MAKES 8 CUPS (12 OZ/375 G)   *Photograph pages 164-165*

Top to bottom: Yam Fries, Idaho Oven Fries

Oregon

DAMN GOOD DILLS

Crisp, garlicky, spicy, tart and—of course—dilly. Bet you can't eat just one.

8 cups (64 fl oz/2 l) white distilled vinegar
8 cups (64 fl oz/2 l) water
1 cup (8 oz/250 g) sugar
1 cup (8 oz/250 g) kosher salt
1 teaspoon ground turmeric
½ cup (4 oz/125 g) pickling spices
24 whole small dried red chili peppers
32 garlic cloves
8 fresh dill heads
5 lb (2.5 kg) well-washed small to medium pickling cucumbers, about 16 cups

◼ In a large nonaluminum stockpot, bring the vinegar, water, sugar, salt, turmeric and pickling spices to a simmer over medium heat. Let cook while preparing the jarred cucumbers.

◼ To each of 4 large 4-cup (31-fl oz/1-l) sterilized glass canning jars (see glossary), add 2 dill sprigs, 8 garlic cloves and 6 chilies. Fill loosely to the shoulder of each jar with the cucumbers. Fill each jar to the top of the shoulder with the hot pickle brine. Clean the rims, screw the lids on snugly, and invert the jars for 3 hours.

◼ Refrigerate for up to 2 months. Use any leftover pickling liquid to pickle other kinds of vegetables.

MAKES 16 CUPS (5 LB/2.5 KG)

Oregon

GARDEN HARVEST PICKLE

This simple, all-purpose pickling recipe is good for a variety of late-summer vegetables. Serve the pickles with sandwiches or as an antipasto before a pasta feast. Use cauliflower, peppers, eggplant, carrots, onions, fennel, celery—whatever strikes your fancy or you planted too much of.

16 cups (3½ lb/1.75 kg) uniformly cut fresh vegetables
6 cups (48 fl oz/1.5 l) white wine vinegar
6 cups (48 fl oz/1.5 l) water
¾ cup (6 oz/185 g) sugar
¾ cup (6 oz/185 g) kosher salt
½ tablespoon ground turmeric
1 cup (8 oz/250 g) pickling spices
4 large fresh thyme sprigs
24 garlic cloves
16 small hot red chili peppers

◼ Loosely pack 4 large 4-cup (31-fl oz/1-l) sterilized glass canning jars (see glossary) with the vegetables.

◼ In a large nonaluminum saucepan, bring the vinegar, water, sugar, salt, turmeric and pickling spices to a steady boil. Place a sprig of thyme, 6 garlic cloves and 4 dried chilies in each jar of vegetables. Pour the hot pickling solution over the vegetables, filling the jars to the shoulder. Wipe the rims and screw the lids on snugly. Invert the jars and allow them to cool to room temperature for 3–5 hours. This pickle will keep in the refrigerator for up to 6 months.

MAKES 16 CUPS (3½ LB/1.75 KG)

Left to right: Damn Good Dills, Garden Harvest Pickle

APPLE-MINT JELLY

Washington is not only famous for apples, it leads the nation in mint production, and this classic jelly is a good way to combine both tastes. Choose Granny Smiths, Criterions, Newtowns or other green apples. The fresh flavor and pale color of homemade mint jelly sets it apart from commercial versions. Serve with roast lamb, curry, pork or venison. Combine with Red Pepper Jelly (recipe on page 173) for a colorful gift.

4–5 lb (2–2.5 kg) green apples
3 cups (24 fl oz/750 ml) water
1 tablespoon fresh lemon juice, strained
7½ cups (3¾ lb/1.8 kg) sugar
½ cup (¾ oz/20 g) chopped fresh mint
3 oz (90 g) liquid fruit pectin

❖ Remove the stems and blossom ends from the apples. Cut the apples into small pieces, but do not peel or core. Place in a large saucepan. Add the water and bring to a boil; lower heat, cover and simmer for 10 minutes. Stir to crush the apples.
❖ Cover the pan and cook for 5–10 minutes longer, or until the apples are completely cooked and smooth when stirred.
❖ Place 3 layers of cheesecloth (muslin) or a jelly bag over a large bowl and pour the cooked apples into the cloth or bag. Tie the ends of the cloth and hang the cloth or bag over the bowl until the dripping stops. Press the cloth or bag very lightly to extract the last few drops of juice without clouding the juice with pulp.
❖ Measure the reserved apple juice, lemon juice and enough water to make 5 cups (40 fl oz/1.2 l) into a large, heavy saucepan. Stir in the sugar and mint and mix well. Bring to a full rolling boil over high heat, stirring constantly, and boil for 2 minutes. Add the pectin and continue boiling for 2 more minutes.
❖ Remove the pan from the heat and skim off any foam. Pour into eight 1-cup (8-oz/250-g) sterilized glass canning jars (see glossary) and seal immediately.
❖ This jelly will keep for several months in the refrigerator.
MAKES 8 CUPS (64 FL OZ/1 L)

PLUMMY PEAR CHUTNEY

In late summer at Old Orchard Farm in Westsound, huge clusters of frosty blue Italian plums ripen in the lingering sun. Any purple plums may be used to make this spicy relish, which is delicious with roast pork or grilled chicken.

1½ cups (12 oz/375 g) chopped onion
6 garlic cloves, crushed
1 teaspoon whole mustard seed
2–3 teaspoons salt
1 tablespoon minced fresh ginger
1 red bell pepper (capsicum), seeded and chopped
1 yellow bell pepper (capsicum), seeded and chopped
1 cinnamon stick
6 whole cloves
1 teaspoon cayenne pepper
1½ cups (12 fl oz/375 ml) cider vinegar
¾ cup (4 oz/125 g) brown sugar, packed
¼ cup (2 fl oz/60 ml) honey
½ cup (4 oz/125 g) sugar
8 Bosc or Bartlett pears, peeled, cored and cut into ½-in (1.5-cm) chunks
15 Italian plums or other purple plums, cut in half and pitted

❖ In a large nonaluminum stockpot, place all of the ingredients except the pears and plums. Bring to a slow boil and cook until the onions are translucent and the mixture is slightly syrupy, about 30–40 minutes. Fold in the cut fruit and cook over medium heat for 15 minutes, or until the fruit is just tender. Fill eight 1-cup (8-oz/250-g) sterilized glass canning jars (see glossary), cover tightly, and refrigerate for up to 3 months.
MAKES 8 CUPS (64 FL OZ/2 L)

Left to right: Apple-Mint Jelly, Plummy Pear Chutney

Sunnyside Pickled Asparagus

Eastern Washington

SUNNYSIDE PICKLED ASPARAGUS

Tart pickled asparagus spears go well with smoked meats or fish and are a tangy addition to any relish tray.

4–5 lb (2–2.5 kg) fresh asparagus
4 garlic cloves
4 dried hot chili peppers, 2–3 in (5–7 cm) long
4 fresh dill sprigs

4 cups (32 fl oz/1 l) water
3 cups (24 fl oz/750 ml) white distilled vinegar
3 tablespoons pickling (pure uniodized) salt

◈ Cut the asparagus to fit into four 2-cup (16-oz/500-g) sterilized glass canning jars (see glossary). To each jar add 1 garlic clove and 1 chili pepper. Pack the asparagus into the jars tips up. Add a sprig of fresh dill to each jar.

◈ In a saucepan, bring the water, vinegar and salt to a boil and boil for 5 minutes. Pour the hot brine into the jars.

◈ Cover and refrigerate for 3 days before serving. This asparagus will keep in the refrigerator for up to 1 month.

MAKES 12–16 CUPS (4–5 LB/2–2.5 KG)

Green Tomato Mincemeat

British Columbia

GREEN TOMATO MINCEMEAT

Pick green tomatoes for this mincemeat in the fall, just before the first frost. Because green tomatoes have tender skin and tiny seeds, it is not necessary to peel or seed them.

4 cups (2 lb/1 kg) chopped green tomatoes
2 tablespoons coarse salt
6 cups (2 lb/1 kg) chopped peeled green apples
5 cups (25 oz/750 g) raisins
6 cups (30 oz/950 g) brown sugar, packed
½ cup (4 fl oz/125 ml) cider vinegar
2 teaspoons salt
1 tablespoon ground cinnamon
2 teaspoons ground cloves
2 teaspoons ground allspice
1 teaspoon ground nutmeg

◙ Place the tomatoes in a nonaluminum container. Sprinkle the tomatoes with the coarse salt, let stand for 12 hours, and drain.
◙ In a large nonaluminum pot, combine the tomatoes with all of the remaining ingredients. Bring to a boil, stirring frequently. Reduce the heat to low and simmer gently, uncovered, stirring occasionally, until thick, about 1 hour.
◙ Pour into six 2-cup (16- fl oz/500-ml) sterilized glass canning jars (see glossary), cover tightly, and refrigerate for up to 6 weeks.

MAKES ABOUT 12 CUPS (96 FL OZ/3 L)

Oregon

PEPPER-PICKLED PEACHES

These cool peppered peaches are just right for hot summer days. Serve them with cured meats, sausages, or as a condiment with grilled meats and seafoods. They're especially good with Coppa-Cured Pork Loin (recipe on page 141) and a glass of good Northwest Chardonnay. The peppercorn mix is available at specialty foods stores.

4 cups (32 fl oz/1 l) white wine vinegar
4 cups (32 fl oz/ 1 l) water
3 cups (1½ lb/625 g) sugar
¾ cup (6 oz/185 g) kosher salt
12 bay leaves
12 garlic cloves
½ cup (2½ oz/75 g) mixed peppercorns (green, pink, white and black)
18 fresh peaches, peeled, halved and pitted, about 5 lb (2.5 kg)

◙ In a large nonaluminum saucepan, bring the vinegar, water, sugar, salt, herbs and spices to a low boil over medium heat. Simmer gently for 10 minutes.
◙ Put the peaches in 2 large 4-cup (32-fl oz/1-l) sterilized glass canning jars (see glossary) with snug-fitting lids. Pour enough of the hot liquid over the peaches to cover them, making sure to transfer all the garlic, bay leaves and peppercorns to the peaches.
◙ Cover tightly, let cool to room temperature (3 hours), and refrigerate.
◙ Chill the pickled peaches for 2–3 days before using. They'll keep for 3–4 weeks in the refrigerator.

MAKES 8 CUPS (5 LB/2.5 KG)   *Photograph pages 164-165*

Pickled Beets

Islands

PICKLED BEETS

A summer's garden bounty can be captured in jars of fruits and vegetables in the pantry. With their scarlet color and spicy tang, beets brighten a winter salad and add a dash of color to a platter of crudités.

6 cups (48 fl oz/1.5 l) water
4 lb (2 kg) beets
1 cinnamon stick
1 teaspoon whole coriander seeds
1 teaspoon whole allspice
6 whole pink peppercorns
6 whole cloves
2 cups (16 fl oz/500 ml) red wine vinegar
½ cup (4 fl oz/125 ml) water
½ cup (4 fl oz/125 ml) honey
½ cup (4 oz/125 g) sugar
6 garlic cloves, crushed

◙ In a large saucepan, bring the water and beets to a boil. Cook for about 20 minutes, or until the beets are tender but still firm.
◙ Rinse the beets in cool water and slide the skins off. Trim the tops and the roots. Cut the beets into 2-in (5-cm) sticks or ¼-in (6-mm) slices, as you prefer.
◙ Tie the spices in a square of cheesecloth (muslin). Heat the vinegar, water, honey, sugar and garlic in a large nonaluminum saucepan. Add the spice bag and cook for 5 minutes. Add the beets and cook for another 5 minutes.

◙ Pack six 2-cup (16-oz/500-g) sterilized glass canning jars (see glossary) with beets and pour the vinegar mixture over beets; cover tightly. The beets may be refrigerated for up to 4 weeks.

MAKES 12 CUPS (4 LB/2 K)

Western Washington

CRANBERRY-SAGE VINEGAR

A unique vinegar to give as a holiday gift. Try using it in Cranberry Vinaigrette (recipe on page 64). If you have access to tri-colored sage, it makes a colorful addition to the vinegar bottle.

1 cup (3 oz/90 g) fresh or frozen cranberries
4 fresh sage sprigs
6 cups (48 fl oz/1.5 l) white wine vinegar or distilled white vinegar
2 teaspoons sugar
½ teaspoon salt

◙ Arrange the cranberries and sage attractively in 2 clean clear-glass wine bottles.
◙ In a nonaluminum pan, bring the vinegar, sugar and salt to a boil. Immediately pour the liquid into the bottles, filling them 1½ in (4 cm) from the top. Let cool to room temperature, then cork. Store in a cool, dark place for 2–3 months, or refrigerate for up to 6 months.

MAKES 6 CUPS (48 FL OZ/1.5 L)

Cranberry-Sage Vinegar

British Columbia

APRICOT MUSTARD

The Okanagan Valley in lush south-central B.C. produces large, juicy apricots of excellent flavor, suitable for eating fresh and for preserving. Serve this apricot mustard with ham, pork or poultry, or with tempura prawns and vegetables.

1 cup (8 oz/250 g) chopped pitted apricots, about 4 large
   apricots
¾ cup (6 fl oz/180 ml) honey
¼ cup (2 oz/60 g) sugar
2 cups (16 fl oz/500 ml) Dijon mustard
salt to taste

◼ In a small saucepan, combine the apricots, honey and sugar, and bring to a simmer over medium heat. Cook, stirring often, for 15–20 minutes, or until thickened to the consistency of preserves. Remove from the heat, stir in the mustard, and add salt.

◼ Pour into three 1-cup (8-fl oz/250-ml) sterilized glass canning jars (see glossary), cover tightly, and refrigerate for up to 6 months.

MAKES ABOUT 3 CUPS (24 FL OZ/750 ML)

Islands

SIX ONION RELISH

Onions grow in abundance in the moist and cool climate of the Pacific Northwest. Walla Walla onions have a rich, sweet flavor, and some claim they can be eaten like an apple. Slow cooking both mellows and enhances their flavor.

1 Walla Walla Sweet onion, or other sweet white onion, diced
4 large leeks, white part only, halved, washed and cut into
   ¼-in (6-mm) slices
8 shallots, cut into ¼-in (6-mm) dice
8 garlic cloves, minced
¼ cup (2 fl oz/60 ml) chicken stock (see glossary)
¼ cup (2 fl oz/60 ml) balsamic vinegar, or 2 tablespoons red
   wine vinegar
2 tablespoons sugar
4 whole cloves
1 bay leaf
1 fresh rosemary sprig
1 fresh thyme sprig
½ cup (3 oz/90 g) golden raisins
3 green (spring) onions, diagonally cut into ¼-in (6-mm)
   pieces
½ cup (¾ oz/20 g) minced fresh chives

◼ Place all of the ingredients except the green onions and chives in a large nonaluminum skillet, making sure the herbs and raisins are submerged in the liquid. Place waxed paper or baking parchment on top of the onion mixture, folding it down inside the edge of the pan so the mixture is covered tightly. (Sealing the onions and herbs tightly concentrates the flavors.) Bring the pot to a very low simmer over the lowest possible heat and cook for 1 hour. Remove the paper and raise the heat to high; boil to reduce for 5 minutes, or until the liquid is syrupy. Remove the bay leaf, cloves, rosemary and thyme. Remove from the heat and stir in green onion and chives.

◼ Let cool, then place in three 1-cup (8-fl oz/250-ml) sterilized glass canning jars (see glossary), cover tightly, and refrigerate for at least 3 weeks before use. The flavor will improve with age. This relish may be refrigerated for up to 2 months.

MAKES 3 CUPS (24 FL OZ/750 ML)

*Top to bottom: Six Onion Relish, Apricot Mustard
and Fraser Valley River Chutney (page 193)*

*Left to right: Fried Green Tomatoes and Grilled Corn on the
Cob with Honey Butter, Ballard Baked Beans*

British Columbia

FRASER VALLEY RELISH

A local favorite for topping grilled frankfurters and hamburgers.

7 large cucumbers, peeled, seeded and minced, about 7 lb (3.5 g)
5 large onions, minced
2 red bell peppers (capsicums), minced
2 green bell peppers (capsicums), minced
¾ cup (6 oz/185 g) pickling (pure uniodized) salt
2½ cups (1¼ lb/625 g) sugar
½ cup (2 oz/60 g) all-purpose (plain) flour
2 teaspoons ground turmeric
1 tablespoon dry mustard
1 tablespoon celery seed
2 cups (16 fl oz/500 ml) distilled white vinegar
1 cup (8 fl oz/250 ml) water

◙ Place the cucumbers, onions and peppers in a large bowl, sprinkle with the pickling salt, and toss well to mix. Cover with plastic wrap and refrigerate overnight.
◙ The next day, drain the vegetables in a colander and rinse well.
◙ Combine the sugar, flour and spices with 1 cup (8 fl oz/250 ml) of the vinegar and set aside.
◙ Combine the drained vegetables, water and the remaining 1 cup vinegar in a large nonaluminum saucepan and boil for 5 minutes. Add the vinegar solution and boil for 5 minutes longer, or until clear.
◙ Immediately ladle into 2 large 4-cup (32-fl oz/1-l) sterilized glass canning jars (see glossary), cover tightly and keep in the refrigerator for up to 6 months.

MAKES 8 CUPS (64 FL OZ/2 L)   *Photograph pages 190-191*

Western Washington

BALLARD BAKED BEANS

Ballard, a neighborhood in north Seattle, is the heart of the local Scandinavian community. Baked beans are a Swedish tradition, and this Americanized version is a favorite of many folks in the Northwest.

1 lb (500 g) dried Great Northern (haricot) beans
6 cups (48 fl oz/1.5 l) water
½ lb (250 g) smoked ham hock
1 large white onion, diced
1 green apple, cored and grated
1 cup (8 fl oz/250 ml) beer
¾ cup (6 fl oz/180 ml) ketchup (tomato sauce)
6 tablespoons brown sugar, packed
4 teaspoons Worcestershire sauce
½ cup (4 fl oz/125 ml) molasses
1 tablespoon dry mustard
1 tablespoon cider vinegar
¼ teaspoon dried red pepper flakes
1 can chopped tomatoes in juice, about 14½ oz (455 g)
1½–2 teaspoons salt

◙ Place the beans in a large pot and cover with the water. Bring to a boil, reduce heat to low, and simmer for 30 minutes. Remove from the heat and let sit for 1 hour. Drain the beans, reserving the cooking water.
◙ Preheat an oven to 300°F (150°C). Mix together all of the remaining ingredients except the salt and stir into the beans. Place in a Dutch oven, cover, and bake in the preheated oven for 1 hour. Reduce the heat to 250°F (130°C) and bake for 4 hours longer.
◙ Uncover the beans, stir in the salt, and bake for 1 more hour. If the beans become dry, add a little of the reserved bean cooking water.

MAKES 8 CUPS (64 FL OZ/2 L); SERVES 10–12

Oregon

MARIONBERRY VINEGAR

Vinegars infused with fruits and herbs are simple to make and elegant to use. Experiment with different berries or herbal infusions depending on the season. Marionberries are a domesticated blackberry with a tart-sweet taste and a dense flesh, also good in pies, cobblers and jams.

8 cups (48 oz/1.5 kg) Marionberries or other fresh berries
½ cup (4 oz/125 g) sugar
4 cups (32 fl oz/1 l) white wine vinegar

◙ Place the berries in large glass jars or a ceramic crock. Pour the sugar and vinegar over them, cover, and let sit at room temperature for 2–3 weeks. Carefully decant the flavored berry vinegar by pouring it through a paper coffee filter, trying not to disturb the fruit sediment. Pour the fruit vinegar into decorative bottles and cork. This vinegar will keep in the refrigerator for up to 6 months.

MAKES ABOUT 4 CUPS (32 FL OZ/1 L)   *Photograph pages 164-165*

Western Washington

GRILLED CORN ON THE COB WITH HONEY BUTTER

Nothing says summer better than fresh sweet corn. Pull back the husks and pull out the silk, then tie back the husks with a strip of husk. This makes for a decorative and useful handle.

4 whole ears (cobs) fresh corn
½ cup (4 oz/120 g) butter at room temperature
2 tablespoons honey
¼ teaspoon salt
¼ teaspoon cayenne pepper
2 teaspoons minced fresh parsley (optional)

◙ Prepare a fire in a charcoal grill. Peel back the corn husks and pull off the corn silk.
◙ To make the honey butter: Beat the butter, honey, salt and cayenne pepper together until blended. Stir in the parsley.
◙ Place the corn over medium-hot coals and cook, turning every few minutes, until the corn is lightly charred and cooked through. Spread the corn with honey butter.

SERVES 4

Western Washington

FRIED GREEN TOMATOES

It's common in western Washington to have lots of green tomatoes at the onset of fall, due to our short growing season. Cornmeal-coated fried green tomatoes are often served with pan-fried oysters and tartar sauce.

1 cup (5 oz/155 g) cornmeal
1 teaspoon paprika
1½ teaspoons salt
¼ teaspoon ground black pepper
4 large green tomatoes, about 2½ lb (1.2 kg), cut into ½-in (1.5-cm) slices
½ cup (4 fl oz/125 ml) vegetable oil or a mixture of oil and bacon drippings

◙ In a large bowl, mix the cornmeal, paprika, salt and pepper. Dip the tomato slices in the mixture to coat them well on both sides.
◙ In a large skillet, preferably made of cast iron, heat half of the oil over medium heat. Fry the tomato slices in batches until golden brown on both sides, a total of about 2–4 minutes, adding more oil as necessary. Serve immediately.

SERVES 6

British Columbia

JAPANESE FIDDLEHEAD FERNS

Fiddleheads should be tightly curled, with short tails. Pick them in the morning when the plants are still crisp, and make sure you pick only ostrich ferns—all others are unsafe to eat. To store, place in a paper bag in the refrigerator crisper for up to 2 days.

8 oz (250 g) fresh fiddlehead ferns, or 1 package frozen
    fiddleheads, about 10 oz (315 g)
3 tablespoons crunchy peanut butter
1 tablespoon soy sauce
1 teaspoon sugar
3–4 teaspoons water
1 carrot, cut into long matchsticks and blanched (optional)

▓ Wash fresh fiddleheads several times in cool water. Trim the dark ends before cooking.
▓ Cook the fiddleheads, uncovered, in a large amount of boiling salted water for 4–6 minutes, or until just tender. Plunge them into cold water, drain, and dry on paper towels; set aside.
▓ In a medium bowl, whisk together all the remaining ingredients except the carrot. Add the fiddleheads and toss gently. Garnish with the carrots, if desired.
▓ Serve at room temperature.

SERVES 4

Eastern Washington

GRILLED VEGETABLES WITH FRESH HERB PESTO

Vegetables brushed with pesto and grilled to sweet perfection will make any meal special. Be sure to brush the skewers with pesto frequently while grilling, to keep the vegetables moist.

1 red (Spanish) onion, cut into wedges
3 small zucchini (courgettes), cut into 1½-in (4-cm) pieces
3 Japanese eggplants (aubergines), cut into 1½-in (4-cm) pieces
1 large red bell pepper (capsicum), seeded and cut into
    8–12 pieces
1 large yellow bell pepper (capsicum), seeded and cut into
    8–12 pieces

Grilled Vegetables with Fresh Herb Pesto

8 oz (250 g) mushroom caps
½ cup (4 fl oz/125 ml) pesto (recipe below), mixed with
    ¼ cup (2 fl oz/60 ml) olive oil

▓ Prepare a fire in a charcoal grill. While the coals are heating, soak 6 wooden skewers in water for 30 minutes.
▓ Thread the vegetables on the skewers, alternating vegetables and colors. Brush generously with pesto. Brush the cooking rack lightly with oil.
▓ Place the vegetables over medium-hot coals and grill them for 4–6 minutes on each side, or until tender, brushing the vegetables with pesto before turning them.

SERVES 4–6

Japanese Fiddlehead Ferns

FRESH HERB PESTO

Pesto is a great way to preserve the bright flavor of your summer herb harvest for a dreary winter's day. Use in soup, salad dressing or homemade bread.

1 cup (2 oz/60 g) fresh basil leaves, packed
4 tablespoons fresh parsley leaves, packed
2 tablespoons chopped fresh herbs of choice
2–3 garlic cloves, minced
⅓ cup (1½ oz/45 g) freshly grated Parmesan cheese
½ cup (4 fl oz/125 ml) olive oil

½ teaspoon salt
¼ cup (1 oz/30 g) pine nuts or walnuts, lightly toasted (see glossary)
pinch of dried red pepper flakes (optional)
olive oil for storing

▧ Coarsely chop all the herbs, then combine with all of the remaining ingredients, except the oil for storing, in a blender or food processor. Process until all of the ingredients are minced and well combined. Pesto also can be pounded by hand in a mortar.
▧ Place the pesto in a glass or plastic container. Pour a thin layer of olive oil over the top of the pesto, cover tightly, and refrigerate for up to 1 week, or freeze.

MAKES ABOUT 1½ CUPS (12 FL OZ/375 ML)

CHUNKY APPLESAUCE

The abundance and variety of apples available in the islands is enough to boggle the mind of any apple-lover. The supply seems endless, but savvy cooks know how to preserve the windfall crop for a later cold and rainy day. Early Duchess and Gravenstein apples are favorites for this sauce. We like to cook the red apples with the skins on; it leaves the sauce a beautiful rosy pink.

¾ cups (6 fl oz/180 ml) water
¼ cup (2 fl oz/60 ml) plus 2 tablespoons fresh lemon juice
¾–1½ cups (6–12 oz/185–375 g) sugar
8 Early Duchess or other red cooking apples, cut into
    2-in (5-cm) chunks
2 Gravenstein or other sweet apples, peeled, cored and cut
    into ½-in (1.5-cm) chunks
¾ cup (4 oz/125 g) raisins
1 teaspoon ground cinnamon

◼ In a large, heavy stockpot, place ½ cup (4 fl oz/125 ml) of the water, sugar and ¼ cup (2 fl oz/60 ml) of the lemon juice. Add the Early Duchess apples to the pot. Bring the pot to a boil and reduce heat to low. Cover and simmer until the apples are tender, about 20 minutes.
◼ Place the Gravenstein chunks, remaining lemon juice, remaining water, raisins and cinnamon in a large saucepan, bring to a boil, and reduce heat to low. Remove the Duchess apples and pass them through a food mill into the saucepan with the Gravenstein chunks. Cook over low heat for 10 minutes, or until the chunks are just tender, stirring frequently. If too much liquid evaporates, add a little water.
◼ Serve warm. Place extra applesauce in sterilized glass canning jars (see glossary), cover tightly, and refrigerate for up to 2 weeks.

MAKES 6–8 CUPS (48–64 FL OZ/1.5–2 L)

SCANDINAVIAN OATMEAL SOUR CREAM COFFEE CAKE

Norwegians came to the Pacific Northwest and found that the Puget Sound reminded them of the fjords of home. Present-day Pacific Northwesterners can thank these hardy pioneers for their legacy of the fabulous pastries and baked goods that line the shelves of neighborhood bakeries.

¾ cup (6 oz/180 g) unsalted butter, at room temperature
1½ cups (12 oz/375 g) sugar
3 eggs, beaten
1½ cups (12 fl oz/375 ml) sour cream
3 cups (12 oz/375 g) all-purpose (plain) flour
1 tablespoon baking powder
¼ teaspoon salt
½ teaspoon baking soda
¾ cup (4 oz/125 g) brown sugar, packed
1 cup (4 oz/125 g) slivered almonds, toasted (see glossary)
1 cup (5 oz/155 g) uncooked oatmeal (rolled oats)
1 tablespoon ground cinnamon
½ teaspoon freshly grated nutmeg

◼ Preheat an oven to 350°F (180°C). In a large bowl, cream the butter with the sugar until fluffy. Add the eggs and beat well, then add the sour cream and beat for about 2 minutes longer.
◼ Sift together the flour, baking powder, salt and baking soda, then beat into the creamed mixture just until blended, being careful not to overbeat. The batter will be thick. In another bowl, blend the brown sugar, almonds, oatmeal and spices.
◼ Butter and flour a 9-by-13-in (23-by-32.5-cm) baking pan. Fill

*Left to right: Scandinavian Oatmeal Sour Cream
Coffee Cake, Chunky Applesauce*

with half of the cake batter, then layer in half of the oatmeal mixture. Layer in the last of the batter and cover with the remaining oatmeal mixture.

◼ Bake in the oven for about 50 minutes, or until a cake tester inserted in the center comes out clean. Let cool for 10 minutes before serving.

SERVES 10–14

STUFFED FRENCH TOAST WITH WILDFLOWER-BERRY BUTTER

A Northwest twist on a breakfast favorite. In summer, garnish with fresh berries or sliced fruit for a sunny brunch.

EGG BATTER

4 eggs
2¼ cups (18 fl oz/560 ml) half & half (half milk and half cream)
1½ teaspoons pure vanilla extract (essence)
⅓ cup (3 oz/90 g) sugar

¼ teaspoon ground cinnamon
¼ teaspoon ground nutmeg

FILLING

⅓ cup (1½ oz/45 g) hazelnuts, lightly toasted, peeled and chopped (see glossary)
8 oz (250 g) cream cheese at room temperature
1 teaspoon grated orange zest
½ teaspoon grated lemon zest
2 tablespoons honey

8 slices hearty sourdough raisin bread or French bread
¼ cup (2 oz/60 g) butter
Wildflower-Berry Butter (recipe follows)
fresh berries (optional)
sifted powdered (icing) sugar (optional)

◘ Place the toasts on warm plates and top with dollops of Wildflower-Berry Butter. Garnish with fresh berries, if desired, and lightly sprinkle with powdered sugar. Serve with warm maple or berry syrup.

SERVES 4

WILDFLOWER-BERRY BUTTER

Borage, Johnny-jump-ups, calendula and rose petals make a pretty combination for this recipe.

½ cup (4 oz/120 g) salted butter, cut into ½-in (1.5-cm) pieces
2 tablespoons seedless berry jam
2 tablespoons sour cream
1½ teaspoons sifted powdered (icing) sugar
dash of ground cinnamon
2 tablespoons lightly chopped unsprayed edible mild-
   flavored flower petals

◘ Whip all the ingredients except the flower petals in a blender, food processor or mixer until well blended. Fold in the flower petals.

MAKES ¾ CUPS (6 OZ /185 G)

British Columbia

SAUTÉED SPINACH WITH PEARS

A quick and easy accompaniment to roasted or grilled lamb.

4 tablespoons (2 oz/60 g) butter
3 shallots, minced
3 lb (1.5 kg) chopped fresh or defrosted frozen spinach
salt and freshly ground pepper to taste
2 ripe pears, peeled, halved, cored, and sprinkled with
   lemon juice

◘ In a large skillet over medium heat, melt the butter and sauté the shallots for 2 minutes, or until translucent. Add the spinach and cook for about 4 minutes, or until the spinach is completely wilted, stirring occasionally. Lower the heat and push the spinach to the side of the skillet. Add salt and pepper.
◘ Slice the pears lengthwise and sauté in the same pan until just tender. Fan the pears out on dinner plates and arrange the spinach alongside.

SERVES 4–6

Sautéed Spinach with Pears

Stuffed French Toast with Wildflower-Berry Butter

warm maple or berry syrup

◘ Preheat an oven to 375°F (190°C). In a medium bowl, whisk together all the egg batter ingredients; set aside.
◘ In a small bowl, mix all the ingredients for the filling together until blended. Spread the filling evenly over 4 bread slices to ½ in (1.5 cm) from the edges. Place the remaining bread slices on top and press together slightly. Place the bread in the egg mixture on both sides for about 1 minute, or until both sides are thoroughly soaked.
◘ Heat the butter in a very large skillet over medium-high heat. Place the soaked bread in the hot skillet and brown on one side, for 2–3 minutes, then turn and cook 2–3 minutes longer.
◘ Place the skillet in the preheated oven for 10–12 minutes, or until the toasts are puffy and lightly browned.

RHUBARB-GINGER COMPOTE

Choose pinkish-red rhubarb that is firm and crisp. Serve this compote with cream cheese and crackers or crusty warm bread.

2 lb (1 kg) rhubarb, trimmed and cut into 1-in (2.5-cm) pieces
3¼ cups (26 oz/300 g) sugar
½ cup (3 oz/90 g) crystallized ginger, chopped
¼ teaspoon Tabasco (hot pepper) sauce
¼ cup (2 fl oz/60 ml) fresh lemon juice

▨ Combine all of the ingredients in a large saucepan and mix well. Place over medium heat and bring to a boil. Stirring frequently, simmer 30 minutes, or until the mixture is thick. Remove any foam with a metal spoon that has been dipped into very hot water.
▨ Ladle into four 1-cup (8-oz/250-g) sterilized glass canning jars (see glossary). Cover tightly and refrigerate for up to 2 months.

MAKES 4 CUPS (32 FL OZ/1 L)

CRIMSON CHERRY CHUTNEY

Plump sun-dried Bing cherries are a sweet contrast to the tart cherries in this chutney, making it an excellent accompaniment to Skagit Valley Duck Sausage (recipe on page 130), poultry or roast pork.

2 lb (1 kg) fresh or frozen pitted tart cherries (not packed in sugar)
1 cup (8 oz/250 g) diced white onion
1 cup (8 oz/250 g) dried pitted Bing cherries, coarsely chopped
2 tablespoons minced fresh ginger
1 tablespoon minced garlic
1½ cups (12 oz/375 g) sugar
1 teaspoon black mustard seeds
1 teaspoon yellow mustard seeds
⅛ teaspoon ground cinnamon
¼ teaspoon celery seed
¼ teaspoon dried red pepper flakes
2 teaspoons salt
⅛ teaspoon ground allspice
½ teaspoon ground coriander
tiny pinch of ground cloves
1½ cups (12 fl oz/375 ml) white wine vinegar or distilled white vinegar
¼ cup (2 fl oz/60 ml) light corn syrup

▨ Place all of the ingredients except the vinegar and corn syrup in a heavy nonaluminum saucepan. Over medium-high heat, bring the mixture to a boil. Cook until reduced to a thick consistency, stirring often, about 20 minutes.
▨ Mix together the vinegar and corn syrup and add to the chutney. Boil down, for about 8 minutes, to a nicely thickened, syrupy consistency. Remove from the heat and let cool. The chutney will thicken slightly as it cools.

MAKES 4 CUPS (32 FL OZ/1 L)

Left to right: Rhubarb-Ginger Compote, Crimson Cherry Chutney

WESTERN OREGON

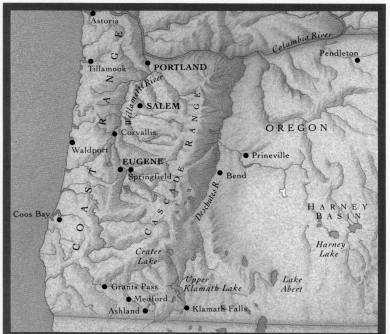

WESTERN OREGON

T here was nothing done or talked of but what had Oregon in it," wrote Keturah Penton Belknap in her diary for 1847. Within the year, she and her family had set off for the Willamette Valley in a wagon train from Iowa, their fourth move westward. For provisions she packed 500 pounds of flour, 125 pounds of corn meal, dried apples and peaches, beans, rice, sugar and coffee. "I have made four nice little tablecloths so am going to live just like I was at home," she wrote optimistically. Buffalo meat supplemented her larder, and the jolting of the wagon turned cream from the train's dairy cows into butter.

Families braved the dangers and uncertainties of the Oregon Trail because the goal was considered worth the risk. Most hoped for land in the Willamette Valley. Fertile, well watered, and moderate in climate, the Willamette was described, with some justification, as a rainy Eden. "The various culinary vegetables are in great profusion, and of the first quality," wrote John Kirk Townsend after a trip to the Oregon Country in 1834. Much has changed

Previous pages: One of the brightest and most beautiful beacons on the Oregon coast, Heceta Head Lighthouse is one of nine sentinels dating from 1857 still standing. Left: Blooming pear orchards cover the countryside around Hood river, Oregon, known as the winter pear (d'Anjou) capital of the world.

in Oregon since then, but Townsend's observation remains accurate. Western Oregon's wonderful produce, available practically year-round, attracts innovative chefs and discriminating diners. Oregon also was one of the first states in the country to certify and promote organic crops, and a network of organic farms and farmers' markets helps further innovation and quality in produce. The annual cycles of seafoods, fruits and vegetables allow for a pleasing variety of meats. "When I find unseasonal items on a menu," says Franz Popperl, a Portland-based chef and member of the Culinary Team USA for 1992, "my heart starts bleeding."

Western Oregon's agriculture is dominated by the Willamette Valley, which stretches, twenty to thirty miles wide, for over 100 hundred miles from its mouth at the Columbia to Roseburg. Vegetables, berries, fruits and nuts all thrive here. The native Oregon hazelnut has been supplanted by commercial varieties—more than three million trees, which have virtually taken over the national hazelnut market. One result is a specialty market in hazelnut products ranging from hazelnut-filled ravioli and hazelnut fudge sauce to hazelnut flour for tortes.

Cane fruits thrive, from familiar raspberries and blackberries to local creations like the Marionberry, bred in and named for Marion County. Vegetables range from the miles and miles of Blue Lake beans and Jubilee corn, grown for processing, to the most rarified radicchios and bibb lettuces for the restaurant trade. The variety of quality foods can make a chef almost giddy with the freedom to invent combinations ranging from salmon with crème fraîche and a dab of raspberry sauce to garlic soup with pesto and lavender. The Willamette Valley is also a center for wine production. The mellow climate is suitable for lighter wines such as Pinot Noirs and Müller-Thurgaus. The valley's substantial German population also is served by bottlings of elderflower wine. The International Pinot Noir Festival, held each year in the farm town of McMinnville, brings in chefs and enologists from as far as Burgundy.

The first farmers in Oregon were not so concerned with gourmet developments, but they were aware of the region's potential. "An immigrant will come in during the autumn," wrote one pioneer, "put himself up a log house with mud and stick chimney, split boards and shingles. His wife has a few cooking utensils, few chairs....You call upon him the next year and he will have a fine field ripe for the sickle. There will be a patch of corn, another of potatoes, and another of garden vegetables. His cattle and horses and dogs will be on the prairie, thriving and increasing."

Still, it took time for the settlers to get the hang of food

This picturesque view of the Columbia River, as seen from Larch Mountain in Oregon, presents a rather tame version of a once powerful whitewater river, now dammed for hydropower.

in the valley. Coming mostly from the Ozarks and Smoky Mountains, the newcomers missed the familiar wild fruits and honey trees of home, and all but the earliest arrivals found game scarce. In a new country, they didn't know which shoots and roots were palatable. The damper lowlands of the Willamette were dense with camas, a member of the lily family whose baked bulbs were a native staple. The blue flowers grew so thick that the men who named Camas Valley, in 1848, at first thought they were looking down at a lake. But the settlers plowed up the sweet walnut-sized bulbs or fed them to the pigs. In their place they planted wheat and corn, the kind of storage crops necessary in a country that had no transportation network for shipping fresh produce. Surrounded by bounty they did not know how to claim, the settlers lived on boiled wheat, potatoes and salt pork until their land was cleared and their own gardens producing.

Wheat—pegged at one dollar a bushel—was declared the legal tender by the provisional government, but it was not really suited to the climate. Potatoes did better, in fact so well that they soon glutted the scant market. While serving as quartermaster at Fort Vancouver in 1853, Ulysses S. Grant tried raising potatoes to supplement his Army pay. "Luckily for us, the Columbia River rose to a great height from the melting of the snow in the mountains in June and overflowed and killed most of our crop," he wrote sardonically in his memoirs. "This saved digging it up, for everybody on the Pacific Coast seemed to have come to the conclusion at the same time that agriculture would be profitable."

Some of the first successful market gardens in the Oregon Country were established on the Clatsop Plain near the mouth of the Columbia. Their customers were the crews of sailing ships, who were desperate for fresh food after weeks at sea. At Astoria, salmon canning was underway by the 1850s. The salmon were so numerous that ocean fishing didn't even require a boat. Fishermen set their nets along the shoreline and drove horses into the surf to haul in the catch.

The main industry along the Oregon coast today is tourism. But the first out-of-towners to winter there, members of the Lewis and Clark Expedition, did not give the area good reviews. They spent a soggy winter at Fort Clatsop south of the Columbia mouth, eating moldy elk meat and conducting surveys of the native flora and fauna. "Snails without covers are numerous," wrote Clark, perhaps the first recorded reference to the infamous Northwest banana slug.

As a break from elk and dried salmon, the expedition made a trade with members of the Tillamook tribe for three hundred pounds of blubber from a whale washed up on the beach. Clark thanked providence for "having sent this Monster to be swallowed by us instead of swallowing us as Jonah's did." He said the blubber was like lard, only grainier.

Blubber has vanished from Oregon menus, but an Indian recipe for clam chowder, including smoked venison, wild onion and wapato root, is echoed in the clam, bacon and potato combination found in coastal cafés today.

By the late nineteenth century, wealthy Portlanders had built summer homes at Seaside, where Lewis and Clark had stood in the downpour, boiling seawater to make salt. Seaside, Cannon Beach, Oceanside and other resort towns now draw visitors from around the country for beachcombing, clam digging, salmon fishing, surfing, hang gliding and hiking. And eating. Restaurants range

Portland is Oregon's largest and most colorful city offering such curious attractions as the Church of Elvis, the Northwest's only coin-operated art gallery.

from bring-the-kids outlets for fish and chips to destination oases concentrating on completely fresh seafood and local lamb, poultry and vegetables. Except for olive oil and balsamic vinegar, William Purdy, the chef at the Bay House in Lincoln City, can get everything for his salmon with wilted basil and tomato topping within a few miles of his kitchen.

Cranberries grew wild in bogs along the southern coast, and were prized by the tribes there as a scarce and therefore valuable trade item. Since conditions clearly were favorable, Charles Dexter McFarlin brought starts for the larger cultivated berries from Cape Cod, and built a bog in Coos County in 1885. Today, the area around Bandon is the center for cranberry production, and locally made condiments—including cranberries in port

The verdant western valleys of Oregon's Columbia River Gorge are full of tumbling cascades and Multnomah Falls is the area's grandest spectacle.

wine and cranberry citrus mustard—are sold in Oregon specialty shops. Another famous Bandon food is cheese. The Cheddars from Bandon are still hand-turned and pressed. Visitors can tour the plant, and on cheese-making days they can buy fresh curds (without the whey) and learn for themselves what Miss Muffett was munching.

Both Bandon cheeses and the larger Tillamook cheese factory to the north reap the benefits of the mild, damp coastal climate. A cow's diet affects her milk and the cheese made from it. Coastal herds graze in green pastures nearly year-round, unlike inland cows which must depend more on hay and fermented silage. Grass-fed cows give sweeter milk and produce a mellower cheese.

Oregon natives, and the settlers who came after them, depended primarily on the seemingly inexhaustible supplies of salmon that returned mostly to the Columbia, but also to the Coos, Rogue and other coastal rivers. But that resource has dwindled from a staple to a treat and less vulnerable rockfish and flatfish, formerly scorned, are now gaining favor in homes and restaurants. Commercial harvesting of bottom fish got a boost during World War II, when fuel was scarce and offshore fishing was restricted. Now lingcods, red snappers and cabazons are welcome at the most up-to-date tables. Though they lack the succulence of a fat salmon, many chefs prefer them because their firm texture and mild flavors are perfect foils for sauces.

South of the Willamette Valley, the Rogue River flows through two ranges of mountains to get to the Pacific. With a greater barrier to the sea, the Rogue has a more continental climate, with blazing summers suitable for heat-loving crops. The area is rugged, and the passionate resistance of tribes there delayed white settlement. But by 1856, the combination of European weapons and European diseases had driven the Rogue River tribes to accept a diminished existence on a reservation. The first whites in the Rogue were looking for gold, but those who came later grew their fortune on trees, especially pear trees. Dessert pears—Comices, Seckels and red-and-gold Forelles—respond especially well to long hot days and cool nights. Peaches, plums and nectarines also thrive here, many in orchards established more than fifty years ago.

Melons, which will take all the heat they can get, are another Rogue Valley treat, and the growing wine industry concentrates on Cabernet Sauvignons, Chardonnays and other heat-loving varietals. In addition to agriculture, southern Oregon lives mostly by timber and tourism. The climate is ideal for outdoor activities ranging from river rafting to open-air theater at the Oregon Shakespeare Festival, an Ashland institution since the 1940s. At the upriver lodges catering to hunters and river runners, the cuisine may run to prime rib from eastern Oregon cattle ranches and homemade hash. In Ashland, theater-goers are likely to critique the performance over a plate of baked chèvre on toast.

Trout fishing is one of the biggest draws in the mountains east of the Rogue and elsewhere in the Oregon Cascades. Oregon trout inspire heroic deeds. In 1888 William Steel hiked forty-nine miles from the Rogue with a bucket full of rainbow trout fingerlings in order to plant them in Crater Lake. The lake was already famous for its beauty, but not for fish; gouged out of a mountaintop by an immense volcanic eruption, it has no outlet along which colonizing species could travel. Most of Steel's little fish spilled en route, but the dozen or so that survived the journey have multiplied fruitfully.

These old fashioned milk cans are a symbol of Oregon's highly developed cheese industry. The coastal town of Tillamook draws thousands of visitors eager to taste some of the over 30 million pounds of cheese produced annually.

Traditional trout recipes assume an ample supply. One, reproduced in the Works Progress Administration's 1951 guide to Oregon, calls for at least fifty pounds of freshly caught trout, calling any smaller quantity "picayune." The catch is to be smoked for twenty-four hours inside a teepee of fresh willow branches over a fire of willow twigs, "a task requiring energy, patience and an optimism that is justified by the results."

While Oregon's farmers came primarily from the Midwest and South, its merchants tended to be Yankees. Portland was named for the Maine hometown of one of its two founders; the other choice was Boston. In any case, the riverside community was known for years as Stumptown. Given its New England roots and its solid commerce based on shipping and shipbuilding, it is not surprising that Portland grew steadily and prudently at the same time that rivals like Seattle, Tacoma and Vancouver took disorienting rides on the boom-bust roller coaster.

A writer in the 1930s asserted that to know how Portland would react in any given situation, it was only necessary to know how Calvin Coolidge would react. That's a recommendation for a quiet life, but it doesn't auger well for great food. Even at the time, however, the assessment was incomplete. Portland's elite liked sedate teas and chafing dish parties, but ethnic neighborhoods spiced up the stew with kosher delis and Chinese noodle houses. A Southern dinner favorite, crawfish boil, was enshrined in Jake's Famous Crawfish Restaurant, which got its catch from the Columbia. Places like Jake's set the stage for the dozens of restaurants that now concentrate on the best local products, prepared with care. While the Portland promoters of the Lewis and Clark Exposition in 1905 went in for quantity, featuring a life-sized cow sculpted of butter, many of their successors have concentrated on quality—and variety. Today, Portland is an international port in a great agricultural valley, where you can order anything from Vietnamese barbecued goat to Columbia River sturgeon saltimbocca.

The proximity of urban centers and farmland is one factor in an explosion of farmers' markets in and around Portland, always a good sign for regional food-lovers, and several small farmers make a living supplying restaurants with edible flowers, European lettuces and other fragile delicacies. In Portland, all the resources of one of the most blessed food-producing areas on the continent come together for the benefit of fortunate diners.

DESSERTS,
COFFEE AND BEVERAGES

Northwestern coffee roasters of national acclaim roast their beans very dark, giving the region's coffee much of its signature flavor and aroma.

DESSERTS, COFFEE AND BEVERAGES

The long gray days have brought about a kind of coffee madness in the Northwest. Known to some now as "latté land," Seattle is also called the coffee capital of the world. The first national coffee-based magazine was founded there; a recent edition even contains a coffee board game in the centerfold! Where other cities have hot dog carts on the corners, Seattle has espresso carts. Not only are there carts galore, but an almost cultlike coffee lingo has developed. Pass by a busy espresso cart in downtown Seattle early some morning and you might hear something like, "I'll have a double decaf, short cappuccino, skinny." To those not in the coffee-lingo know, that means, a double shot of espresso topped with a short topping of low-fat steamed-milk foam. You can even get your favorite espresso drink without leaving your car at drive-through carts or stands, positioned by heavy traffic commuter areas.

In 1971 Starbucks Coffee opened its first store in the Pike Place Public Market, bringing Seattle dark-roasted whole beans and influencing the future of that city's coffee culture. It was those dark-roasted beans that started the love affair with the rich dark cup of "joe" that Northwesterners are so passionate about. The Northwest's nationally acclaimed coffee roasters roast their beans very dark, which changes the sugar and starches in green coffee beans into volatile oils that give coffee much of its rich flavor and aroma.

Not only do Northwesterners like caffeine for a quick rainy-day pick-me-up, but they also like their desserts.

Home-style fruit-based desserts such as cobblers made with the prized tiny wild blackberries and fresh juicy peach crisps are the most popular. When it comes to chocolate they like it on the dark bittersweet side, like their coffee.

Granville Island Market is one of Vancouver's best spots to buy locally-grown apples, like the Granny Smith shown here in a favorite autumn dessert.

Fresh fruits and berries are the basis for wonderful Northwest summer sweets such as tarts, pies, shortcake, cobblers, and ice cream.

Holiday cookie exchanges bring a variety of sweets to the table: old-fashioned oatmeal cookies studded with jewel-like nuggets of dried cherries, apricots and blueberries in place of raisins; Italian-influenced hazelnut biscotti; rich Scandinavian almond butter spritz cookies. British Columbia made a big cookie hit in the forties with the Nanaimo bar, an easy-to-prepare, sinfully delicious three-layer bar. Sweet-toothers raved over them then and still do. And what better to go with holiday cookies than apple cider simmered with cinnamon, or hot steaming cups of cocoa made the old-fashioned way and topped with brandied whipped cream and chocolate-covered espresso beans or shaved bittersweet chocolate for the adults, and mini-marshmallows for the little ones. A favorite beverage, especially in the winter after a long day of skiing, is mulled red wine, whose spicy aroma wafts through the air at winter cabins and holiday parties. When driving through the wine country of eastern Washington in the fall, you can smell the apples being pressed for cider, and the aroma will fill your head with sweet holiday memories.

While American Northwesterners are not much interested in British-influenced sweets such as fruitcakes, mincemeat pies and steamed puddings, to Canadian British Columbians the holidays would not be the same without them.

All visitors to Victoria, B.C., must make a stop for afternoon tea at one of the popular tea spots such as the grand Empress Hotel. Here steaming cups of Earl Grey are poured and accompanied with such traditional afternoon sweets as freshly baked scones served with Devonshire cream and fresh berries, and Banbury tarts stuffed with raisins and candied lemon peel.

In the summer it's berries galore, for the Northwest has a bounty of varieties: strawberries; red, black and golden yellow raspberries; tiny wild blackberries; and big juicy Himalaya blackberries growing along railroad tracks and country roads. There are red and black currants, Marionberries, boysenberries, loganberries and tayberries, a cross between the loganberry and black raspberry, as well as brilliant green gooseberries, blueberries and pink and purple huckleberries. Native Americans have long picked the wild peach-colored salmon berries and bittersweet soapberries, the latter used to make soapberry froth, otherwise known as Indian ice cream. This treat is traditionally made by whipping fresh soapberries and water in a deep bowl with a tree branch until thick and frothy.

The Fourth of July is also a celebration of sweet, juicy strawberries: shortcakes, scones or angelfood cake slices smothered with fresh berries and topped with lightly sweetened whipped cream end the traditional picnic with a bang!

It seems that no region is safe from those peculiar vegetable cakes, mostly devised out of self-defense from the monster vegetables from over-abundant gardens. Zucchini cake is a true-blue standby recipe, both the nut-studded chocolate and the cinnamony spiced version. Adding grated zucchini to a quick-bread batter makes an ultra-moist cake.

The ongoing bounty of summer fruit brings county fair pie-baking contests with such favorites as rhubarb-strawberry, blueberry-apple and mile-high peachy-plum pie. On hot summer days they like to eat a slice of pie with a refreshing glass of iced sun tea: good black tea leaves, fresh sprigs of mint, slices of lemon and rose hips placed in a big jar filled with water, then slowly brewed by the heat of the sun.

In the fall, when the sagging fruit-laden branches of apple and pear trees have been picked, desserts such as Bartlett pears poached in a good Oregon Pinot Noir, or warm apple-cranberry pie topped with a slice of melting sharp Tillamook Cheddar cheese, warm the heart as crisp fall leaves drift down.

Oregon

RHUBARB CHEESECAKE TART

Make extra walnut pastry dough to keep in the freezer—this will make baking a fresh tart much more convenient. When rhubarb is at the peak of its season, make extra compote topping too, as it also freezes well.

WALNUT PASTRY CRUST

½ cup (2 oz/60 g) ground walnuts
1¾ cup (7 oz/220 g) all-purpose (plain) flour
1 tablespoon ground cinnamon
2 tablespoons sugar
½ teaspoon salt
⅔ cup (5 oz/155 g) butter
⅓ cup (2.5 fl oz/75 ml) cold water

FILLING

12 oz (375 g) cream cheese at room temperature
3 tablespoons sugar
3 tablespoons all-purpose (plain) flour
2 eggs
1½ teaspoons vanilla extract (essence)
1 teaspoon grated lemon zest

TOPPING

4 cups (20 oz/625 g) diced fresh rhubarb
1⅓ cups (11 oz/340 g) sugar
¼ cup (2 fl oz/60 ml) water

◫ To make the crust: In a medium bowl or a food processor, combine all of the dry ingredients. Cut in the butter with a pastry cutter, 2 knives, or the processor. Mix in the water until it is just combined. Shape the dough into a ball, flatten, wrap in plastic, and refrigerate for 1–1½ hours.

◫ Preheat an oven to 375°F (190°C). Meanwhile, roll the dough out on a lightly floured board. Fit into a 10-in (25-cm) tart shell, crimping the edges. Prick the bottom with a fork, line with aluminum foil, and fill with pie weights or dried beans. Bake in the preheated oven until set but not browned. Remove from the oven and let cool, leaving the oven at 375°F (190°C).

◫ To make the filling: Beat all of the ingredients together until smooth, about 5–7 minutes. Fill the partially baked tart shell ¼–½ in (6 mm–1.5 cm) from the rim with this mixture. Bake in the preheated oven for 20–25 minutes, or until the cheese filling puffs a bit and is just firm to the touch. Remove from the oven and let cool.

◫ To make the topping: Combine all of the ingredients in a saucepan. Bring the mixture to a boil over medium heat and continue cooking until the rhubarb is tender and the liquid is reduced to a thick, syrupy compote, about 10–12 minutes. Set aside.

◫ Spread the rhubarb compote evenly over the cooled tart. Refrigerate until the topping is set.

SERVES 6–8

Western Washington

CASCADE BERRY SHORTCAKE

There's no better ending to a long Northwest summer day than a backyard barbecue with a finale of a luscious berry shortcake, especially if you have picked the berries yourself. The Northwest has a large variety of wild berries, from big, plump Himalaya blackberries to tiny pink and purple huckleberries.

4 cups (1½ lb/750 g) fresh berries in season, such as strawberries, raspberries, blueberries or blackberries
¼–½ cup (2–4 oz/60–125 g) sugar, depending on the tartness of the berries
2 tablespoons berry liqueur (optional)

Rhubarb Cheesecake Tart

Cascade Berry Cheesecake

SHORTCAKE

2 cups (8 oz/250 g) all-purpose (plain) flour
2½ teaspoons baking powder
1 teaspoon salt
¼ cup (2 oz/60 g) sugar
⅓ cup (2½ oz/80 g) vegetable shortening (vegetable lard)
¼ cup (1 oz/30 g) sliced almonds, lightly toasted (see glossary)
¾–1 cup (6–8 fl oz/180–250 ml) milk

1 cup (8 fl oz/250 ml) heavy (double) cream
⅓ cup (2 oz/60 g) sifted powdered (icing) sugar
2 tablespoons amaretto liqueur
fresh mint sprigs (optional)
sifted powdered (icing) sugar for dusting
mild-tasting unsprayed edible flowers, such as johnny-jump-ups (optional)

◼ Preheat an oven to 375°F (190°C). In large bowl, lightly toss the berries with the sugar and liqueur. Chill.
◼ Meanwhile, to make the shortcake: Into a large bowl, sift together the flour, baking powder, salt and sugar. Cut in the shortening with a pastry cutter or 2 knives, then stir in the nuts. Lightly stir in as much milk as is needed to make a soft, moist dough.
◼ Turn the dough out onto a lightly floured surface. Lightly pat the dough out ½ in (1.5 cm) thick. Cut the dough into 2½-in (6.5-cm) rounds with a biscuit cutter. Place the biscuits, sides touching, on a baking sheet.
◼ Bake the biscuits in the preheated oven for about 18–20 minutes, or until they are lightly browned. Let cool.
◼ Right before serving, whip the cream in a deep bowl until soft peaks form. Whisk in the powdered sugar and liqueur, and a spoonful of berry juice, if desired. Split the biscuits in half crosswise.
◼ On each of 6 large chilled plates, place a split biscuit bottom, spoon berries over it, and top with a dollop of whipped cream. Place the biscuit top on slightly askew. Garnish with mint sprigs, if you like. Dust the rims of the plates with powdered sugar shaken from a sieve or a shaker can. And, for the ultimate presentation, top off with edible flowers, if desired.

SERVES 6

Islands

CARAMEL-WALNUT PIE

Old walnut and filbert trees, planted by Scots pioneers, dot the landscape of Vancouver Island. One of the best uses for a fall bumper crop is this pie, sweet with caramel and crunchy with toasted nuts.

½ recipe basic pie pastry (see glossary)
1 cup (8 oz/250 g) sugar
2 cups (16 fl oz/500 ml) half & half (half milk and
    half cream)
⅓ cup (1½ oz/45 g) all-purpose (plain) flour
2 teaspoons butter
3 egg yolks, beaten
1 vanilla bean (pod) or 1 teaspoon vanilla extract (essence)
1 cup (4 oz/125 g) toasted walnuts
¼ teaspoon freshly grated nutmeg

◨ Prepare the pie pastry dough. On a lightly floured surface, roll out the dough. Fit the pastry into a 9-in (23-cm) pie pan. Flute the edges and set the shell aside.

◨ In a large, heavy saucepan, caramelize the sugar by stirring it over high heat until the sugar turns golden brown, about 10 minutes; take care not to burn it. Remove the syrup from the heat immediately, as it will continue to cook. Bring the half & half to a low boil in another saucepan. Warm the caramelized sugar to low heat and gradually stir the hot half & half into it, using a long-handled wooden spoon. If the caramel balls up in the cream, continue stirring until it melts into the sauce. Remove from the heat and let cool to room temperature, about 30 minutes.

◨ Whisk the flour, butter and egg yolks into the cooled caramel. Slit the vanilla bean lengthwise and scrape the seeds into the mixture. Stir in the walnuts.

◨ Sprinkle the nutmeg over the pastry shell, pour in the filling mixture and bake in the oven for 10 minutes. Reduce the heat to 325°F (170°C) and bake for 30 minutes longer, or until a knife inserted in the center comes out clean.

SERVES 6

Islands

MULLED WINTER CIDER

Many orchard-loving farmers in the San Juans have managed to keep their eighty- and ninety-year-old fruit trees healthy. The hard work pays off in the fall when antique varieties of apples hang heavy on the fragile limbs. Every October on Orcas Island, the Boy Scouts sell orchard-pressed cider for their fall fund-raiser.

8 cups (64 fl oz/2 l) fresh apple cider
15 whole cloves
½ cup (4 oz/125 g) sugar
6 cinnamon sticks
10 allspice berries
10 juniper berries

◨ Combine all of the ingredients in a large nonaluminum stockpot. Bring to a boil, then reduce heat to a simmer for 15 minutes. Remove from the heat, cover, and let steep for at least 1 hour or up to 12 hours. Strain the cider to remove the spices and reheat to serve.

SERVES 8–10   *Photograph page 230*

Caramel-Walnut Pie

Oregon

FIG TART WITH WALNUTS

Fresh figs are the ultimate summer fruit. Try them with the Coppa-Cured Pork Tenderloins (recipe on page 141), and in this tart, sweet conclusion to a meal in the garden.

1 recipe Walnut Pastry Crust (see Rhubarb Cheesecake Tart on page 214)
1 cup (8 fl oz/250 ml) milk
2 cups (1 lb/500 g) sugar
1 tablespoon vanilla extract (essence)
3 tablespoons cornstarch (cornflour)

½ teaspoon salt
4 egg yolks
1 cup (8 fl oz/250 ml) half & half (half milk and half cream)
2 cups (16 oz/500 ml) Pinot Noir
12 fresh figs, halved
1 cup (4 oz/125 g) toasted and coarsely chopped walnuts (see glossary)

▨ Prepare the dough for the pastry crust following the instructions on page 214.
▨ To make the pastry cream: In a heavy saucepan over medium-low heat, combine the milk, 1 cup (8 oz/ 250 g) sugar, vanilla, cornstarch and salt. Bring to a simmer and cook for

Preheat an oven to 375°F (190°C). Meanwhile, roll the pie dough out on a lightly floured board to a 14-in (35-cm) circle. Line a 10-in (25-cm) fluted tart pan with the crust, allowing it to hang evenly over the edge. Tuck the edges of the dough completely down inside the rim of the pan, crimp the border, and prick the bottom evenly with a fork. Line the shell with aluminum foil, fill with pie weights or dried beans, and bake in the preheated oven for about 15–20 minutes, or until golden brown and crisp, pressing down any spots that arise unevenly during baking. Remove from the oven and let cool completely.

Pour the pastry cream into the tart and smooth it with a spatula. Arrange the poached fig halves in a decorative manner on top of the cream and brush them with the topping. Top with the toasted walnuts.

SERVES 8

Western Washington

SPARKLING BERRY KIR

Raspberries are suggested, but any sweet, ripe berries such as strawberries or blackberries will do nicely. Or you may want to experiment with other seasonal fruits and their respective liqueurs, such as juicy apricots paired with apricot brandy.

1 cup (6 oz/185 g) fresh or frozen raspberries
2 tablespoons sugar
¼ cup (2 fl oz/ 60 ml) berry liqueur
2 bottles chilled sparkling wine or champagne
fresh whole raspberries for garnish
fresh mint sprigs for garnish (optional)

In a blender, place the raspberries, sugar and liqueur. Blend on low speed for 30 seconds, then increase to high until smoothly puréed. Press through a fine strainer and refrigerate until needed.

To serve: Spoon about 1 tablespoon of the berry purée into each of 12 chilled champagne glasses. Fill with sparkling wine or champagne, add 2–3 fresh berries, and garnish with mint, if desired. Serve immediately.

SERVES 12

Sparkling Berry Kir

Fig Tarts with Walnuts

5 minutes, stirring frequently. Beat the egg yolks into the half & half and gradually whisk this mixture into the pan. Continue stirring and heating until the pastry cream is smooth and thick. Remove the pastry cream from the heat and pour into a cold bowl. Stir the pastry cream until it cools to room temperature, cover, and refrigerate.

To make the topping: Combine the remaining 1 cup (8 oz/250 g) sugar and Pinot Noir in a nonaluminum saucepan and bring to a simmer over medium heat. Add the figs and poach until tender, 7–10 minutes. Remove the figs with a slotted spoon and set them aside on a plate. Cook the wine over medium heat for about 20–25 minutes, or until reduced to a thick syrup. Remove from the heat and set aside.

Eastern Washington

SUN TEA WITH ROSE HIPS AND FRESH MINT

A jug of tea brewing on the deck or the back porch is a sure sign of summer. Rose hips and dried hibiscus may be purchased in spice shops or natural foods stores. Rose hips are high in vitamin C, and, combined with the hibiscus flower, they give tea a rich rosy color.

4 tablespoons good black tea tied in a square of cheesecloth (muslin)
3–4 tablespoons dried rose hips or dried hibiscus flowers, or a mixture of both
3–4 fresh mint sprigs
1 lemon, cut into slices
lemon slices and mint sprigs for garnish

 Place the tea, rose hips, mint and lemon in a large 16-cup (128-fl oz/4-l), clear-glass jug. Fill with cool water, cover, and place in a sunny spot for 2–3 hours, or until the tea is a rich color.
 Strain and serve over ice, garnished with lemon and mint.

MAKES 14–16 CUPS (112–128 FL OZ/3.5–4 L)

Oregon

BAKED BLUEBERRY CLAFOUTI

This Northwest version of the French clafouti is easy to make for a picnic or barbecue dinner. Any summer berry or chopped soft fruit may be used in place of the blueberries.

4 eggs
2 cups (16 fl oz/500 ml) milk
½ cup (2 oz/60 g) all-purpose (plain) flour
1 tablespoon ground cinnamon
1 cup (5 oz/155 g) sifted powdered (icing) sugar
½ teaspoon salt
2 cups (12 oz/375 g) blueberries
2 tablespoons butter

 Preheat an oven to 375°F (190°C). Meanwhile, in a large bowl, beat the eggs and milk together, then gradually stir in the flour, cinnamon, ¾ cup (4 oz/125 g) of the powdered sugar and the salt. Beat until smooth. Gently fold in the blueberries.
 Generously butter a large, heavy skillet or 12-in (30-cm) fluted flan dish. Pour in the batter and bake in the oven until golden brown and set, about 45 minutes. Let cool and sprinkle with the remaining powdered sugar to serve.

SERVES 6-8   *Photograph page 210*

Eastern Washington

OATMEAL FRUIT GEMS

This variation on the classic oatmeal cookie uses dried cherries or apricots in place of raisins. Crisp and chewy, these cookies are perfect with a glass of milk or a cup of tea. Store in a covered container.

1½ cups (12 oz/375 g) butter at room temperature
1½ cups (8 oz/250 g) brown sugar, packed
1½ cups (12 oz/375 g) granulated sugar
3 eggs
2¼ cups (9 oz/280 g) all-purpose (plain) flour
½ teaspoon salt
1½ teaspoons baking soda (bicarbonate of soda)
1 teaspoon vanilla extract (essence)
4½ cups (14 oz/440 g) uncooked oatmeal (rolled oats)
1½ cups (8 oz/250 g) coarsely chopped dried cherries or apricots

Sun Tea with Rose Hips and Fresh Mint, Oatmeal Fruit Gems

⬛ In a large bowl, cream the butter and sugars until light. Add the eggs and mix until well combined. Add the flour, salt, baking soda, vanilla and oatmeal, and mix at low speed until thoroughly combined. Add the dried fruit and stir to distribute the fruit evenly.

⬛ Place the dough in the refrigerator to chill for 20 minutes. Meanwhile, preheat an oven to 400°F (200°C).

⬛ Drop spoonfuls of dough 2 in (5 cm) apart on greased baking sheets and flatten each spoonful with your fingertips.

⬛ Bake in the preheated oven for 8–10 minutes, or until the edges of the cookies are browned (the centers may appear slightly underbaked). Let cool on the pans for 5 minutes before removing to wire rack to cool completely.

MAKES 42–48 COOKIES

221

Western Washington

MILE-HIGH FRESH PLUM CAKE

Italian plum trees abound in western Washington backyards, usually producing bumper crops. These plums, sometimes called prunes, are popular stewed and served as a breakfast fruit or used in desserts.

PLUM COMPOTE

1½ lb (750 g) purple plums, pitted and cut into quarters,
 about 4 cups
2 tablespoons water
1 cup (8 oz/250 g) sugar
½ teaspoon ground cinnamon

CAKE

¾ cup (6 oz/180 g) butter
2 cups (1 lb/500 g) sugar
1 teaspoon vanilla extract (essence)
2 teaspoons grated orange zest
3 cups (12 oz/375 g) all-purpose (plain) flour
1 tablespoon baking powder
¼ teaspoon salt
1 cup (8 fl oz/250 ml) milk
6 egg whites

Rhubarb-Strawberry Fool

ORANGE CREAM

1½ cups (12 fl oz/375 ml) heavy (double) cream
¼ cup (1½ oz/45 g) sifted powdered (icing) sugar
2 teaspoons grated orange zest
3 tablespoons orange juice

☒ To make the compote: Place the plums in a large pan, add water, and sprinkle with sugar and cinnamon. Cook over medium heat until the plums release some juice, then cover with a lid and cook for 15 minutes. Uncover the plums and cook 10 minutes longer, or until they are nicely thickened to a jamlike consistency. Remove from the heat and let cool.

☒ To make the cake: Preheat an oven to 350°F (180°C). Butter and flour three 8-in (20-cm) round cake pans. Cream the butter and 1½ cups (12 oz/375 g) of the sugar with the vanilla and orange zest. Then sift together the flour, baking powder and salt. Add alternately with the milk to the creamed mixture, stirring until smooth, then transfer to a large bowl.

☒ In a large bowl, whip the egg whites until soft peaks form, then gradually sprinkle in the remaining ½ cup (4 oz/125 g) sugar and beat until stiff but not dry. Mix one fourth of the whites into the cake batter to lighten it, then gently fold in the remaining whites.

☒ Divide the cake batter evenly among the prepared cake pans. Top each cake with ¼ cup (2 fl oz/60 ml) of the cooled plum compote, swirling it over the batter. Bake in the preheated oven for 30 minutes. Let cool for 5 minutes, then remove and let cool on a rack.

☒ To make the orange cream: In a deep bowl, whip the cream and powdered sugar until soft peaks form. Whisk in the orange zest and orange juice.

☒ To assemble: On the first layer of cake place one half of the remaining plum compote and spread it ½ in (1.5 cm) from the edge of the cake. Top with a second cake layer and repeat with remaining the plum compote. Top with the remaining cake layer. Frost the cake with the orange whipped cream and chill until ready to serve.

SERVES 8–10

British Columbia

RHUBARB-STRAWBERRY FOOL

This dessert is as easy as it is delicious. Originally served in a Granville Island restaurant as a rhubarb fool, the addition of strawberries makes it even better.

1 lb (500 g) rhubarb, trimmed
1 cup (8 oz/250 g) sugar, according to tartness of rhubarb
2 tablespoons fresh lemon juice
1½ cups (12 fl oz/375 ml) heavy (double) cream
1 cup (6 oz/185 g) sliced fresh strawberries
¼ cup (1 oz/30 g) slivered almonds, toasted (see glossary)
4 whole strawberries for garnish

☒ Preheat an oven to 350°F (180°C). Cut the rhubarb into 1-in (2.5-cm) pieces and place in a baking dish; sprinkle with the sugar. Cover and bake in the preheated oven for about 35 minutes, or until the rhubarb is tender.

☒ Drain off the liquid. Add the lemon juice to the rhubarb and chill in the refrigerator.

☒ Whip the cream until stiff and fold it into the rhubarb, reserving a little of the whipped cream for garnish. Fold in the sliced strawberries.

☒ Serve in stemmed glasses, garnished with whipped cream, almonds and whole strawberries.

SERVES 4

Mile-High Fresh Plum Cake

Oregon

BING CHERRY FRITTERS

Fruit fritters dusted in powdered sugar are special for either breakfast or dessert. You can use almost any of your favorite fruits in place of the cherries.

2 cups (8 oz/250 g) all-purpose (plain) flour
1 tablespoon baking powder
½ teaspoon salt
2 tablespoons sugar
1 tablespoon ground cinnamon
1⅓ cups (10.5 fl oz/325 ml) milk
4 eggs, separated
1 tablespoon vegetable oil
1 tablespoon fresh lemon juice
2 cups (12 oz/375 g) Bing cherries, pitted
oil for frying
sifted powdered (icing) sugar and whole Bing cherries for garnish

▨ Into a large bowl, sift together the flour, baking powder, salt, sugar and cinnamon. Add the milk, egg yolks, oil and lemon juice and beat until smooth.
▨ In a large bowl, whip the egg whites until soft peaks form, then gently fold them into the batter. Fold in the pitted cherries.
▨ In a deep, heavy saucepan, heat 3 in (7.5 cm) of the oil to 375°F (190°C). Drop a few tablespoonfuls of the batter into the hot oil and fry for 3–5 minutes, or until golden brown. Drain on paper towels and keep warm in a very low oven. Repeat until all the batter is cooked. Serve at once, topped with powdered sugar and garnished with cherries.

MAKES 18–24 FRITTERS; SERVES 6

Oregon

SPICED PANCAKES WITH WHIPPED CREAM AND SUMMER FRUIT

These gingery flapjacks are natural partners for luscious summer fruits and whipped cream. .

1 cup (4 oz/125 g) all purpose (plain) flour
1 cup (4 oz/125 g) buckwheat flour
1 tablespoon baking powder
3 tablespoons sugar
½ teaspoon salt
½ teaspoon ground allspice
1 teaspoon ground ginger
½ teaspoon ground nutmeg
½ teaspoon ground white pepper
2 eggs
1 cup (8 fl oz/250 ml) milk
¼ cup (2 oz/60 g) butter, melted
whipped cream, lightly sweetened with sugar
4 cups (1½ lb/750 g) pitted and sliced summer fruits such as peaches, plums and nectarines

▨ Into a large bowl, sift together the flours, baking powder, sugar, salt and spices. In another bowl, whisk the eggs, milk and melted butter together, then beat them into the dry ingredients, making a smooth batter.
▨ Cook the pancakes on an oiled griddle or skillet, turning them when bubbles appear on the top of the cakes, 3–5 minutes. Cook 1 minute on the second side, or until lightly browned.
▨ Place on individual plates, top with whipped cream and fresh fruit, and serve at once.

SERVES 6   *Photograph page 12*

Bing Cherry Fritters

British Columbia

CRANBERRY BREAD PUDDING

British Columbians like homey foods for dessert, and nothing is more comforting than warm cranberry bread pudding topped with ice cream. Cranberries are grown in Richmond, B.C.—in fact, this area accounts for much of the commercial supply in North America.

6 cups (12 oz/375 g) toasted diced sourdough or whole-wheat bread, packed
1 cup (3 oz/90 g) fresh or frozen cranberries
2 cups (16 fl oz/500 ml) raspberry-cranberry juice
1 cup (8 fl oz/250 ml) honey
½ cup (4 oz/125 ml) butter
1 teaspoon ground cinnamon
½ teaspoon ground nutmeg
1 cup (5 oz/155 g) dried currants

◙ Preheat an oven to 350°F (180°C). Place the bread cubes in a greased 8-cup (64-fl oz/2-l) baking dish. Set aside.
◙ Combine all of the remaining ingredients in a large saucepan and bring to a boil over medium heat. Boil gently just until the cranberries begin to pop. Pour the cranberry mixture over the bread cubes, mixing gently, and let sit for 15 minutes.
◙ Bake the pudding in the preheated oven for 45 minutes, or until bubbly.

SERVES 10

British Columbia

BLUEBERRY BAKED APPLES

You can use either wild or cultivated blueberries for this dessert. The combination of apples and blueberries makes a wonderful plum-colored sauce.

4 Roma or other baking apples, cored
3–4 tablespoons brown sugar, packed
½ teaspoon ground cinnamon

Left to right: Blueberry Baked Apples, Okanagan Apple Cake with Maple Cream

½ teaspoon freshly grated nutmeg
2 cups (12 oz/375 g) blueberries
grated zest of 1 lemon
2 tablespoons chopped walnuts
¼ cup (2 fl oz/60 ml) hot water
1 cup (8 fl oz/250 ml) crème fraîche (recipe follows) or whipped cream

◙ Preheat an oven to 325°F (170°C). Peel the upper quarter of each apple. Mix together all of the ingredients except the hot water and crème fraîche or whipped cream. Place the apples in a baking dish.
◙ Fill the cavities of the apples with the blueberry mixture, allowing some of it to fall into the baking dish.
◙ Pour the hot water around the apples and bake in the preheated oven, basting occasionally, for 35–40 minutes, or until just tender. Remove from the oven and let cool for 10 minutes.
◙ Serve warm with crème fraîche or whipped cream.

SERVES 4

CRÈME FRAÎCHE

Served over fresh fruits and berries, this thick French-style cream is perfect for soups and sauces because it does not curdle.

1 cup (8 fl oz/250 ml) sour cream
2 cups (16 fl oz/500 ml) heavy (double) cream
1 tablespoon fresh lemon juice

◙ Place the sour cream in a large bowl. Slowly whisk in the heavy cream until thoroughly mixed. Cover with plastic wrap and put in a warm place for 8–24 hours or until the mixture has thickened.
◙ Place a plastic coffee filter holder in a mixing bowl and insert a coffee filter paper. Pour the thickened cream mixture into the filter. Cover with plastic wrap, refrigerate and drain for 24–36 hours.
◙ Stir the lemon juice into the thickened cream.

MAKES 2 CUPS (16 FL OZ/500 ML)

British Columbia

OKANAGAN APPLE CAKE WITH MAPLE CREAM

Apple orchards produce abundantly in the Okanagan Valley of south-central British Columbia, and the local roadside stands offer a great variety of apples. Serve this simple apple cake recipe with powdered sugar or maple cream.

1½ cups (6 oz/185 g) unbleached all-purpose (plain) flour
2 teaspoons baking soda (bicarbonate of soda)
½ teaspoon salt
1 teaspoon ground cinnamon
½ teaspoon ground nutmeg
½ cup (4 oz/125 g) butter at room temperature
1 cup (8 oz/250 g) sugar
2 eggs
4 cups (8 oz/250 g) grated peeled apples
1 cup (4 oz/125 g) miller's bran
Maple Cream (recipe follows) or sifted powdered (icing) sugar

◙ Preheat an oven to 350°F (180°C). In a medium bowl, combine the flour, baking soda, salt, cinnamon and nutmeg.
◙ In a large bowl, beat the butter and sugar together until blended. Beat in the eggs. Stir in the apples, bran and dry ingredients and mix well.
◙ Spread the batter evenly in a greased 9-in (23-cm) baking pan. Bake in the preheated oven for 40–45 minutes, or until the center is set and springs back when lightly touched. Let cool.
◙ Serve with maple cream or sprinkle with powdered sugar.

MAKES 8–10 SERVINGS

Cranberry Bread Pudding

MAPLE CREAM

1 cup (8 fl oz/250 ml) maple syrup
½ cup (4 fl oz/125 ml) water
1 tablespoon butter
2 teaspoons flour
½ cup (4 fl oz/125 ml) half & half (half milk and half cream)
1 cup (8 fl oz/250 ml) heavy (double) cream

▨ In a small saucepan, combine the maple syrup and water.

Place over medium heat and boil to reduce to ¾ cup (6 fl oz/180 ml), about 15 minutes.

▨ Melt the butter in a large saucepan. Blend in the flour and half & half and add the reduced maple syrup. Boil, uncovered, until reduced to 1 cup (8 fl oz/250 ml), about 10 minutes. Let cool.

▨ While the mixture cools, whip the heavy cream. Fold the whipped cream into the cooled mixture.

MAKES 1½ CUPS (12 FL OZ/375 ML)

MT. ST. HELENS CRATER COOKIES

Fill the thumbprint in each of these rich nut cookies with your favorite jam, jelly or homemade Himalaya Blackberry Preserves (recipe on page 174).

¼ cup (2 oz/60 g) butter at room temperature
¼ cup (2 oz/60 g) vegetable shortening (vegetable lard)
¼ cup (1½ oz/45 g) brown sugar, packed
1 egg, separated
1 teaspoon pure vanilla extract (essence)
½ teaspoon grated lemon zest
pinch of ground nutmeg
¼ teaspoon salt
1 cup (4 oz/125 g) all-purpose (plain) flour
1 cup (4 oz/125 g) minced hazelnuts
about 6 tablespoons (3 fl oz/80 ml) jam or preserves

▨ Preheat an oven to 350°F (180°C). In a large bowl, cream together the butter, shortening, sugar, egg yolk, vanilla and lemon zest.
▨ Mix together the dry ingredients and stir into the creamed mixture. Roll heaping teaspoonfuls of the dough into balls, dip in the reserved egg white, then coat with the nuts. Place 1½ in (4 cm) apart on an ungreased baking sheet. Press your thumb gently into the center of each cookie. Fill each indentation with jam or preserves.
▨ Bake in the preheated oven for 10–12 minutes, or until just set. Let cool on a rack.

MAKES ABOUT 36 COOKIES

JAVA CITY ICED MOCHA

Seattle has been called the "espresso capital of the nation," as it seems to have an espresso cart on practically every corner. Refreshing iced mochas are favorites during the warm summer months.

1 cup (8 fl oz/250 ml) cold strong espresso
1 teaspoon pure vanilla extract (essence)
1 tablespoon sugar
2 oz (60 g) bittersweet (plain) chocolate, cut into small chunks

BITTER CHOCOLATE BRANDY CREAM

2 teaspoons unsweetened cocoa powder
1 tablespoon sugar
¼ cup (2 fl oz/60 ml) heavy (double) cream
1 tablespoon brandy (optional)

1 cup (8 fl oz/250 ml) half & half (half milk and half cream)
shaved dark chocolate for garnish (optional)

▨ In a small saucepan, heat the espresso, vanilla and sugar over medium heat and whisk in chocolate. Remove from heat and stir until chocolate is melted. Let cool, then chill.
▨ Meanwhile, to make the brandy cream: In a small bowl, whisk together the cocoa and sugar. Add the cream and whip until soft peaks form. Stir in the brandy.
▨ Fill 4 tall 8-oz (20-cm) glasses with ice. Divide the cold espresso mixture among the glasses. Drizzle in the half & half evenly among them, then top with the brandy cream. Sprinkle the tops with shaved chocolate, if desired.

SERVES 4

Left to right: Mt. St. Helens Crater Cookies, Java City Iced Mocha

Eastern Washington

PUMPKIN-PECAN CAKE

This beautifully flavored and textured cake stays moist for several days. The cream cheese icing adds just the right touch of sweetness.

CAKE

3 cups (12 oz/375 g) all-purpose (plain) flour
3 cups (24 oz/750 g) sugar
3 teaspoons baking soda (bicarbonate of soda)
2 teaspoons ground cinnamon
½ teaspoon ground cloves
¼ teaspoon ground nutmeg
1½ cups (12 fl oz/375 ml) corn oil
4 eggs
2 teaspoons vanilla extract (essence)
2 cups (16 fl oz/500 ml) cooked pumpkin purée
8 oz (250 g) crushed pineapple, drained
1½ cups (6 oz/185 g) chopped pecans

ICING

8 oz (250 g) cream cheese at room temperature
⅓ cup (3 oz/90 g) unsalted butter at room temperature
3 cups (15 oz/ 470 g) sifted powdered (icing) sugar
1 teaspoon vanilla extract (essence)

◻ Preheat an oven to 350°F (180°C). Butter and flour two 9-in (23-cm) round cake pans.
◻ To make the cake: In a large bowl, combine the flour, sugar, baking soda and spices. Add the oil, eggs and vanilla; beat well. Add the pumpkin, pineapple and pecans and mix to combine well.
◻ Pour the batter into the prepared pans and bake in the oven for 30–35 minutes, or until a toothpick inserted in the center of each layer comes out clean. Let cool for 5 minutes, remove from the pans, and let cool completely on a wire rack before icing.
◻ To make the icing: In a small bowl, cream the cream cheese and butter until light and smooth. Add the powdered sugar gradually and beat until smooth and creamy. Stir in the vanilla.

Pumpkin-Pecan Cake, Mulled Winter Cider (page 216)

If the icing is too soft, gradually add more sugar until the icing is a spreadable consistency.

◙ Spread some icing on top of one layer and place the second layer on top. Ice the sides and top of the cake with the remaining icing. Let sit until the icing is set before cutting into wedges to serve.

SERVES 12

Oregon
NECTARINE ICE CREAM

Homemade ice cream—what could be better? Especially ice cream made from ripe nectarines. You can also use peaches, plums or berries in place of the nectarines.

ICE CREAM BASE

8 egg yolks
1 cup (8 oz/250 g) sugar
3 cups (24 fl oz/750 ml) milk
2 cups (16 fl oz/500 ml) heavy (double) cream

COMPOTE

1 cup (8 oz/250 g) sugar
3–4 tablespoons fresh lemon juice, depending on tartness
    of fruit
6 fresh nectarines, pitted, peeled and diced, about 1½ lb (750 g)

◙ To make the ice cream base: In a large mixing bowl, beat the egg yolks until they are pale and thick. Gradually beat in the sugar until the mixture is light and fluffy. Gradually whip in the milk and then the cream.

◙ Transfer the mixture to a saucepan and stir with a wooden spoon over low heat until lightly thickened, 7–10 minutes, taking care not to scorch.

◙ Pour the mixture into a large bowl and let cool to room temperature, stirring frequently. Place in the freezer for 3–5 hours, or until partially frozen, stirring every 30 minutes to prevent ice crystals from forming, or partially freeze in an ice cream maker according to the manufacturer's instructions.

◙ Meanwhile, to make the compote: In a medium nonaluminum saucepan, heat the sugar and lemon juice over low heat. When the sugar dissolves and the mixture begins to boil, add the nectarines and simmer until tender, 4–6 minutes.

◙ Chill the compote completely in the refrigerator, then mix it thoroughly into the partially frozen ice cream base. Let the ice cream mixture freeze to the desired texture, continuing to stir every 30 minutes if freezing it in a bowl. To finish freezing in an ice cream maker, follow the manufacturer's instructions.

MAKES 6 CUPS (48 FL OZ/1.5 L)

Islands
NANAIMO BARS

This three-layer bar originated in the village of Nanaimo, on the northern end of Vancouver Island, and has achieved fame (or infamy) over the islands for its richness. This recipe comes from April Point lodge, British Columbia's premier salmon-fishing resort, on Quadra Island.

BOTTOM LAYER

½ cup (4 oz/125 g) butter
1 teaspoon vanilla extract (essence)
5 tablespoons (1½ oz/45 g) unsweetened cocoa
¼ cup (2 oz/60 g) sugar
1 egg, beaten
2 cups (8 oz/250 g) crushed graham crackers
½ cup (1½ oz/45 g) shredded coconut
½ cup (2 oz/60 g) chopped walnuts

Top to bottom: Nectarine Ice cream, Nanaimo Bars

MIDDLE LAYER

2 cups (12 oz/375 g) sifted powdered (icing) sugar
4 tablespoons (2 oz/60 g) unsalted butter at room temperature
2 tablespoons instant vanilla pudding mix
2 tablespoons milk
1 teaspoon vanilla extract (essence)

TOP LAYER

4 oz (125 g) semisweet (plain) chocolate
¼ cup (2 oz/60 g) butter

◙ To make the bottom layer: In a large double boiler over barely simmering water, slowly melt the first 4 ingredients together. Add the egg and whisk until blended. Remove from the heat and let cool.

◙ Stir in the graham cracker crumbs, coconut and chopped walnuts. Press the mixture into a 9-in (23-cm) square cake pan.

◙ To make the middle layer: Blend together the powdered sugar and butter. Mix together the instant pudding, milk and vanilla. Add this to the sugar mixture and pour over the bottom layer. Chill.

◙ To make the top layer: Stir the chocolate and the butter in a double boiler over barely simmering water until smooth. Spread on top of the middle layer and chill for at least 1 hour before slicing.

MAKES TWELVE 1½-IN (4-CM) SQUARES

Eastern Washington

HUCKLEBERRY SLUMP

Native huckleberries are the reward for many a hiker throughout the timberline areas of the Cascade Mountains, and for some families a trip to the huckleberry fields in the shadow of Mt. Adams is a yearly ritual. Huckleberry slump, or "huckle buckle," as it's sometimes called, is a favorite campfire treat, but it's just as good at home.

4 cups (1½ lb/750 g) huckleberries or blueberries
1 cup (8 oz/250 g) sugar
2 cups (16 fl oz/250 ml) water
juice of 1 lemon
2 cups (8 oz/250g) all-purpose (plain) flour
1 tablespoon baking powder
¼ cup (2 oz/60 g) sugar
½ teaspoon salt
grated zest of 1 lemon
¼ cup (2 oz/60 g) butter
1 cup (8 fl oz/250 ml) canned evaporated milk or half & half
   (half milk and half cream)
heavy (double) cream or crème fraîche

❖ In a large nonreactive Dutch oven or heavy saucepan, cook the berries, sugar and water over medium heat, stirring frequently, until the mixture boils. Boil for 5 minutes. Add the lemon juice and keep hot.
❖ Mix the flour, baking powder, sugar, salt and lemon zest together in a bowl. Cut in the butter with a pastry cutter or 2 knives until the mixture resembles coarse meal. Add the milk or half & half all at once, and stir with a fork until the ingredients are barely mixed.
❖ Drop the batter by spoonfuls into the hot huckleberry mixture. When the dumplings rise to the surface, cover and cook over medium heat until the dough is cooked through, about 10–15 minutes. Serve warm with heavy cream or crème fraîche.

SERVES 8

Eastern Washington

PEACH UPSIDE-DOWN GINGERBREAD CAKE WITH LEMON CREAM

Old-fashioned gingerbread and fresh peaches are a winning combination. The lemon cream is a lovely addition.

CAKE

3 large peaches
7 tablespoons (3½ oz/105 g) unsalted butter at room temperature
¾ cup (5 oz/150 g) plus 1 tablespoon brown sugar, packed
1 egg
½ cup (4 fl oz/125 ml) unsulfured molasses
1¼ cups (5 oz/155 g) all-purpose (plain) flour
½ teaspoon baking soda (bicarbonate of soda)
1 teaspoon ground cinnamon
½ teaspoon ground nutmeg
½ teaspoon ground cloves
1 teaspoon ground ginger
½ cup (4 fl oz/125 ml) buttermilk

LEMON CREAM

2 cups (16 fl oz/500 ml) heavy (double) cream
¼ cup (2 oz/60 g) sugar
3 egg yolks, lightly beaten
grated zest of 1 lemon

❖ Preheat an oven to 350°F (180°C). Meanwhile, to make the cake: Drop the peaches into boiling water for 5 seconds. Let cool slightly and remove the skins.
❖ In a 10-in (25-cm) cast-iron or ovenproof skillet, melt 3 tablespoons of the butter. Remove from the heat and sprinkle ½ cup (3 oz/90 g) of the brown sugar evenly over the bottom of the pan. Cut the peaches in half, remove the pits, and cut into ¼-in (6-mm) slices. Arrange the slices in a clockwise direction, overlapping them slightly to cover the bottom of the skillet; set aside.
❖ In a medium bowl, beat the remaining 4 tablespoons (2 oz/60 g) of butter and the remaining ¼ cup (1½ oz/45 g) plus 1 tablespoon brown sugar until well combined. Add the egg, then the molasses, and mix until blended.
❖ Sift the dry ingredients together and add alternately with the buttermilk to the batter, mixing until smooth. Pour the batter over the peaches.
❖ Bake in the oven for 35–40 minutes, or until a toothpick inserted in the center comes out clean. Let cool for 5 minutes, then turn upside down on a serving platter.
❖ While the cake is baking, make the lemon cream: In a heavy saucepan, mix together all of the ingredients. Stirring constantly with a wooden spoon, cook over medium heat until the mixture thickens and coats the back of the spoon, about 10 minutes. Strain the sauce and let cool. Cover with plastic and refrigerate until cold.
❖ Serve the sauce over slices of the cake or on the side.

SERVES 8

Eastern Washington

CAMPFIRE COFFEE

"Boiled" coffee can rival good espresso, especially when served around a campfire or by a wood stove in a farm kitchen. It is important to have the coffee coarsely ground to avoid a muddy brew. Anise or caraway seed is sometimes added to the pot, and a shot of brandy is served alongside each cup. The eggshell helps to settle the grounds.

8 tablespoons (2 oz/60 g) coarsely ground coffee
1 eggshell
1¼ cups (10 fl oz/300 ml) cold water
4 cups (32 fl oz/1 l) boiling water
1 teaspoon aniseed or caraway seed (optional)

❖ Combine the coffee, eggshell and 1 cup (8 fl oz/250 ml) of the cold water in a flameproof coffeepot or saucepan. Add the boiling water and simmer over low heat for several minutes. Remove from the heat. Add the anise or caraway seed if desired, cover, and let steep in a warm place for about 10 minutes.
❖ Just before serving, splash the remaining ¼ cup (2 fl oz/60 ml) cold water into the pot to settle the grounds.

SERVES 4

Clockwise from top left: Huckleberry Slump, Campfire Coffee, Peach Upside-Down Gingerbread Cake with Lemon Cream

Pinot Noir-Poached Pears with Chocolate Sabayon

PINOT NOIR-POACHED PEARS WITH CHOCOLATE SABAYON

These luxurious pears are ideal for the finale of a special dinner party. A chilled glass of Oregon's Clear Creek pear brandy is the perfect companion.

6 ripe pears (2½ lb/1.2 kg), peeled, left whole, and cored from the bottom, leaving stem intact, preferably Comice or D'Anjou
3 cups (24 fl oz/750 ml) Oregon Pinot Noir
1 cup (8 oz/250 g) sugar
CHOCOLATE SABAYON

6 egg yolks
¾ cup (6 fl oz/180 ml) crème de cacao
1 tablespoon unsweetened cocoa powder
⅓ cup (3 oz/90 g) sugar
6 fresh mint sprigs for garnish (see glossary)
½ cup (4 fl oz/125 ml) crème fraîche or sour cream

In a medium nonaluminum saucepan, gently simmer the peeled pears with the Pinot Noir, sugar and enough water to cover until tender, 30–40 minutes. Remove the pears with a slotted spoon, increase the heat to medium, and cook to reduce the poaching liquid to a syrup, taking care not to burn it, 30–45 minutes. Ladle the syrup over the pears and set aside.

To make the chocolate sabayon: In a double boiler, whisk the egg yolks, liqueur, cocoa and sugar over simmering water, constantly whipping until the mixture is light and fluffy and will retain the mark of the whisk on its surface for a moment.

Remove the sabayon from the heat. Pour it equally into the center of each of 6 dessert plates. Rim the outer edge of the sabayon with the Pinot Noir syrup and place a pear on each plate. Drizzle with crème fraîche or sour cream and serve at once, garnished with a mint sprig.

SERVES 6

STRAWBERRY ICE CREAM

Wild strawberries are abundant in the meadows and wood-lands of the San Juan Islands, but they are not an easy crop to harvest. The locals get there first: birds, deer and ground squirrels, even eagles, can spot the bright red berries from above. The cultivated Shuksan and Quinalt strawberries, or other flavorful local varieties, are a more practical choice for this beautiful ice cream.

4 cups (1½ lb/750 g) fresh ripe strawberries
1–1¾ cups (8–14 oz/250–440 g) sugar, depending on sweetness of berries
1 teaspoon vanilla extract (essence)
1 tablespoon Grand Marnier
4 egg yolks
1½ cups (12 fl oz/375 ml) half & half (half milk and half cream)
2½ cups (20 fl oz/625 ml) heavy (double) cream
½ cup (4 fl oz/125 ml) plain yogurt

Wash and hull the strawberries gently in cool water, being careful not to bruise them. In a large bowl, place the berries, sugar, vanilla and Grand Marnier. Using 2 table knives, cut across the berries in rows, then turn the bowl and cut across the berries again in the other direction. Let the berries sit for 30 minutes.

Meanwhile, place 2 of the egg yolks in a large bowl and whisk until pale yellow. In a medium saucepan, whisk the remaining 2 egg yolks with 1 cup (8 fl oz/250 ml) of the half & half. Bring to a simmer over medium heat, whisking constantly, and cook just until the cream begins to bubble at the edges, about 8 minutes.

Pour the hot cream mixture into the bowl of egg yolks, whisking constantly. Add the remaining half & half, yogurt, cream and berries. Stir gently. Chill for 30 minutes, then freeze in an ice cream freezer according to the manufacturer's instructions.

MAKES 8 CUPS (64 FL OZ/2 L)

Strawberry Ice Cream

LEMON-RASPBERRY MERINGUE TART

A bit more special than traditional lemon meringue pie, this tart has a nut crust and a lemon curd filling speckled with fresh raspberries.

PASTRY

5 oz (155 g) hazelnuts, walnuts or almonds
3 tablespoons sugar
¼ teaspoon ground nutmeg

1½ cups (6 oz/185 g) all-purpose (plain) flour
½ cup (4 oz/125 g) butter
1 egg, beaten

FILLING AND MERINGUE

8 eggs
1 cup plus 6 tablespoons (11 oz/340 g) sugar
2 teaspoons grated lemon zest
pinch of salt
½ cup (4 oz/125 ml) fresh lemon juice
¼ cup (2 oz/60 g) cold butter

the dough with a fork. Line the shell with aluminum foil and fill with pie weights or dried beans. Bake in the preheated oven for about 25–30 minutes, or until golden. Let cool on a rack.

To make the filling: In a large stainless steel bowl, place 4 eggs, 4 egg yolks (reserve the 4 whites for the meringue), 1 cup (8 oz/250 g) of the sugar, lemon zest, salt and lemon juice. Place the bowl over but not touching a pan of simmering water. Vigorously beat with a whisk or hand-held mixer until the mixture is nicely thickened, about 9 minutes. Beat in the butter and remove the bowl from the heat. Do not overcook the mixture or it will curdle.

Pour the lemon filling into the baked tart shell. Let cool to room temperature, then arrange the raspberries evenly on top of the filling.

Turn the oven temperature up to 400°F (200°C). To make the meringue: Beat the 4 reserved egg whites and cream of tartar in a large bowl until frothy. Gradually beat in the remaining 6 tablespoons of sugar a little at a time, and continue beating until stiff and glossy but not dry. Pile the meringue onto the tart, sealing it onto the edge of the crust to keep the meringue from shrinking. Swirl the meringue decoratively with a spoon and bake the pie in the preheated oven for 8–10 minutes, or until lightly browned. Let cool completely on a rack.

SERVES 8–10

Lemon-Raspberry Meringue Tart

1½ cups (9 oz/280 g) fresh raspberries
¼ teaspoon cream of tartar

Preheat an oven to 350°F (180°C). To make the pastry: Place the nuts and sugar in a blender or food processor and process until the nuts are chopped fine. In a medium bowl, combine the nut mixture, nutmeg and flour. With a pastry cutter or 2 knives, cut in the butter and then stir in the egg. Refrigerate for 20 minutes.

Meanwhile, butter and flour a fluted 11-in (28-cm) tart pan.

When the dough is chilled, press it evenly into the bottom and sides of the pan. Trim the edges and prick the bottom of

Islands

TRIPLE-CHOCOLATE BOAT BROWNIES

On Puget Sound it can get cold fast, even in summer, and on fall fishing trips the chill comes off the water and into the boat. When restoratives are in order, chocolate provides quick energy. Three kinds of chocolate are used to make these moist brownies glazed with white chocolate. They transport well for picnics, wrapped in plastic or waxed paper.

3 oz (90 g) unsweetened (bitter cooking) chocolate
1 oz (30 g) bittersweet (plain) chocolate
1 cup (8 oz/250 g) butter, cut into small pieces
2 eggs
1½ cups (12 oz/375 g) sugar
1 teaspoon vanilla extract (essence)
¾ cup (3 oz/90 g) all-purpose (plain) flour
¾ cup (4½ oz/140 g) semisweet (plain) chocolate chips
2 oz (60 g) white chocolate
¾ cup (6 fl oz/180 ml) half & half (half milk and half cream)

In a double boiler, melt the unsweetened and bittersweet chocolates over barely simmering water. As the chocolate begins to melt, add the butter in small pieces, stirring well. When the chocolate is completely melted and all the butter is incorporated, set aside to cool.

Preheat an oven to 350°F (180°C). Beat the eggs and sugar together in a large bowl. Add the vanilla, then fold the chocolate mixture into the eggs and sugar, blending completely. Stir in the flour gently until just blended. Do not overmix. Fold in the chocolate chips.

Grease and flour a 9-by-13-in (23-by-32.5-cm) baking pan, spread the batter in the pan with a spatula, and bake in the preheated oven for 25 minutes, or until the brownies are set and begin to pull away from the sides of the pan. Remove from the oven and let cool.

In a double boiler, melt the white chocolate with the half & half over simmering water and stir until smooth. Drizzle the white chocolate mixture over the cooled brownies. Let the glaze set for 30 minutes or so before slicing the brownies into squares.

MAKES 24 LARGE BROWNIES   *Photograph pages 238-239*

British Columbia

BUTTER TARTS

A truly Canadian confection! If you stroll around the market on Granville Island in British Columbia, you will notice lots of happy people with these melt-in-the-mouth tarts.

PASTRY

5–6 cups (20 oz/625 g) all-purpose (plain) flour
2 teaspoons salt
2 teaspoons baking powder
1 lb (500 g) lard, cut into quarters and chilled
1 egg, slightly beaten
1 tablespoon distilled white vinegar

FILLING

2 cups (10 oz/315 g) brown sugar, packed
2 cups (16 fl oz/500 ml) light corn syrup
1 cup (8 oz/250 g) butter
6 large eggs
2 teaspoons vanilla extract (essence)
1½ cups (8 oz/250 g) raisins

☒ To make the pastry: Place the flour, salt and baking powder in the bowl of a food processor. Distribute the lard evenly over the flour mixture and process until the mixture resembles coarse meal.

☒ Place the egg and vinegar in a measuring cup and add enough water to make 1 cup (8 fl oz/250 ml) of liquid. Add to the processor and process just until well incorporated.

☒ To make the pastry by hand, place the flour and salt in a large bowl and mix. Cut in the lard with a pastry blender or 2 knives until the mixture resembles course meal. Place the egg and vinegar in a measuring cup and add enough water to make 1 cup of liquid. Gradually stir the liquid into the flour-lard mixture, adding only enough liquid to make the dough cling together.

☒ Transfer the dough to a lightly floured work surface and shape into 3 flat discs. Cover with plastic wrap and chill for 1 hour, or until the pastry is firm enough to roll out.

☒ On a lightly floured board, roll the dough out to a ⅛-in (3-mm) thickness. Cut into 4-in (10-cm) rounds and fit into 24 muffin cups. Prick the bottoms and sides with a fork.

☒ Preheat an oven to 400°F (200°C). To make the filling: In a large saucepan, stir together the sugar and syrup, bring to a boil, and cook for 5 minutes. Remove from the heat and add the butter.

☒ In a large bowl, beat the eggs and gradually add the hot liquid, beating constantly. Add the vanilla.

☒ Add 1 tablespoon of the raisins to each tart shell and pour the hot mixture almost to the top of each shell.

☒ Bake in the preheated oven for 15–30 minutes, or until pastry is browned. Let cool before removing from pans.

MAKES 24 TARTS

Western Washington

RICE PUDDING WITH CHERRIES

Sweet Bing cherries soaked in amaretto are a colorful new touch for this home-style dessert.

2 tablespoons amaretto liqueur
1½ cups (12 oz/375 g) pitted fresh Bing cherries
⅔ cup (5½ oz/155 g) short-grain rice
4½ cups (36 fl oz/1.2 l) milk
⅓ cup (3 oz/90 g) granulated sugar
½ teaspoon ground cinnamon
¼ teaspoon ground nutmeg
1 egg

2 tablespoons brown sugar, packed
1 teaspoon vanilla extract (essence)
¼ teaspoon almond extract (essence)
1 tablespoon cornstarch (cornflour)
¼ cup (1 oz/30 g) chopped pitted dried cherries or
    dried currants
2 tablespoons butter
½ cup (4 fl oz/125 ml) heavy (double) cream
2 tablespoons sugar
⅓ cup (1½ oz/45 g) sliced almonds, lightly toasted (see glossary)

Clockwise from top left: Butter Tarts, Rice Pudding with Cherries,
Triple-Chocolate Boat Brownies (page 237)

⊠ In a small bowl, mix the amaretto and cherries together; set aside.

⊠ In a large, heavy saucepan, combine the rice, milk and half of the granulated sugar. Bring to a boil, then reduce heat to a low simmer. Cook, stirring occasionally, for 40 minutes, or until the rice is tender.

⊠ Meanwhile, in a small bowl, whisk together the remaining granulated sugar, cinnamon and nutmeg. Then whisk in the egg, brown sugar, vanilla extract, almond extract and cornstarch.

⊠ After the rice has cooked for 40 minutes, stir in the dried cherries or currants. Cook for 5 minutes longer. Turn off the heat, and immediately and vigorously whisk in the egg mixture. The pudding mixture should be thick and creamy. Whisk in the butter, then remove from heat and let cool to room temperature.

⊠ In a deep bowl, whip the cream until frothy, add the sugar, and whip until soft peaks form. Mix the soaked cherries into the cooled rice pudding. Fold in the whipped cream and almonds.

SERVES 6–8

239

HAZELNUT AND APRICOT BISCOTTI

The thing to remember when making biscotti is to make plenty. They keep well, make wonderful gifts, and get eaten quickly, so you might want to double—or triple—this recipe.

4 cups (16 oz/500 g) all-purpose (plain) flour
2½ cups (20 oz/625 g) sugar
1 teaspoon baking powder
½ teaspoon salt
6 eggs
2 egg yolks
1 tablespoon vanilla extract (essence)
1 cup (4 oz/125 g) hazelnuts, toasted, peeled and coarsely chopped (see glossary)
1½ cups (4 oz/125 g) finely diced dried apricots
2 tablespoons water

▦ Preheat an oven to 350°F (180°C). Meanwhile, into a large bowl, sift together the flour, sugar, baking powder and salt. In another bowl, beat together 5 of the eggs, 2 yolks and vanilla. Mix the beaten eggs with the flour mixture and add the hazelnuts and apricots.
▦ On a lightly floured board, knead the dough for 5–7 minutes, or until evenly blended. If the dough is too crumbly to hold together, add a little water.
▦ Divide the dough into 4 parts and roll each of these into a cylinder 2 in (5 cm) in diameter. Place 2 cylinders 3 in (7.5 cm) apart on each of 2 well-greased baking sheets and flatten slightly. Beat the remaining egg with the water and brush each cylinder with the mixture. Bake in the preheated oven for 35 minutes, or until set.
▦ Remove from the oven and reduce the heat to 325°F (165°C). Diagonally slice the biscotti ¾ in (2 cm) thick. Spread the slices out on the baking sheets and return to the oven for 10 minutes, or until just beginning to color. Let cool and store in an airtight jar. Biscotti will keep for up to 2 weeks.
MAKES ABOUT 48 BISCOTTI

GREEN TOMATO MINCEMEAT PIE

Tart-sweet green tomato mincemeat makes a delicious pie. Serve this with ice cream or crème fraîche.

1 recipe basic pie pastry (see glossary)
4 cups (32 fl oz/1 l) Green Tomato Mincemeat (recipe on page 187)
1 tablespoon flour
2 tablespoons cold butter, cut in small pieces
milk and sugar for topping (optional)

▦ Preheat an oven to 450°F (230°C).
▦ Prepare the pastry dough. On a lightly floured surface, roll out 1 ball of dough to fit a 9-in (23-cm) pie pan.
▦ Line the pan with the pastry. Stir the flour into the green tomato mincemeat and mound the mincemeat evenly into the pastry-lined pan. Dot with butter. Roll out the second ball of dough and place the pastry over the mincemeat. Seal and flute the edges with your fingertips. Make several slits in the top crust to allow steam to escape. (For a shiny, sweet top, brush the top crust lightly with milk or water and sprinkle with sugar.)
▦ Bake in the oven for 10 minutes, then reduce the heat to 350°F (180°C) and bake for another 30 minutes, or until golden.
▦ Remove from the oven and let cool for 20 minutes, then cut into wedges and serve.
SERVES 8

Hazelnut and Apricot Biscotti

Green Tomato Mincemeat Pie

Islands

RASPBERRIES WITH WHITE CHOCOLATE–SOUR CREAM SAUCE

In the rich farmland of Lopez Island, raspberries ripen earlier than almost anywhere else in the Pacific Northwest. Madrona Farm on the island trucks its raspberries to Seattle's Pike Place Market daily during the season. As big as a thumb, these berries are dark and tart, with juice as sweet as syrup.

8 cups (2½ lb/1.25 kg) fresh ripe raspberries
5 oz (155 g) white chocolate
1 cup (8 fl oz/250 ml) sour cream
¼ cup (2 fl oz/60 ml) Grand Marnier, Cointreau or other
  fruit liqueur
½ cup (4 fl oz/125 ml) heavy (double) cream

▨ Wash the berries very gently in a bowl of cold water. Drain and set aside.
▨ In a double boiler, warm all of the remaining ingredients over barely simmering water until the chocolate is just melted, whisking occasionally. Do not let this mixture boil.
▨ When the sauce is warm and smooth, pour over the raspberries in individual bowls and serve at once.

SERVES 8

British Columbia

CHOCOLATE PÂTÉ WITH RASPBERRY SAUCE

This exceptionally good pâté is adapted from one of Chef John Bishop's most popular desserts, Death by Chocolate. The pâté may be made ahead and frozen for up to 1 month.

1 cup (8 oz/250 g) butter at room temperature
2 cups (7 oz/220 g) unsweetened cocoa
6 oz (185 g) high-quality bittersweet (plain) chocolate,
  broken into ½-in (1.5-cm) pieces
1 cup (8 fl oz/250 ml) heavy (double) cream
8 large egg yolks
¾ cup (6 oz/185 g) sugar
¼ cup (2 fl oz/60 ml) Scotch whisky
Raspberry sauce (recipe follows)

▨ Line the long sides and bottom of an 8½-by-4½-in (21.5-by-11.5-cm) loaf pan with a sheet of parchment paper or waxed paper extending 3 in (7.5 cm) over each side. Spray or brush the paper and insides of the pan with oil and set aside.
▨ Place the butter and cocoa in a food processor or bowl and process or mix with a wooden spoon until very smooth. Set aside.
▨ Place the chocolate in a double boiler over barely simmering water and stir until just melted. Set aside to cool.
▨ Whip the cream in a deep bowl and set aside.
▨ Combine the egg yolks and sugar in a large bowl. With an electric beater, beat at medium speed until the mixture is thick and pale yellow, 3–5 minutes.
▨ Add the melted chocolate to the egg mixture and beat until well blended. Add the butter-cocoa mixture and beat until smooth. Stir in the Scotch whisky, then gently fold in the whipped cream.
▨ Transfer the mixture to the loaf pan and smooth the top evenly with a spatula. Gently tap the container on the counter to eliminate any air bubbles. Cover and freeze overnight.
▨ To serve: Remove the chocolate pâté from the freezer and let sit at room temperature for 30 minutes. Run a knife along each

short side of the pan and lift the pâté out by the paper wings. Invert on a rectangular platter and carefully peel off the paper.
▨ Place 2 tablespoons of raspberry sauce on each of 16 large dessert plates. With a knife dipped in hot water, cut the pâté into ½-in (1.5-cm) slices and place a slice on each plate.

SERVES 16

Top to bottom: Chocolate Pâté with Raspberry Sauce,
Raspberries with White Chocolate–Sour Cream Sauce

RASPBERRY SAUCE

2 lb (1 kg) frozen sweetened raspberries, thawed
1 tablespoon cornstarch (cornflour)
¼ cup (2 fl oz/60 ml) raspberry liqueur, kirsch or brandy

▨ In a food processor or in 2 batches in a blender, blend the thawed raspberries with their syrup at high speed until thoroughly puréed and slightly frothy. Place a strainer over a saucepan and strain the berries to remove the seeds.

▨ In a small bowl, dissolve the cornstarch in the liqueur. Stir into the raspberry purée. Stir constantly over medium heat until the sauce comes to a boil and thickens. Let cool.

MAKES ABOUT 2 CUPS (16 FL OZ/500 ML)

British Columbia

GREEN APPLE CRÈME BRULÉE

Crème brulée baked in an apple cup: a Northwest angle on a classic custard from Chef John Bishop. You can eat this dessert dish and all.

6 Granny Smith or other tart apples
1 lemon slice
1 vanilla bean (pod), split
1½ cups (12 fl oz/375 ml) heavy (double) cream
6 egg yolks
¼ cup (2 oz/60 g) sugar
pinch salt
1 teaspoon grated orange zest
¼ cup (1½ oz/45 g) sugar

☒ Slice the bottom of each apple so it will stand upright. Cutting crosswise, slice off the top of the apple, leaving at least 1¾–2 in (4.3–5 cm). Using a melon baller, carefully scoop out each apple 1-in (2.5-cm) down and so that the side walls remaining are no more than ⅓ in (8 mm) thick. Rub the top of each apple with the lemon slice to prevent browning and set aside.
☒ Preheat an oven to 325°F (170°C). In a small saucepan over moderate heat bring the vanilla bean and cream to a low simmer. Immediately remove from the heat. Remove the vanilla bean from the cream and scrape out the seeds with a small knife, returning them to the cream. Whisk the egg yolks in a bowl and gradually whisk in the remaining cream. Pour through a fine sieve into a picture or large bowl, add the sugar, salt and orange zest, and stir to combine. Place the apples in a shallow baking pan. Fill the apples with custard.
☒ Bake in the preheated oven for about 25–30 minutes or until a knife comes out almost clean when inserted into custard.
☒ Remove apples from pan, let cool to room temperature and refrigerate until chilled.
☒ Before serving, preheat a broiler (griller). Push brown sugar through a small sieve to evenly cover each custard with a thin layer of brown sugar.
☒ Broil about 3 in (7.5 mm) from the heat for 2–3 minutes, or until

part of the sugar is golden brown, melted and bubbling. Remove from the heat and set aside for 5 minutes for the sugar to harden.
☒ Serve immediately, or refrigerate up to 1 hour.
SERVES 6

Western Washington

APPLE-CRANBERRY PIE

Granny Smith or other tart apples make the tastiest pies, and fresh cranberries add a beautiful splash of color. Serve warm, topped with vanilla ice cream.

1 recipe basic pie pastry (see glossary)
1¼–1½ cups (10–12 oz/310–375 g) sugar
¾ teaspoon ground cinnamon
¼ teaspoon ground nutmeg
3 tablespoons flour
7–8 cups thinly sliced apples (about 2–2½ lb/1.2 kg)
¾ cup (2 oz/60 g) coarsely chopped fresh or frozen
    cranberries
2 tablespoons cold butter, cut into small pieces
milk and sugar for topping (optional)

☒ Preheat an oven to 400°–425°F (200°–220°C). Prepare the pastry dough. Roll out 1 ball to fit a 9-in (23-cm) pie pan. Line a pie pan with the dough.
☒ In a large bowl, toss together the sugar, cinnamon, nutmeg, flour, apples and cranberries. Mound the apple mixture evenly into the pastry-lined pan.
☒ Roll out the second ball of dough for the top crust. Dot the apple mixture with butter and cover with the top crust. Seal and flute the edges with your fingertips. Make several slits in the top crust to allow steam to escape. (For a shiny, sugary top, brush the top crust lightly with milk or water and sprinkle with sugar.)
☒ Bake in the preheated oven until the crust is nicely browned and the apples are cooked through, about 50–60 minutes.
SERVES 8

Green Apple Crème Brulée

Apple-Cranberry Pie

CROW VALLEY PEAR CRISP WITH VANILLA CREAM

In autumn, golden leaves cover the ground in the Northwest pear orchards, and the trees are bare except for pears swaying in the wind. The sturdy Bartlett pear, one of the major varieties grown in

Crow Valley and elsewhere on the islands, is perfect for this country-style dessert.

12 pears, peeled, cored and cut into thin wedges
1 cup (8 oz/250 g) granulated sugar
¾ cup (6 fl oz/180 ml) dry red wine or apple juice
½ cup (4 fl oz/125 ml) pure maple syrup
2 tablespoons fresh lemon juice

❖ Preheat an oven to 350°F (180°C). In a large bowl, combine the pears, granulated sugar, wine or apple juice, syrup, lemon juice and cornstarch. Let sit for 15 minutes.

❖ Meanwhile, combine the oats, brown sugar, flour and cinnamon in a medium bowl. Using a fork, crumble the butter into the mixture. It will be quite dry.

❖ Grease a 9-by-13-in (23-by-32.5-cm) baking pan and fill with the pears. Sprinkle the oatmeal mixture over the top, pressing gently to even it out. Bake in the preheated oven for 35–40 minutes, or until bubbly and golden. Let cool for 30 minutes before serving.

❖ Serve with vanilla cream.

SERVES 12

VANILLA CREAM

1½ cups (12 fl oz/375 ml) heavy (double) cream
3 tablespoons sifted powdered (icing) sugar
2 tablespoons brandy
1 vanilla bean (pod), or 1 tablespoon pure vanilla extract
   (essence)

❖ Combine the cream, sugar and brandy in a chilled deep bowl. Split the vanilla bean lengthwise and scrape the seeds into the bowl (reserve the bean for another use).

❖ Whisk all the ingredients together until soft peaks begin to form. Chill until ready to use.

MAKES ABOUT 3 CUPS (24 FL OZ/750 ML)

Islands

BLACKBERRY COBBLER

The Himalayan blackberry has escaped from garden plots and run amok all over the Pacific Northwest. Considered a pest by some, this prolific vine produces buckets of large berries at the end of every summer. For those intrepid enough to brave the blackberry jungles, the rewards are sweet.

4 cups (1½ lb/750 g) blackberries
1½ cups (12 oz/375 g) plus 3 tablespoons sugar
1 teaspoon vanilla extract (essence)
2 tablespoons cornstarch (corn flour)
½ cup (4 fl oz/125 ml) lemonade, orange juice, ginger ale or
   water
2 cups (8 oz/250 g) all-purpose (plain) flour
2 teaspoons baking powder
¼ cup (2 oz/60 g) unsalted butter
¾ cup (6 fl oz/180 ml) half & half (half milk and half cream)

❖ Preheat an oven to 350°F (180°C). In a large bowl, combine the berries, 1½ cups (12 oz/375 g) of the sugar, vanilla, cornstarch and lemonade. Let the berries sit for 10 minutes.

❖ Meanwhile, sift the flour and baking powder together into a medium bowl. Add the remaining 3 tablespoons of sugar, then cut in the butter with a pastry cutter or 2 knives (or use a food processor to crumble the flour and butter together). Mix in the half & half.

❖ Turn the dough out onto a lightly floured board. Knead lightly for just 1 minute. Pat the dough out gently to ½-in (1.5-cm) thickness and cut into 12 rounds with a 3-in (7.5-cm) biscuit cutter.

❖ Grease a 9-by-13-in (23-by-32.5-cm) baking pan and fill with the berry mixture. Place 3 shortbread rounds on top of the berries across one short end, and 4 in 3 lengthwise rows.

❖ Bake in the oven for about 30 minutes, or until the berries bubble around the edges and the pastry is golden. Let the cobbler cool for 30 minutes before serving.

SERVES 12

Top to bottom: Blackberry Cobbler, Crow Valley Pear Crisp with Vanilla Cream

2 tablespoons cornstarch (cornflour)
1 cup (5 oz/155 g) uncooked oatmeal (rolled oats)
1 cup (5½ oz/170 g) brown sugar, packed
¼ cup (1 oz/130 g) all-purpose (plain) flour
1 tablespoon ground cinnamon
½ cup (4 oz/125 g) butter, cut into pieces
Vanilla Cream (recipe follows)

Vashon Ferry Coffee

Islands

VASHON FERRY COFFEE

Fresh-roasted coffee beans now are available almost everywhere in the United States, but the taste for fresh beans and specialty coffees is a tradition in the Northwest. The Vashon Ferry, part of the old Blackball Line, plied the waters between Anacortes and the islands for more than fifty years. In winter, the galley closed during the long stormy crossings, and passengers brought their own Thermoses of flavored varietal coffee drinks like this one.

7 cups (56 fl oz/1.75 l) water
8 tablespoons (2½ oz/75 g) freshly drip-ground fresh-roasted coffee
¾ cup (6 fl oz/180 ml) dark Jamaican rum or other dark rum
¾ cup (6 fl oz/180 ml) Kahlúa
½ teaspoon vanilla extract (essence)

▨ Bring the water to a boil, let it sit off the heat for a moment, then pour it over the coffee grounds in a drip-style coffee maker. Pour the hot coffee at once into a large Thermos-style carafe and add the rum, Kahlúa and vanilla.

MAKES TEN 6-OZ (180-ML) CUPS

Western Washington

CHOCOLATE ZUCCHINI CAKE

This is a perfect recipe for using up those 20-lb zucchini that hang around your kitchen in the summer. Grated apple or carrot can be substituted for the zucchini. This moist cake freezes exceptionally well.

CAKE

½ cup (4 oz/125 g) butter at room temperature
½ cup (4 fl oz/125 ml) vegetable oil
1 cup (8 oz/250 g) granulated sugar
½ cup (3 oz/90 g) brown sugar, packed
2 eggs
1 teaspoon vanilla extract (essence)
½ cup (4 fl oz/125 ml) buttermilk
½ teaspoon ground cinnamon
½ teaspoon salt
½ teaspoon baking powder
½ teaspoon baking soda (bicarbonate of soda)
2½ cups (10 oz/300 g) all-purpose (plain) flour
¼ cup (1 oz/30 g) unsweetened cocoa powder

½ cup (2 oz/60 g) chopped walnuts
2 cups (8 oz/250 g) grated zucchini (courgettes)
1 cup (4 oz/125 g) semisweet (plain) chocolate chips

GLAZE

1 cup (6 oz/185 g) semisweet (plain) chocolate chips
¼ cup (2 fl oz/60 ml) heavy (double) cream
2 tablespoons strong coffee or espresso

◫ Preheat an oven to 350°F (180°C). To make the cake: Cream together the butter, oil and sugars. Beat in the eggs, vanilla and buttermilk until smooth.

◫ Sift together the dry ingredients; mix into the creamed ingredients a little at a time until incorporated. Stir in the walnuts, zucchini and chocolate chips.

◫ Butter and flour a large (10-cup or 80-fl oz/2.5-l) bundt pan and pour in the batter. Bake in the preheated oven for about 1 hour and 15 minutes, or until a toothpick inserted in the cake comes out clean.

◫ Let the cake cool in the pan for 5 minutes or so, then remove it from the pan and place on a rack to cool.

◫ To make the glaze: In a small pan, heat the chocolate, cream and coffee over low heat until smooth and just melted. Pour over the cake. Let sit for 15 minutes before serving.

SERVES 12

Chocolate Zucchini Cake

AUTHOR INFORMATION

Kathy Casey, a native of Seattle, received her first acclaim as executive chef at Fullers restaurant in Seattle and now heads up her own consulting firm, Kazzy & Associates, specializing in creative food, beverage and concept development. A champion of Northwest bounty, Kathy is host of a companion public television program taking viewers on culinary adventures throughout the beautiful Northwest. Also a freelance writer, her work has appeared in *Food & Wine* and *Simply Seafood.* A high-ranking member of the food chain, Kathy resides in Seattle with her husand John, where they enjoy foraging for wild foods and edible mushrooms.

Gwenyth Caldwell Bassetti moved to Seattle in 1958 soon after graduating from Smith College. In 1972 she and two partners founded The Bakery, a popular luncheon restaurant in Seattle's Pioneer Square. She left Seattle five years later for a new life on a farm outside Goldendale, Washington, where she raised a large family and earned a national reputation as a breeder of Columbia Sheep. Returning to Seattle in 1989, she joined the newly christened Grand Central Bakery, which has introduced rustic European-style breads to the Northwest. She is partner and General Manager of Grand Central Bakery, Inc. which operates a restaurant, deli and retail bakery in the original Pioneer Square location, as well as an independent wholesale division.

Donna Boechler is a North Dakota native. She is a graduate of the California Culinary Academy in San Francisco. In 1984, she opened Great American Food, in San Francisco, which she ran and operated until 1990. Donna and her husband, who is also a chef, are currently part of the management staff of the Grand Central Bakery in Seattle.

Born into a large family in a farming community in up state New York, **Greg Higgins** was raised with an appreciation for the cultivation and traditional presentation of American foods. His culinary apprenticeship and training as a cheese and sausage maker sharpened his appetite for kitchen lore and knowledge. Greg is the Executive Chef of the Heathman Hotel, a member of Preferred Hotels in Portland, Oregon, and the designer and driving force behind B. Moloch/The Heathman Bakery & Pub. An avid organic gardener, Greg raises many heirloom herbs and vegetables that find their way into the emerging regional cuisine of The Heathman.

Seattle-born **Christina Reid Orchid** is the owner and chef of Christina's, a twelve-table restaurant on Orcas Island where she has honed her culinary skills for over twelve years. Her restaurant has drawn attention from many quarters: *The Zagat Survey, Lifestyles of the Rich and Famous, Gourmet, Food & Wine, Travel and Leisure, Vogue, Bazaar, Sunset* and others. A member of a third-generation Washington farming family, she is a champion of the foods and wines of the Northwest region and a popular guest on radio and television. A member of Les Dames d'Escoffier she makes her home at Westbound on Orcas Island.

Kasey Wilson is a Vancouver-based food and wine columnist, restaurant reviewer, travel writer and contributor to several cookbooks and magazines, and author of *The Granville Island Cookbook, Gifts from the Kitchen, Done like Dinner* and *Spirit and Style.* She has studied at La Varenne in Paris and with Julia Child in California, and has attended cooking classes in Japan, Thailand, Hong Kong and Europe. She is a proponent of food safety and was Foodsafe Spokesperson for the Ministry of Health, Government of British Columbia. She has judged cooking competitions such as the National Bread Contest, the Jack Daniels Barbecue Cook-off and the Vancouver Playhouse Wine Festival Dessert Competition. She is a member of the Newspaper Food Editors and Writers Association, and the Vancouver American Wine Society.

ACKNOWLEDGMENTS

Kathy Casey would like to thank the following: Ann Manly for her wondrous and invaluable assistance on everything; John T. Casey, a wonderful husband, helper and taster; Pat Boone and Mike and Ron Rosella of Rosella's Fruit and Produce Co.; Charmaine Eads; Rebecca Naccarato, Dessert Works; Melanie Annin; David Madayag, Sr., Seattle Central Community College Culinary Arts Program; Patrice Benson, Puget Sound Mycological Society; Jon Rowley of Fish Works!; Harry Yoshimura, Mutual Fish Co.; Mike Bakeman, K&N Meats; Jan Grant, County Food and Nutrition Agent, WSU Cooperative Extension, King County; Therese Harvey, Alaska Seafood Marketing Institute; Mary Lou Mills, Washington State Department of Fisheries, Marine Fish and Shellfish Program. She would also like to thank Jane Fraser and Anne Dickerson for their patient guidance and support.

Kasey Wilson would like to thank: Stephen Wong for his wonderfully innovative ideas, Sue Kelly for testing recipes, and Ruy Paes-Braga of the Four Seasons Hotel for his generous support.

Christina Reid Orchid would like to thank: her mother, horticultural expert Emily Snyder Reid, for sharing her knowledge of plant and fruit varieties and giving generous support in the pursuit of her culinary career.

Lane Morgan wishes to thank the following people for farm tours and hospitality: Eunice Farmilant; John Thompson; Rick, Lora Lea and Willow Misterly; Randy and Patty Brown; Barb Mohagen; Loyalty, Victory, Success and Maia Isreal. Also and always, her family for their patience and support, especially her daughter Laurel who is a great traveling companion.

The publishers and the photographers would like to thank the following people and organizations for their assistance in the preparation of this book: Robert Cave-Rogers, Wendely Harvey, Richard VanOosterhout, Dawn Low, Sigrid Chase, Janique Poncelet, Tori Ritchie Bunting, Tara Brown, Fee-ling Tan, Laurie Wertz, Jim Obata, Stuart Laurence, Ken Dellapenta, Beverley Sharpe, Bruce Bailey, Bob Firken; Pinnacle Publishing Services. Yvonne Pederson for helping with props; Michael Reynolds Moroccan Imports; Willie Greens Farms, Monroe Washington; Grand Central Bakery, Seattle, Washington.

GLOSSARY

AL DENTE: An Italian cooking term meaning "to the tooth." It refers to food that is barely tender, with a slight resistance to the teeth when bitten.

ANISE HYSSOP: Sometimes called fragrant giant hyssop, or licorice mint, this ancient herb was used in the Middle East centuries before Christ. Hyssop is one of the flavorings in the liqueur Chartreuse. The anise-mint flavor of hyssop gives an unusual tang to green salads and vegetable soups and is sometimes used with fruits in pies and preserves, stewed peaches and tarts. It is good with cranberries. Substitute: fresh anise leaves or sweet cicely.

ARUGULA: Also known as rocket, *rucolo,* or Italian cress. A nutty, peppery green that grows wild in eastern Washington and is also commercially grown. The blossoms also are edible. Substitute: other peppery greens such as watercress.

BLACK MUSTARD SEED: Most commonly used in Middle Eastern and Indian cooking. Substitute: yellow mustard seed.

BLACK SESAME SEED: Jet black and used as a dramatic garnish. It is earthier tasting than white sesame seed. Available in Asian markets.

CALAMATA OLIVES: Salty, brined Greek olives available in specialty foods markets and well-stocked delis. Substitute: any other salty-brined black olive.

CAPERS: The pickled buds of the caper bush are used in sauces, dressings and other dishes where a piquant flavor is wanted. Available packed in brine or salted.

CASINGS: Cleaned hog or sheep intestines are used in making link sausages; available dry-salted or brined from specialty butcher shops. Store frozen or refrigerated until ready to use; wash salted casings well in cold water before using.

CHÈVRE: A soft fresh goat's milk cheese, tangy in flavor.

CHILI PASTE WITH GARLIC: Lan Chi Chili Paste with Garlic is a recommended brand. Available in Asian markets.

CHINESE BROCCOLI: This vegetable resembles ordinary broccoli but is longer, with larger leaves and more slender stalks. It is harvested just as the flower buds begin to open. Substitute: ordinary broccoli.

CILANTRO: Also called Chinese parsley, Mexican parsley and fresh coriander. The leaves have a bold taste with sharp citrus notes.

CLAMS
Geoduck: This odd-looking king clam reaches sizes up to 3 ft (1 m) including its protruding siphon; it averages 1–3 lbs (500 g–15 kg). After cleaning it is thinly sliced and served raw as sashimi or quickly sautéed or steamed and paired with a flavorful sauce such as black bean. It is also chopped or ground for clam chowder.
Littleneck: Hard-shelled native littlenecks and Manila clams. The littleneck clam was introduced to Northwest waters from Japan and is best prepared steamed. Clams are fresh if the shells are tightly closed or if they close quickly after being tapped. Discard any that fail to open after cooking. Substitute: any small, hard-shelled clam.
Razor: (*Siliqua patula*) a long, narrow, square-edged shell clam from the west coast, 2–10 inches (5–25 cm) in length, with tender ivory meat. They are typically dredged in flour and quickly fried. Substitute: eastern razor clams.

CLARIFIED BUTTER: Best for sautéing because it can be heated to a fairly high temperature without burning. To clarify butter, melt it in a small saucepan over low heat without stirring, then skim and discard any white foam. Spoon the clear butter into a container discarding the milky residue or use it in soups and sauces. Keeps up to 2 months refrigerated in an air tight container.

COCONUT MILK, UNSWEETENED: Unsweetened coconut milk is available in cans and frozen in Asian markets. Thai brands are the best.

CRÈME FRAÎCHE: Culture-thickened cream available in some supermarkets, or you can make your own. Recipe on page 226. Substitute: sour cream.

DUNGENESS CRAB: A West Coast crab averaging 2 lbs (1 kg) in weight and prized for its sweet-flavored meat. The back shell, averaging 7 in (18 cm) across, turns bright reddish-orange when cooked. Available fresh in summer and fall from Alaska, in winter from Washington and Oregon; available frozen year round. Substitute: any high-quality crab meat.

FENNEL: This vegetable has feathery foliage that makes a beautiful garnish, and a crisp celerylike bulb with an aniseed flavor.

FIDDLEHEAD FERNS: The tightly curled young shoot of the ostrich fern (*Matteuccia struthiopteris*) is available frozen and sometimes fresh. Never eat mature fronds of any fern species; be certain of your identification before sampling fresh fiddleheads. Fiddleheads are best steamed or sautéed. Substitute: asparagus.

FISH SAUCE: This flavorful Southeast Asian style sauce is made by layering fresh anchovies with salt in wooden barrels and fermenting them for several months. Vietnamese fish sauce is known as *nuoc mam;* Thai fish sauce is called *nam bla.* They are available in Asian markets.

FRESH GINGERROOT: The fresh, spicy flavor of this tropical rhizome (underground stem) makes it a prized ingredient in Asian-influenced dishes. Fresh ginger is usually peeled before slicing or mincing. The ground dried ginger used in baking is not interchangeable with fresh ginger.

HAZELNUT: Also known as cobnuts or filberts, hazelnuts are a versatile, aromatic nut used to enhance baked goods or delicate savory foods such as fish or poultry. Hazelnuts are cultivated in Europe and North America and must be roasted to remove the skin from the kernel. To roast hazelnuts, spread the nuts in a single layer on a shallow pan or baking tray with edges and bake at 350°F (180°C) for 10–15 minutes or until golden brown. Wrap the warm nuts in a towel or course textured cloth. Rub the nuts briskly in the cloth to loosen the skins.

JULIENNE: To cut into even, matchstick-size strips.

JUNIPER BERRIES: The aromatic berries of the juniper tree or shrub, often used in pickling spices and in game cookery. Juniper berries provide the characteristic flavor of gin.

LEMON BALM: This plant, with its refreshing lemon-scented leaves, is frequently grown in herb gardens; use the leaves in salads, iced tea or with fish.

LEMON GRASS: Fresh lemon grass is sold by the stalk, which averages 1½–2 ft (45–60 cm) in length. Only the lower 8 in (20 cm) of the stalk are used, for the outer and top leaves are tough. Cut the stalk into thin rounds or coarsely chop it to add its delicate lemon perfume to foods. Substitute: dried shredded (not ground) lemon grass soaked in hot water.

LEMON THYME: A fresh herb with dark green, glossy leaves; strong in lemon scent and flavor. Substitute: fresh thyme.

LOP CHANG SAUSAGE: Dried red Chinese sweet pork sausage, available in Chinese groceries and other Asian markets.

LOVAGE: This celerylike herb enjoyed great popularity in the Middle Ages. The leaves are used fresh or dried in soups and sauces, the stems can be used like celery stalks, and the seeds are added to pickling brines, salad dressings and sauces. Substitute: celery leaves.

MIRIN: A sweet Japanese rice wine used for light dressings, sauces and marinades; it is available in Asian markets. Substitute: sweet sherry.

MUSHROOMS
Enoki: A small white clumping Japanese mushroom with very slender stems, available in supermarkets that stock gourmet produce. Cut off the roots before using.
Shiitake: Also called Chinese black mushrooms, they are widely available in dried form in Asian markets, and are becoming more available fresh. Soak in hot water for 30 minutes and cut off the tough stem before using.
Wild: Wild, edible mushrooms, include chanterelles, morels, boletus, hedgehogs (also called cèpes and porcini), matsutakes, oysters, and so on. *Warning:* Always be sure purchased wild mushrooms come from a reliable source, or go with a mycology expert to identify mushrooms when picking your own.

MUSSELS: Most West Coast mussels have a mild flavor. Use only live mussels, which are tightly closed or close quickly when tapped. Rinse fresh mussels thoroughly, then scrub the shells and debeard them by grasping the fuzzy beard firmly and pulling it out of the shell.

PANKO BREADING: Japanese bread crumbs used to coat food for frying, producing a light, crispy breading. Substitute: cracker meal, dried bread crumbs.

PEPPERCORNS, GREEN; PINK: Green peppercorns are usually available canned or freeze-dried; pink peppercorns are available dried. Available at specialty foods stores.

PEPPERS, HOT CHILI: Handle hot chilies with rubber gloves; or take care not to touch face or other sensitive skin before washing your hands. Jalapeños are about 2 in (5 cm) long, with a very hot, dark green meaty flesh; they are widely available fresh or pickled. The ancho, a large, dark mahogany dried chili called Poblano when fresh, is medium to hot in strength; always cook before eating.

PEPPERS, ROASTED: Roast peppers over a gas flame under a broiler, on a grill over hot coals, or in a 475°F (240°C) oven, turning as necessary till the skin is charred black on all sides. Immediately place in a paper bag, close the bag and let cool for 15 minutes, then peel off the skin and remove the seeds and core. Substitute: canned or jarred roast peppers.

PICKLING SALT: Also known as dairy salt, it's free from additives which cloud pickles. It comes in granulated and flaked forms. For volume measurement, allow fifty percent more of flaked form.

PIE PASTRY, BASIC: For a 9-in (23-cm) double-crust pie:
2½ cups (10 oz/315 g) all-purpose (plain) flour
1 teaspoon sugar
½ teaspoon salt
½ cup (4 oz/125 g) cold unsalted butter
½ cup (4 oz/125 g) cold solid vegetable shortening (vegetable lard)
¼ cup (2 fl oz/60 ml) cold water
Combine the flour with the sugar and salt in a bowl. Cut in the butter and shortening until the texture of coarse crumbs. Add the water, a tablespoon at a time, and mix gently with a fork to form a soft dough. Chill for 1 hour or until ready to use.

PORK FAT/BACK FAT: The firm fat from the back of a hog, rather than the soft, rendered belly fat; available from specialty butchers and well-stocked meat departments in supermarkets.

PRESERVING, CANNING: Home preserves and canned goods must be put up in sterilized jars. To sterilize canning jars, boil them gently in water to cover for 10 minutes; leave them in the water until you are ready to fill them. In order to process any of these preserves for shelf-stable storage, further important steps must be followed for the safety of the product. Please contact your local County Cooperative Extension Office found under your County Listings. This office provides current information from the USDA and the Land Grant University System for safe home preserving procedures.

ROSE HIPS: The dried ripened fruits of rose bushes. Rich in vitamin C and tart in flavor, they are packaged to use as an herbal tea and sold in natural foods stores. Or pick and dry your own wild rose hips. Fresh rose hips are used to make rose hip jelly.

SAKE: Japanese rice wine. Widely available. Substitute: dry sherry.

SAKE LEES: Called *kasu* in Japanese, which means "remnants." This flavoring is the remnants from making sake (rice wine) and is used to make Japanese fish marinade, also called *kasu*. Available in well-stocked Japanese groceries.

SALMON
Pink salmon: Also known as humpback or humpies, has a silvery skin; during spawning season this fish develops a large hump on its back. Its flesh is moderately fatty, fine textured, and pale pink.
Silver salmon: Also known as aka coho, has fatty, light pink meat.
King salmon: Also called chinook or spring salmon, has fatty meat ranging in color from vivid red to white; those weighing over 50 lbs (25 kg) are called Tyee. This king of salmon has dark spots on its back and a silver belly, is rich-tasting and favored for grilling.
Chum salmon: Silver-bodied with pale pink flesh that is moderately fatty is often used for smoking.
Sockeye salmon: Has the most vivid red meat of all and is moderately fatty; it is available frozen year round.

SAMBAL OELEK: A hot Southeast Asian chili condiment. Substitute: one-quarter the amount of dried red chili flakes or chili oil.

SAUTÉ: To cook quickly in a hot pan with a small amount of butter or oil.

SCALLOPS
Alaskan weathervane: Found only in Pacific Northwest waters, this is the largest free-swimming scallop in the world. It grows up to 8–10 in (20–25 cm) across. Substitute: sea scallops.
Swimming: Also known as singing pink scallops, they have an oysterlike brininess and a nutty flavor, and their shells seldom grow larger than 3 in (7.5 cm) across. They open and close their translucent pink shell rapidly in order to swim through the water. Steam them in the shell as you would tiny clams, with mild herbs and dry white wine.

SEASONED FLOUR: Combine 1 cup (4 oz/125 g) all-purpose flour, 1 teaspoon salt, ½ teaspoon black pepper and ¼ teaspoon paprika. Mix all together well and store in an air-tight container until needed.

SEMOLINA: Also known as pasta flour, is hard-wheat flour prized for pasta making.

ASIAN (TOASTED) SESAME OIL: This oil is made from toasted sesame seeds and is used primarily for its nutty flavor.

SMELT: Tiny silver-sided fish ranging from 4–6 in (10–15 cm) long. Northwest varieties include the silver saltwater variety, and the spring-running Columbia River smelt, also called candlefish, which is traditionally prized by Northwest Indians for its high oil content.

SPOT PRAWNS: This sweet-tasting prawn, named for the white spots behind its head on each side comes from Alaska, the San Juan Channel and Hood Canal. It is sometimes available with its bright orange roe in late spring and early summer. Substitute: any other medium prawns.

SQUID: Also known as calamari, squid is available fresh and frozen. The tender squid's edible tentacles and body toughen if cooked too long and is best quickly sautéed, fried or marinated.

STAR ANISE: The beautiful, eight-pointed star-shaped pod of a small evergreen that grows in southwestern China and northern Vietnam. One of the components in Chinese five-spice powder, star anise is available in Asian markets.

STOCKS: Homemade stocks are easy to make and can be frozen for future use.

Canned broth may be substituted for stock in most recipes, but it should be used with discretion because most of these products are very salty.

To make beef or lamb stock: Roast 4 lbs (2 kg) beef or lamb bones (with some meat on them) in a 450°F (230°) oven in a roasting pan for 30 minutes, turning once. Place the bones in a large pot and add 2 onions, peeled and halved, 3 whole carrots, 3 whole celery stocks, a bay leaf, a handful of parsley sprigs, 1 teaspoon salt and ½ teaspoon cracked peppercorns. Discard the fat from the roasting pan and deglaze the pan with 2 cups of water. Add to the pot with 3 additional quarts of water. Bring to a boil, then reduce the heat and simmer very gently, partially covered, for about 5 hours, skimming off any foam that rises to the surface for the first 30 minutes or so. Strain through several thicknesses of cheesecloth and let cool, uncovered. Makes about 3 quarts.

To make chicken stock: Place about 4 lbs (2 kg) chicken pieces (backs, wings, necks, and the remains of a roast chicken) in a large pot. Add 2 onions peeled and halved, 2 whole carrots, 2 whole celery stalks, a handful of parsley sprigs, 1 bay leaf, 6 crushed peppercorns, 1 teaspoon dried thyme, and 1 teaspoon salt. Pour in about 4 quarts of water, or enough to cover the ingredients by 1 inch. Bring to a boil and reduce heat and simmer gently, partially covered for about 4 hours, skimming off any foam that rises to the surface for the first 30 minutes or so. Strain through several thicknesses of cheesecloth and let cool, uncovered. Makes 3 quarts.

To make fish stock: Rinse about 4 lbs (2 kg) combined white-fleshed fish heads and meaty skeletons under running water and place in a large pot. Add 2 onions, peeled and sliced, 2 carrots, peeled and thinly sliced, 2 stalks celery, sliced, 1 bay leaf, 8 crushed peppercorns and 1 teaspoon salt. Add 2 cups dry white wine and about 3 quarts of water, or enough to cover the ingredients by 1 inch. Bring to a boil, and reduce the heat and simmer, uncovered, for about 45 minutes, skimming any foam that forms on the surface. Strain through several thicknesses of cheesecloth and cool uncovered. Makes 3 quarts.

STURGEON: A prehistoric fish ranging from 3–8 ft (1–2.4 m) long and weighing up to 200 lbs (90 kg). A firm, fatty fish it is best sautéed, smoked or braised. Substitute: shark, marlin or swordfish.

SURIMI: A cooked product made of white fish and formed to resemble crab, shrimp or other seafoods.

SWEAT: To cook in a small amount of fat at low temperature so that the food softens but does not brown; generally a preliminary cooking procedure.

TERIYAKI SAUCE: A sweet and salty Japanese soy-based sauce or marinade. Available in bottles in Asian markets.

THAI RED CURRY PASTE: This Asian curry, more complex in flavor and hotter in taste than Indian curry powders, is available in Asian markets.

TOASTING NUTS : Toasting nuts brings out their rich flavor, deepens their color and increases their crunchiness. To toast nuts: Spread the nuts in a single layer on a shallow baking pan with edges and place under the broiler (griller) about 6 in (15 cm) from the heat. Turn the nuts frequently until they are golden, 3–5 minutes.

VINEGAR
Balsamic: An Italian wine vinegar aged up to fifty years in wooden barrels. The dark-colored liquid is sweet, smooth and mellow, excellent for salad dressings or as a condiment.
Rice wine: White or pale-colored, this mild-flavored Japanese vinegar comes in seasoned and unseasoned varieties.

WILD RICE: Unrelated botanically to cultivated rice, wild rice is actually the seed from a grass growing wild in northern North America. Wild rice contains twice as much protein as white rice. Use 1 cup (5 oz/155 g) of wild rice to 3½ cups (28 fl oz/875 ml) of water; cook about 40–45 minutes.

WON TON SKINS: Egg noodle wrappers made with wheat flour, usually 3½ in (9 cm) square. Wonton skins freeze well, both before and after being stuffed.

ZEST: The flavorful colored skin of the citrus fruits, minus the white underlying pith, which is bitter. It may be grated, or peeled and then minced or cut into julienne. Peel very finely with a knife.

INDEX

aïoli. *See* sauces
Anise Hyssop Mayonnaise 52-53, *52-53*
apples
  Apple-Cranberry Pie 244, *245*
  Apple-Mint Jelly 184, *184*
  Blueberry Baked Apples 226, *226*
  Braised Pheasant with Yakima Valley Hard Cider and Apples 128, *129*
  Chunky Applesauce 196, *196-197*
  Granny Smith Apple and Yakima Gouda Tartlets 32-33, 38
  Green Apple Crème Brulée 244, *244*
  Mulled Winter Cider 216, 230
  Okanagan Apple Cake with Maple Cream 226, *226-227*
  Roasted Mustard Rabbit with Spiced Apple Rings 145, *145*
  Winter Greens with Spicy Walnuts, Apples and Cranberry Vinaigrette 64, *64-65*
apricots
  Apricot and Green Peppercorn Relish 142, *143*
  Apricot Mustard 190, *190-191*
  Hazelnut and Apricot Biscotti 241, *241*
  Oatmeal Fruit Gems 220-221, *220-221*
Artichokes, Baked Pacific Oysters with Bay Shrimp and 84, *84*
asparagus
  Fettuccine with Dungeness Crab and Asparagus 85, *85*
  Spring Asparagus Soup 42, *42*
  Sunnyside Pickled Asparagus 185, *185*

Baked Blueberry Clafouti *210-211,* 220
Baked Ham Omelet 154, *154*
Baked Pacific Oysters with Bay Shrimp and Artichokes 84, *84*
Ballard Baked Beans 192, 193
Barbecued Pork Tenderloin with Plum Sauce 65, *65*
Barbecued Ribs with Apricot Glaze 148, *149*
Barbecued Salmon with Wine Country Butter Baste 76-77, 82
Basque Onions in Sour Cream 171, *171*
beans
  Ballard Baked Beans 192, 193
  Blue Lake Green Beans with Country Almond Butter 176, *179*
  Northern White Bean Soup with Chipotle Crème Fraîche 32-33, 38
beef
  Beef Short Ribs with Root Vegetables 124-125, *124-125*
  Grilled Picnic Burgers 148, *148*
  Peninsula Cranberry Pot Roast 124, *124-125*
  Peppered Flank Steak with Oregon Blue

Cheese Sauce 150, *150-151*
  Rib Eye Steak with Ha Cha Cha Barbecue Sauce and Frizzled Onions *10-11*, 128
  Roast Prime Rib of Beef with Herbed Popovers 152, 153
  Stout-Braised Beef with Onions and Sour Cream 128, *129*
Beer-Battered Walla Walla Onion Rings 44-45, 45
Beets, Pickled 188, *188*
berries. *See also* blackberries; blueberries; cranberries; raspberries; strawberries
  Cascade Berry Shortcake 214-215, *215*
  Huckleberry Slump 232, *233*
  Poppy Seed-Berry Vinaigrette 59, *59*
  Sparkling Berry Kir 219, *219*
beverages
  Bloody Caesar Cocktail 55, *55*
  Campfire Coffee 232, *233*
  Java City Iced Mocha 228, *228-229*
  Mulled Winter Cider 216, 230
  Sparkling Berry Kir 219, *219*
  Sun Tea with Rose Hips and Fresh Mint 220, *220-221*
  Vashon Ferry Coffee 248, *248*
Bing Cherry Fritters 224, *224-225*
Biscotti, Hazelnut and Apricot 241, *241*
Biscuits, Mini Scallion, with Smoked Salmon Spread and Pickled Onions 52, *52-53*
Bitter Chocolate Brandy Cream 228
blackberries
  Blackberry Cobbler *246-247*, 247
  Himalaya Blackberry Preserves 174, *174-175*
  Steamed Halibut with Blackberry Butter 104-105, *105*
Black Cod with Six Onion Relish and Savory Vinaigrette 99, *99*
Bloody Caesar Cocktail 55, *55*
blueberries
  Baked Blueberry Clafouti *210-211,* 220
  Blueberry Baked Apples 226, *226*
  Blue Lake Green Beans with Country Almond Butter 176, *179*
Braised Pheasant with Yakima Valley Hard Cider and Apples 128, *129*
Braised Sausage and Lentils *138-139*, 139
breads
  Herbed Popovers *152*, 153
  Indian Fry Bread *172-173*, 173
  Mini Scallion Biscuits with Smoked Salmon Spread and Pickled Onions 52, *52-53*
  Rosemary-Garlic Buns 148-149, *149*
  Sheepherder's Bread 174, *174-175*
  Walnut-Stout Bread 176, *176-177*
Broccoli, Steamed, and Cheddar Rarebit 170-171, *170-171*
Brownies, Triple-Chocolate Boat 237, *238-239*

Brulée, Green Apple Crème 244, *244*
butter
  Butter Tarts 238, *238-239*
  Citrus-Rosemary Butter 81, *81*
  Country Almond Butter 176, *179*
  Wildflower-Berry Butter 199, *199*
  Wine Country Butter Baste 76-77, 82
cakes
  Cascade Berry Shortcake 214-215, *215*
  Chocolate Zucchini Cake 249, *249*
  Mile-High Fresh Plum Cake 222, 223
  Okanagan Apple Cake with Maple Cream 226, *226-227*
  Peach Upside-Down Gingerbread Cake with Lemon Cream 232, *233*
  Pumpkin-Pecan Cake 230, *230-231*
  Scandinavian Oatmeal Sour Cream Coffee Cake 196-197, *196-197*
Calamari with Lemon Aïoli 47, *47*
Calves' Liver and Bacon with Orange-Leek Sauce *126*, 127
Campfire Coffee 232, *233*
Caramel-Walnut Pie 216, *216-217*
Carrots, Scalloped Potatoes with 168, *168*
Cascade Berry Shortcake 214-215, *215*
cherries
  Bing Cherry Fritters 224, *224-225*
  Chilled Bing Cherry Soup 42, *42*
  Crimson Cherry Chutney 200-201, 201
  Oatmeal Fruit Gems 220-221, *220-221*
  Rice Pudding with Cherries 238-239, *238-239*
chicken
  Chicken with Herbed Dumplings 127, *127*
  Grilled Chicken with Pico de Gallo 154-155, *155*
  Market Pot au Feu 136, *137*
  Roast Chicken Stuffed with Autumn Fruits 120-121, 135
  Thai-Flavored Chicken Skewers 147, *147*
  Walnut-Crusted Chicken Breast with Rhubarb-Onion Chutney 142, *143*
Chilled Bing Cherry Soup 42, *42*
Chipotle Crème Fraîche 32-33, 38
Chive Flower Sabayon 88-89, *88-89*
chocolate
  Chocolate Pâté with Raspberry Sauce 242-243, *242-243*
  Chocolate Sabayon 234, 235
  Chocolate Zucchini Cake 249, *249*
  Triple-Chocolate Boat Brownies 237, *238-239*
chowders
  Granville Island Chowder *36-37*, 37
  Manila Clam Chowder 36-37, *36-37*
Chunky Applesauce 196, *196-197*
chutneys. *See also* relishes; salsas; sauces
  Chutney Lime Dressing 56, *56-57*
  Crimson Cherry Chutney 200-201, 201
  Plummy Pear Chutney 184, *184*
  Rhubarb-Onion Chutney 142, *143*

Tomato-Ginger Chutney 96-97, *96-97*
Citrus-Rosemary Butter 81, *81*
Clafouti, Baked Blueberry *210-211,* 220
clams
  Cliff Island Clambake with Five Pounds of Garlic and a Case of Wine 82-83, *82-83*
  Geoduck and Green Onion Hash 90-91, *90-91*
  Granville Island Chowder *36-37*, 37
  Manila Clam Chowder 36-37, *36-37*
  Pan-Fried Razor Clams with Citrus-Rosemary Butter 81, *81*
  Steamed Clams in a Thai Curry Broth 81, *81*
Cliff Island Clambake with Five Pounds of Garlic and a Case of Wine 82-83, *82-83*
Cobbler, Blackberry *246-247*, 247
Cocktail, Bloody Caesar 55, *55*
cod
  Black Cod with Six Onion Relish and Savory Vinaigrette 99, *99*
  Sake Kasu Cod 92, *92-93*
coffee
  Campfire Coffee 232, *233*
  Java City Iced Mocha 228, *228-229*
  Vashon Ferry Coffee 248, *248*
coleslaw
  Salmon Cakes with Ginger Aïoli and Sesame Vegetable Slaw 92, 93
Columbia River Sturgeon with Chanterelles, Sun-Dried Tomatoes and Basil 108, *109*
Compote, Rhubarb-Ginger 200-201, 201
cookies
  Mt. St. Helens Crater Cookies 228, *228-229*
  Oatmeal Fruit Gems 220-221, *220-221*
Coppa-Cured Pork Tenderloin with Pickled Peaches 141, *141*
corn
  Green Chili Corn Cakes with Sturgeon Caviar 54, *54*
  Grilled Corn on the Cob with Honey Butter 192, *193*
Cornish Game Hens with Lemongrass 136, *136*
Country Almond Butter 176, *179*
Country Bread Salad with Roasted Vegetables 64, *64*
crab
  Crab-Stuffed Morel Mushrooms 50, *51*
  Dungeness Crab and Bay Shrimp Cakes 86, *86*
  Fettuccine with Dungeness Crab and Asparagus 85, *85*
  Hot Crab Melt with Two Cheeses 98, *98*
  Pacific Northwest Crab Pot with Dipping Sauces 106, *106-107*
  Pacific Rim Stuffed Salmon 94, 95
  Seattle Crab Louis 60, *60-61*
  Spinach and Crab-Stuffed Baked Prawns 102-103, *103*

Tojo's Shrimp Dumplings with Hot
    Mustard Sauce 65, 65
cranberries
    Apple-Cranberry Pie 244, 245
    Cranberry Bread Pudding 226, 227
    Cranberry Relish 110, 110
    Cranberry-Sage Vinegar 188, 189
    Cranberry Vinaigrette 64, 64
    Peninsula Cranberry Pot Roast 124, 124-125
cream
    Bitter Chocolate Brandy Cream 228
    Crème Fraîche 226
    Lemon Cream 232, 233
    Maple Cream 226, 226-227
    Orange Cream 222
    Vanilla Cream 246-247, 246-247
Crimson Cherry Chutney 200-201, 201
croutons 56-57
    Goat Cheese Croutons 63, 63
Crow Valley Pear Crisp with Vanilla Cream
    246-247, 246-247
cucumbers
    Cucumber-Yogurt Sauce 106
    Damn Good Dills 182-183, 183
    Thai Cucumber Salad 56, 56-57

Damn Good Dills 182-183, 183
Deep-Fried Smelts, Chinese Style 96, 96-97
dressings
    Chutney Lime Dressing 56, 56-57
    Cranberry Vinaigrette 64, 64
    Lemon Thyme-Apple Vinaigrette 104, 105
    Louis Dressing 60, 60-61
    Poppy Seed-Berry Vinaigrette 59, 59
    Red Wine Vinaigrette 32-33, 50
    Roasted Shallot Vinaigrette 58, 59
    Rogue River Blue Cheese Dressing 60-61,
        60-61
    Savory Vinaigrette 99, 99
    Sesame Dressing 56-57
duck
    Duck Breast with Wild Blackberries and
        Ginger 140, 140
    Market Pot au Feu 136, 137
    Mt. Bachelor Duck Confit 145, 146
    Roast Duckling with Pressed Cider and
        Sage 134-135, 135
    Skagit Valley Duck Sausage 130-131, 130-
        131
dumplings
    Chicken with Herbed Dumplings 127, 127
    Tojo's Shrimp Dumplings with Hot
        Mustard Sauce 65, 65
Dungeness Crab and Bay Shrimp Cakes 86,
    86

Eggplant Caponata and Roasted Garlic 32-33,
    66
eggs
    Baked Ham Omelet 154, 154

Fettuccine with Dungeness Crab and
    Asparagus 85, 85
Fiddlehead Ferns, Japanese 194, 194-195
Fig Tart with Walnuts 218-219, 218-219
fish
    Barbecued Salmon with Wine Country
        Butter Baste 76-77, 82
    Black Cod with Six Onion Relish and
        Savory Vinaigrette 99, 99
    Columbia River Sturgeon with
        Chanterelles, Sun-Dried Tomatoes and
        Basil 108, 109
    Deep-Fried Smelts, Chinese Style 96, 96-97
    Halibut with Hazelnut Crust and Lemon
        Thyme-Apple Vinaigrette 104, 105
    Halibut with Strawberry Mint Salsa 108,
        108
    Microbrew Beer-Battered Fish 98, 98
    New Westminster Salmonbellies 54, 54-55
    Pacific Rim Stuffed Salmon 94, 95
    Pan-Fried Cornmeal-Dusted Idaho Trout
        90, 90-91
    Pan-Fried Walleye with Romesco Sauce
        100-101, 100-101
    Pan-Roasted Steelhead with Apples, Onions
        and Sage 100-101, 101
    Pickled Herring with Sour Cream and
        Cucumber 48-49, 49
    Pickled Salmon 48-49, 49
    Planked White King Salmon with
        Cranberry Relish 110, 110
    Sake Kasu Cod 92, 92-93
    Salmon Cakes with Ginger Aïoli and
        Sesame Vegetable Slaw 92, 93
    Sautéed Sturgeon with Pinot Noir and
        Ginger Glaze 108, 109
    Smoked Salmon Benedict with Sour

Cream-Chive Hollandaise 102-103, 102-
    103
Smoked Salmon Risotto with Chanterelles
    and Roasted Garlic 85, 85
Smoked Salmon Spread 52, 52-53
Steamed Halibut with Blackberry Butter
    104-105, 105
Summer Ceviche 62, 62
Teriyaki Yelloweye Rockfish with
    Pineapple Salsa 92, 93
Fraser Valley Relish 190-191, 193
French Toast, Stuffed, with Wildflower-Berry
    Butter 198-199, 199
Fresh Herb Pesto 194, 195
Fried Green Tomatoes 192, 193
fries
    Idaho Oven Fries 180, 180-181
    Yam Fries 180, 180-181
Fritters, Bing Cherry 224, 224-225
Frizzled Onions 10-11, 128

Garden Greens with Bay Shrimp and Rogue
    River Blue Cheese Dressing
    60-61, 60-61
Garden Harvest Pickle 182-183, 183
garlic
    Cliff Island Clambake with Five Pounds of
        Garlic and a Case of Wine 82-83, 82-83
    Garlic Whipped Potatoes 124, 124-125
    Roasted Garlic 32-33, 66
    Smoked Salmon Risotto with Chanterelles
        and Roasted Garlic 85, 85
Geoduck and Green Onion Hash 90-91, 90-
    91
Ginger Aïoli 92, 93
Granny Smith Apple and Yakima Gouda
    Tartlets 32-33, 38
Granville Island Chowder 36-37, 37
gravies 124
    Wild Turkey Gravy 152, 152-153
Green Apple Crème Brulée 244, 244
Green Chili Corn Cakes with Sturgeon
    Caviar 54, 54
green onions. See onions
Green Tomato Mincemeat 186-187, 187
Green Tomato Mincemeat Pie 240, 241
Grilled Chicken with Pico de Gallo 154-155,
    155
Grilled Corn on the Cob with Honey Butter
    192, 193
Grilled Picnic Burgers 148, 148
Grilled Vegetables with Fresh Herb Pesto 194,
    194
Ha Cha Cha Barbecue Sauce 10-11, 128
halibut
    Halibut with Hazelnut Crust and Lemon
        Thyme-Apple Vinaigrette 104, 105
    Halibut with Strawberry Mint Salsa 108,
        108
    Microbrew Beer-Battered Fish 98, 98
    Steamed Halibut with Blackberry Butter
        104-105, 105
    Summer Ceviche 62, 62
hamburgers
    Grilled Picnic Burgers 148, 148
    Lamb Burgers on Rosemary-Garlic Buns
        148-149, 149
hash
    Geoduck and Green Onion Hash 90-91, 90-
        91
    Wild Turkey Hash 154, 154
hazelnuts
    Hazelnut and Apricot Biscotti 241, 241
    Hazelnut Crust 104
Herb Butter Sauce 106
Herbed Bread Crumbs 103
Herbed Dumplings 127, 127
Herbed Popovers 152, 153
Herring, Pickled, with Sour Cream and
    Cucumber 48-49, 49
Himalaya Blackberry Preserves 174, 174-175
Hot Crab Melt with Two Cheeses 98, 98
Hot Mustard Sauce 65, 65
Howdy Beach Cocktail Sauce 46, 46
Huckleberry Slump 232, 233

ice cream
    Nectarine Ice Cream 231, 231
    Strawberry Ice Cream 235, 235
Idaho Oven Fries 180, 180-181
Indian Fry Bread 172-173, 173
Island Picnic Potato Salad 66, 67

Japanese Fiddlehead Ferns 194, 194-195
Java City Iced Mocha 228, 228-229
jellies
    Apple-Mint Jelly 184, 184

Red Pepper Jelly 172-173, 173

lamb
    Lamb Burgers on Rosemary-Garlic Buns
        148-149, 149
    Lamb Chops, Basque Style 144, 144-145
    Minted Lamb with Pear Relish 133, 133
    Roast Leg of Lamb with Merlot Marinade
        120-121, 150-151
    Scotch Broth 43, 43
    Shepherd's Pie 120-121, 134
    Spanish Lamb Stew 132, 132-133
lemons
    Lemon Cream 232, 233
    Lemon Pasta 88-89, 89
    Lemon-Raspberry Meringue Tart 236-237,
        236-237
    Lemon Thyme-Apple Vinaigrette 104, 105
lentils
    Braised Sausage and Lentils 138-139, 139
    Palouse Lentil Soup 42, 43
Liver and Bacon with Orange-Leek Sauce
    126, 127
Louis Dressing 60, 60-61

Manila Clam Chowder 36-37, 36-37
Maple Cream 226, 226-227
Marinated Walla Walla Sweets with Tomato
    Wedges 66, 67
Marionberry Vinegar 164-165, 193
Market Pot au Feu 136, 137
mayonnaise
    Anise Hyssop Mayonnaise 52-53, 52-53
    Roasted Red Pepper Mayonnaise 148-149
melons
    Mint-Pickled Melons 164-165, 180
    Summer Melon and Prawn Salad with
        Chutney Lime Dressing 56, 56-57
Microbrew Beer-Battered Fish 98, 98
Mile-High Fresh Plum Cake 222, 223
mincemeat
    Green Tomato Mincemeat 186-187, 187
    Green Tomato Mincemeat Pie 240, 241
Mini Scallion Biscuits with Smoked Salmon
    Spread and Pickled Onions 52, 52-53
Minted Lamb with Pear Relish 133, 133
Mint-Pickled Melons 164-165, 180
Mt. Bachelor Duck Confit 145, 146
Mt. St. Helens Crater Cookies 228, 228-229
Mulled Winter Cider 216, 230
mushrooms
    Columbia River Sturgeon with
        Chanterelles, Sun-Dried Tomatoes and
        Basil 108, 109
    Crab-Stuffed Morel Mushrooms 50, 51
    Smoked Salmon Risotto with Chanterelles
        and Roasted Garlic 85, 85
    Wild Mushroom Filo Packets 50, 51
    Wild Mushroom Ragout 178, 178
Mussels with Leeks and Tarragon Cream 99, 99
mustard
    Apricot Mustard 190, 190-191
    Hot Mustard Sauce 65, 65

Nanaimo Bars 231, 231
Nectarine Ice Cream 231, 231
New Westminster Salmonbellies 54, 54-55
Northern White Bean Soup with Chipotle
    Crème Fraîche 32-33, 38
Northwest Hangtown Fry 90, 90-91
nuts
    Caramel-Walnut Pie 216, 216-217
    Hazelnut and Apricot Biscotti 241, 241
    Pumpkin-Pecan Cake 230, 230-231
    Roasted Spicy Northwest Nuts 44, 44-45
    Spicy Walnuts 64, 64-65
    Walnut-Stout Bread 176, 176-177

Oatmeal Fruit Gems 220-221, 220-221
Okanagan Apple Cake with Maple Cream
    226, 226-227
onions
    Basque Onions in Sour Cream 171, 171
    Beer-Battered Walla Walla Onion Rings 44-
        45, 45
    Frizzled Onions 10-11, 128
    Geoduck and Green Onion Hash 90-91, 90-
        91
    Marinated Walla Walla Sweets with
        Tomato Wedges 66, 67
    Mini Scallion Biscuits with Smoked Salmon
        Spread and Pickled Onions 52, 52-53
    Six Onion Relish 190, 190-191
    Spiced Onion and Ale Soup 38, 39
oranges
    Orange Cream 222
    Orange-Leek Sauce 126, 127
    Orange Scones 103

Oregon Blue Cheese Sauce 150, 150-151
oysters
    Baked Pacific Oysters with Bay Shrimp and
        Artichokes 84, 84
    Northwest Hangtown Fry 90, 90-91
    Oyster-Corn Bread Stuffing 152, 152-153
    Oysters on the Half Shell with Howdy
        Beach Cocktail Sauce 46, 46
    Pan-Fried Oysters with Rock Island Tartar
        111, 111
    Wasp Passage Oyster Stew 84, 84-85

Pacific Northwest Crab Pot with Dipping
    Sauces 106, 106-107
Pacific Northwest Seafood Stew 86, 87
Pacific Rim Stuffed Salmon 94, 95
Palouse Lentil Soup 42, 43
pancakes
    Spiced Pancakes with Whipped Cream and
        Summer Fruit 12, 224
    Wild Rice Cakes 179, 179
Pan-Fried Cornmeal-Dusted Idaho Trout 90,
    90-91
Pan-Fried Oysters with Rock Island Tartar
    111, 111
Pan-Fried Razor Clams with Citrus-Rosemary
    Butter 81, 81
Pan-Fried Walleye with Romesco Sauce 100-
    101, 100-101
Pan-Roasted Steelhead with Apples, Onions
    and Sage 100-101, 101
pasta
    Fettuccine with Dungeness Crab and
        Asparagus 85, 85
    Spot Prawns with Lemon Pasta and Chives
        88-89, 89
peaches
    Peach Upside-Down Gingerbread Cake
        with Lemon Cream 232, 233
    Pepper-Pickled Peaches 164-165, 187
pears
    Crow Valley Pear Crisp with Vanilla Cream
        246-247, 246-247
    Pear Relish 133, 133
    Pears, Prosciutto and Bitter Greens with
        Roasted Shallot Vinaigrette 58, 59
    Pinot Noir-Poached Pears with Chocolate
        Sabayon 234, 235
    Plummy Pear Chutney 184, 184
Peas, Spicy Sesame Snap 168, 169
Peninsula Cranberry Pot Roast 124, 124-125
Peppered Flank Steak with Oregon Blue
    Cheese Sauce 150, 150-151
Pepper-Pickled Peaches 164-165, 187
Pesto, Fresh Herb 194, 195
Pheasant, Braised, with Yakima Valley Hard
    Cider and Apples 128, 129
Pickled Herring with Sour Cream and
    Cucumber 48-49, 49
Pickled Salmon 48-49, 49
pickles
    Damn Good Dills 182-183, 183
    Garden Harvest Pickle 182-183, 183
    Mint-Pickled Melons 164-165, 180
    Pepper-Pickled Peaches 164-165, 187
    Pickled Beets 188, 188
    Sunnyside Pickled Asparagus 185, 185
Pico de Gallo 154-155, 155
pies
    Apple-Cranberry Pie 244, 245
    Caramel-Walnut Pie 216, 216-217
    Green Tomato Mincemeat Pie 240, 241
    Tourtière Christmas Pie 152, 153
Pineapple Salsa 92, 93
Pinot Noir-Poached Pears with Chocolate
    Sabayon 234, 235
Planked White King Salmon with Cranberry
    Relish 110, 110
plums
    Mile-High Fresh Plum Cake 222, 223
    Plummy Pear Chutney 184, 184
    Plum Sauce 65, 65
Polenta 4, 104
Popovers, Herbed 152, 153
Poppy Seed-Berry Vinaigrette 59, 59
pork
    Baked Ham Omelet 154, 154
    Barbecued Pork Tenderloin with Plum
        Sauce 65, 65
    Barbecued Ribs with Apricot Glaze 148,
        149
    Coppa-Cured Pork Tenderloin with Pickled
        Peaches 141, 141
    Pears, Prosciutto and Bitter Greens with
        Roasted Shallot Vinaigrette 58, 59
    Portuguese Pork Chops 155, 155
    Roast Pork Tenderloin with Red Currant
        Sauce 132, 132

Tourtière Christmas Pie 152, 153
Portuguese Pork Chops 155, *155*
potatoes
 Garlic Whipped Potatoes 124, *124-125*
 Idaho Oven Fries 180, *180-181*
 Island Picnic Potato Salad 66, *67*
 Scalloped Potatoes with Carrots 168, *168*
prawns. See also shrimp
 Spinach and Crab-Stuffed Baked Prawns 102-103, 103
 Spot Prawns with Lemon Pasta and Chives 88-89, 89
 Summer Melon and Prawn Salad with Chutney Lime Dressing 56, *56-57*
 Tempura Prawns with Vietnamese Dipping Sauce 94, 95
 Whiffin Spit Spot Prawns with Anise Hyssop Mayonnaise 52-53, *52-53*
Preserves, Himalaya Blackberry 174, *174-175*
Prunes, Venison Stew with 138-139, 139
puddings
 Cranberry Bread Pudding 226, 227
 Rice Pudding with Cherries 238-239, *238-239*
Pumpkin-Pecan Cake 230, 230-231

quail
 Roast Quail with Apricot and Green Peppercorn Relish 142, *143*

rabbit
 Roasted Mustard Rabbit with Spiced Apple Rings 145, *145*
raspberries
 Lemon-Raspberry Meringue Tart 236-237, *236-237*
 Raspberries with White Chocolate-Sour Cream Sauce 242, *242-243*
 Raspberry Sauce 242-243, *242-243*
Red Currant Sauce 132, *132*
Red Pepper Jelly 172-173, 173
relishes. See also chutneys; salsas; sauces
 Apricot and Green Peppercorn Relish 142, *143*
 Cranberry Relish 110, *110*
 Fraser Valley Relish 190-191, 193
 Pear Relish 133, *133*
 Six Onion Relish 190, *190-191*
rhubarb
 Rhubarb Cheesecake Tart 214, *214*
 Rhubarb-Ginger Compote 200-201, 201
 Rhubarb-Onion Chutney 142, *143*
 Rhubarb-Strawberry Fool 222, 222
Rib Eye Steak with Ha Cha Cha Barbecue Sauce and Frizzled Onions 10-11, 128
ribs
 Barbecued Ribs with Apricot Glaze 148, *149*
 Beef Short Ribs with Root Vegetables 124-125, *124-125*
 Roast Prime Rib of Beef with Herbed Popovers 152, 153
rice
 Rice Pudding with Cherries 238-239, *238-239*
 Smoked Salmon Risotto with Chanterelles and Roasted Garlic 85, *85*
 Vancouver Fried Rice 94, 95
 Wild Rice Cakes 179, *179*
Roast Chicken Stuffed with Autumn Fruits 120-121, 135
Roast Duckling with Pressed Cider and Sage 134-135, 135
Roasted Garlic 32-33, 66
Roasted Mustard Rabbit with Spiced Apple Rings 145, *145*
Roasted Pepper, Corn and Arugula Salad with Goat Cheese Croutons 63, *63*
Roasted Red Pepper Mayonnaise 148-149
Roasted Shallot Vinaigrette 58, 59
Roasted Spicy Northwest Nuts 44, 44-45
Roast Leg of Lamb with Merlot Marinade 120-121, 150-151
Roast Pork Tenderloin with Red Currant Sauce 132, *132*
Roast Prime Rib of Beef with Herbed Popovers 152, 153
Roast Quail with Apricot and Green Peppercorn Relish 142, *143*
Roast Turkey with Oyster-Corn Bread Stuffing and Wild Turkey Gravy 152, 152-153
Rock Island Tartar Sauce 111, *111*
Rogue River Blue Cheese Dressing 60-61, *60-61*
Romesco Sauce 100-101, *100-101*
Rosemary-Garlic Buns 148-149, *149*

sabayon. See sauces

Sake Kasu Cod 92, 92-93
salads
 Country Bread Salad with Roasted Vegetables 64, *64*
 Garden Greens with Bay Shrimp and Rogue River Blue Cheese Dressing 60-61, *60-61*
 Island Picnic Potato Salad 66, *67*
 Pears, Prosciutto and Bitter Greens with Roasted Shallot Vinaigrette 58, 59
 Roasted Pepper, Corn and Arugula Salad with Goat Cheese Croutons 63, *63*
 Seattle Crab Louis 60, *60-61*
 Sesame Caesar Salad 56-57, *56-57*
 Spinach Salad with Strawberries and Poppy Seed-Berry Vinaigrette 59, *59*
 Summer Ceviche 62, *62*
 Summer Melon and Prawn Salad with Chutney Lime Dressing 56, *56-57*
 Thai Cucumber Salad 56, *56-57*
 Wild Greens with Red Wine Vinaigrette 32-33, 50
 Winter Greens with Spicy Walnuts, Apples and Cranberry Vinaigrette 64, 64-65
salmon
 Barbecued Salmon with Wine Country Butter Baste 76-77, 82
 New Westminster Salmonbellies 54, 54-55
 Pacific Rim Stuffed Salmon 94, 95
 Pickled Salmon 48-49, 49
 Planked White King Salmon with Cranberry Relish 110, *110*
 Salmon Cakes with Ginger Aïoli and Sesame Vegetable Slaw 92, 93
 Smoked Salmon Benedict with Sour Cream-Chive Hollandaise 102-103, *102-103*
 Smoked Salmon Risotto with Chanterelles and Roasted Garlic 85, *85*
 Smoked Salmon Spread 52, 52-53
salsas. See also chutneys; relishes; sauces
 Pico de Gallo 154-155, *155*
 Pineapple Salsa 92, 93
 Strawberry Mint Salsa 108, *108*
 Yakima Beefsteak-Tomato Salsa with Fresh Tortilla Chips 44, 44-45
sauces. See also chutneys; relishes; salsas
 Chive Flower Sabayon 88-89, *88-89*
 Chocolate Sabayon 234, 235
 Cucumber-Yogurt Sauce 106
 Ginger Aïoli 92, 93
 Ha Cha Cha Barbecue Sauce 10-11, 128
 Herb Butter Sauce 106
 Hot Mustard Sauce 65, 65
 Howdy Beach Cocktail Sauce 46, *46*
 Lemon Aïoli 47, 47
 Orange-Leek Sauce 126, 127
 Oregon Blue Cheese Sauce 150, *150-151*
 Plum Sauce 65, 65
 Raspberry Sauce 242-243, *242-243*
 Red Currant Sauce 132, *132*
 Rock Island Tartar Sauce 111, *111*
 Romesco Sauce 100-101, *100-101*
 Sour Cream-Chive Hollandaise 102, *102-103*
 Thai Curry Broth 81, *81*
 Vietnamese Dipping Sauce 94, 95
 White Chocolate-Sour Cream Sauce 242, *242-243*
sausages
 Braised Sausage and Lentils 138-139, 139
 Skagit Valley Duck Sausage 130-131, *130-131*
 Venison Sausage 120-121, 142
Sautéed Spinach with Pears 198-199, 199
Sautéed Sturgeon with Pinot Noir and Ginger Glaze 108, *109*
Savory Vinaigrette 99, *99*
scallions. See onions
Scalloped Potatoes with Carrots 168, *168*
scallops
 Scallop Wontons with Tomato-Ginger Chutney 96-97, *96-97*
 Seared Sea Scallops with Roasted Peppers and Polenta 4, 104
 Sooke Harbour House Singing Scallops with Chive Flower Sabayon 88-89, *88-89*
 Summer Ceviche 62, *62*
Scandinavian Oatmeal Sour Cream Coffee Cake 196-197, *196-197*
Scones, Orange 103
Scotch Broth 43, *43*
seafood. See also clams; crab; fish; oysters; prawns; scallops; shrimp
 Calamari with Lemon Aïoli 47, *47*
 Geoduck and Green Onion Hash 90-91, *90-91*
 Green Chili Corn Cakes with Sturgeon Caviar 54, *54*
 Mussels with Leeks and Tarragon Cream 99, *99*
 Pacific Northwest Seafood Stew 86, 87
 Summer Ceviche 62, *62*

Vancouver Fried Rice 94, 95
Seared Sea Scallops with Roasted Peppers and Polenta 4, 104
Seattle Crab Louis 60, *60-61*
Sesame Caesar Salad 56-57, *56-57*
Sesame Vegetable Slaw 92, 93
shallots
 Roasted Shallot Vinaigrette 58, 59
Sheepherder's Bread 174, *174-175*
Shepherd's Pie 120-121, 134
shrimp. See also prawns
 Baked Pacific Oysters with Bay Shrimp and Artichokes 84, *84*
 Dungeness Crab and Bay Shrimp Cakes 86, *86*
 Garden Greens with Bay Shrimp and Rogue River Blue Cheese Dressing 60-61, *60-61*
 New Westminster Salmonbellies 54, 54-55
 Shrimp Wonton Soup with Vegetable Flowers 40, 40-41
 Tojo's Shrimp Dumplings with Hot Mustard Sauce 65, *65*
Six Onion Relish 190, *190-191*
Skagit Valley Duck Sausage 130-131, *130-131*
Smoked Salmon Benedict with Sour Cream-Chive Hollandaise 102-103, *102-103*
Smoked Salmon Risotto with Chanterelles and Roasted Garlic 85, *85*
Sooke Harbour House Singing Scallops with Chive Flower Sabayon 88-89, *88-89*
soups. See also chowders; stews
 Chilled Bing Cherry Soup 42, *42*
 Northern White Bean Soup with Chipotle Crème Fraîche 32-33, 38
 Palouse Lentil Soup 42, 43
 Scotch Broth 43, *43*
 Shrimp Wonton Soup with Vegetable Flowers 40, 40-41
 Spiced Onion and Ale Soup 38, *39*
 Spicy Squash Bisque with Root Vegetables 41, *41*
 Spring Asparagus Soup 42, *42*
Sour Cream-Chive Hollandaise 102, *102-103*
Spanish Lamb Stew 132, 132-133
Sparkling Berry Kir 219, *219*
Spiced Onion and Ale Soup 38, *39*
Spiced Pancakes with Whipped Cream and Summer Fruit 12, 224
Spicy Sesame Snap Peas 168, *169*
Spicy Squash Bisque with Root Vegetables 41, *41*
spinach
 Sautéed Spinach with Pears 198-199, 199
 Spinach and Crab-Stuffed Baked Prawns 102-103, 103
 Spinach Salad with Strawberries and Poppy Seed-Berry Vinaigrette 59, *59*
Spot Prawns with Lemon Pasta and Chives 88-89, 89
spreads
 Anise Hyssop Mayonnaise 52-53, *52-53*
 Roasted Red Pepper Mayonnaise 148-149
 Smoked Salmon Spread 52, *52-53*
Spring Asparagus Soup 42, 42
Squash Bisque with Root Vegetables, Spicy 41, *41*
squid
 Calamari with Lemon Aïoli 47, *47*
Steamed Broccoli and Cheddar Rarebit 170-171, *170-171*
Steamed Clams in a Thai Curry Broth 81, *81*
Steamed Halibut with Blackberry Butter 104-105, *105*
stews
 Pacific Northwest Seafood Stew 86, 87
 Spanish Lamb Stew 132, 132-133
 Venison Stew with Prunes 138-139, 139
 Wasp Passage Oyster Stew 84, 84-85
Stout-Braised Beef with Onions and Sour Cream 128, *129*
strawberries
 Rhubarb-Strawberry Fool 222, 222
 Spinach Salad with Strawberries and Poppy Seed-Berry Vinaigrette 59, *59*
 Strawberry Ice Cream 235, *235*
 Strawberry Mint Salsa 108, *108*
Stuffed French Toast with Wildflower-Berry Butter 198-199, *199*
Stuffing, Oyster-Corn Bread 152, 152-153
sturgeon
 Columbia River Sturgeon with Chanterelles, Sun-Dried Tomatoes and Basil 108, *109*
 Sautéed Sturgeon with Pinot Noir and Ginger Glaze 108, *109*
Summer Ceviche 62, *62*
Summer Melon and Prawn Salad with Chutney Lime Dressing 56, *56-57*

Sunnyside Pickled Asparagus 185, *185*
Sun Tea with Rose Hips and Fresh Mint 220, *220-221*

tarts
 Butter Tarts 238, *238-239*
 Fig Tart with Walnuts 218-219, *218-219*
 Granny Smith Apple and Yakima Gouda Tartlets 32-33, 38
 Lemon-Raspberry Meringue Tart 236-237, *236-237*
 Rhubarb Cheesecake Tart 214, *214*
tea
 Sun Tea with Rose Hips and Fresh Mint 220, 220-221
Tempura Prawns with Vietnamese Dipping Sauce 94, 95
Teriyaki Yelloweye Rockfish with Pineapple Salsa 92, 93
Thai Cucumber Salad 56, *56-57*
Thai Curry Broth 81, *81*
Thai-Flavored Chicken Skewers 147, *147*
Tojo's Shrimp Dumplings with Hot Mustard Sauce 65, *65*
tomatoes
 Columbia River Sturgeon with Chanterelles, Sun-Dried Tomatoes and Basil 108, *109*
 Fried Green Tomatoes 192, 193
 Green Tomato Mincemeat 186-187, 187
 Green Tomato Mincemeat Pie 240, *241*
 Tomato-Ginger Chutney 96-97, *96-97*
 Yakima Beefsteak-Tomato Salsa with Fresh Tortilla Chips 44, 44-45
Tourtière Christmas Pie 152, 153
Triple-Chocolate Boat Brownies 237, 238-239
trout
 Pan-Fried Cornmeal-Dusted Idaho Trout 90, *90-91*
 Pan-Roasted Steelhead with Apples, Onions and Sage 100-101, 101
turkey
 Roast Turkey with Oyster-Corn Bread Stuffing and Wild Turkey Gravy 152, 152-153
 Wild Turkey Hash 154, *154*

Vancouver Fried Rice 94, 95
Vanilla Cream 246-247, *246-247*
Vashon Ferry Coffee 248, *248*
veal
 Market Pot au Feu 136, *137*
 Tourtière Christmas Pie 152, 153
vegetables. See also individual vegetables
 Fraser Valley Relish 190-191, 193
 Grilled Vegetables with Fresh Herb Pesto 194, *194*
venison
 Venison Sausage 120-121, 142
 Venison Stew with Prunes 138-139, 139
Vietnamese Dipping Sauce 94, 95
vinegar
 Cranberry-Sage Vinegar 188, *189*
 Marionberry Vinegar 164-165, 193

walnuts
 Fig Tart with Walnuts 218-219, *218-219*
 Walnut-Crusted Chicken Breast with Rhubarb-Onion Chutney 142, *143*
 Walnut-Stout Bread 174, 176-177
Wasp Passage Oyster Stew 84, 84-85
Whiffin Spit Spot Prawns with Anise Hyssop Mayonnaise 52-53, *52-53*
White Chocolate-Sour Cream Sauce 242, *242-243*
Wildflower-Berry Butter 199, *199*
Wild Greens with Red Wine Vinaigrette 32-33, 50
Wild Mushroom Filo Packets 50, *51*
Wild Mushroom Ragout 178, *178*
Wild Rice Cakes 179, *179*
Wild Turkey Gravy 152, 152-153
Wild Turkey Hash 154, *154*
Wine Country Butter Baste 76-77, 82
Winter Greens with Spicy Walnuts, Apples and Cranberry Vinaigrette 64, 64-65
wontons
 Scallop Wontons with Tomato-Ginger Chutney 96-97, *96-97*
 Shrimp Wonton Soup with Vegetable Flowers 40, 40-41

Yakima Beefsteak-Tomato Salsa with Fresh Tortilla Chips 44, 44-45
Yam Fries 180, *180-181*

zucchini
 Chocolate Zucchini Cake 249, *249*